Course   Accounting Information Systems

Course Number   **ACTG 335**

PORTLAND STATE UNIVERSITY

ACCOUNTING & INFORMATION SYS

http://create.mheducation.com

ISBN-10: 1307115705   ISBN-13: 9781307115703

Contents

   i. About the Authors 1
  ii. Preface 3
 iii. AIS 2e Content Updates 5
 iv. Main Features 8
  v. Acknowledgments 14
  1. Accounting Information Systems and Firm Value 16
  2. Accountants as Business Analysts 44
  3. Data Modeling 74
  4. Relational Databases and Enterprise Systems 96
  5. Sales and Collections Business Process 132
  6. Purchases and Payments Business Process 164
  7. Conversion Business Process 190
  8. Integrated Project 212
  A. Glossary of Models 222
  B. Glossary 236
  C. Index 245

Credits

i. About the Authors: *Chapter from Accounting Information Systems, Second Edition by Richardson, Chang, Smith, 2018* 1

ii. Preface: *Chapter from Accounting Information Systems, Second Edition by Richardson, Chang, Smith, 2018* 3

iii. AIS 2e Content Updates: *Chapter from Accounting Information Systems, Second Edition by Richardson, Chang, Smith, 2018* 5

iv. Main Features: *Chapter from Accounting Information Systems, Second Edition by Richardson, Chang, Smith, 2018* 8

v. Acknowledgments: *Chapter from Accounting Information Systems, Second Edition by Richardson, Chang, Smith, 2018* 14

1. Accounting Information Systems and Firm Value: *Chapter 1 from Accounting Information Systems, Second Edition by Richardson, Chang, Smith, 2018* 16

2. Accountants as Business Analysts: *Chapter 2 from Accounting Information Systems, Second Edition by Richardson, Chang, Smith, 2018* 44

3. Data Modeling: *Chapter 3 from Accounting Information Systems, Second Edition by Richardson, Chang, Smith, 2018* 74

4. Relational Databases and Enterprise Systems: *Chapter 4 from Accounting Information Systems, Second Edition by Richardson, Chang, Smith, 2018* 96

5. Sales and Collections Business Process: *Chapter 5 from Accounting Information Systems, Second Edition by Richardson, Chang, Smith, 2018* 132

6. Purchases and Payments Business Process: *Chapter 6 from Accounting Information Systems, Second Edition by Richardson, Chang, Smith, 2018* 164

7. Conversion Business Process: *Chapter 7 from Accounting Information Systems, Second Edition by Richardson, Chang, Smith, 2018* 190

8. Integrated Project: *Chapter 8 from Accounting Information Systems, Second Edition by Richardson, Chang, Smith, 2018* 212

A. Glossary of Models: *Chapter from Accounting Information Systems, Second Edition by Richardson, Chang, Smith, 2018* 222

B. Glossary: *Chapter from Accounting Information Systems, Second Edition by Richardson, Chang, Smith, 2018* 236

C. Index: *Chapter from Accounting Information Systems, Second Edition by Richardson, Chang, Smith, 2018* 245

About the Authors

Vernon J. Richardson   *University of Arkansas; Xi'an Jiaotong Liverpool University*
Vernon J. Richardson is Professor of Accounting and the S. Robson Walton Distinguished Chair in the Sam M. Walton College of Business at the University of Arkansas. He also serves as Accounting Department chair. He is also a research fellow at the International Business School Suzhou, Xi'an Jiaotong Liverpool University. He received his BS, MAcc, and MBA from Brigham Young University and has a PhD in accounting from the University of Illinois at Urbana-Champaign. He has taught students at the University of Arkansas, University of Illinois, Brigham Young University, Aarhus University, University of Kansas, Xi'an Jiaotong Liverpool University, and the China Europe International Business School (Shanghai).

Dr. Richardson is a member of the American Accounting Association. He has served as president of the American Accounting Association Information Systems section. He was formerly editor at the *Accounting Review* and is currently an editor at *Accounting Horizons*. He also served as associate editor at *MIS Quarterly* and the *Journal of Information Systems*. He has published articles in the *Accounting Review, Journal of Information Systems, Journal of Accounting and Economics, Contemporary Accounting Research, MIS Quarterly, Journal of Management Information Systems, Journal of Operations Management,* and *Journal of Marketing*.

C. Janie Chang   *San Diego State University*
C. Janie Chang is the Vern Odmark Professor of Accounting in the Charles W. Lamden School of Accountancy at San Diego State University (SDSU). She received her PhD from the University of California, Irvine. Before coming to SDSU, Dr. Chang served as Professor of Accounting Information Systems (AIS) at San Jose State University (SJSU). At SJSU, she established the undergraduate AIS program. She also taught students at University of California–Davis, University of California–Irvine, and California State University–San Marcos. Dr. Chang's teaching interests in AIS include information systems audit, data modeling, issues in e-business, and business networks and controls.

Dr. Chang is a member of the American Accounting Association and Information Systems Audit and Control Association (ISACA). She was formerly a co-editor at the *Review of Accounting and Finance*. Dr. Chang has studied issues in auditing, accounting, and information systems to investigate information processing of experts in addition to cross-cultural issues related to professional judgments and decisions. Her studies have been published in *Abacus, Auditing: A Journal of Practice and Theory, Behavioral Research in Accounting, Data Base, International Journal of Accounting, International Journal of Accounting Information Systems, Journal of Accounting Literature, Journal of Accounting and Public Policy,* and *Review of Accounting and Finance,* among others.

Rod Smith   *California State University, Long Beach*
Rod Smith is Professor of Accountancy at California State University, Long Beach. He received his BS in Mathematics from the University of Oregon; MS in Financial Management from the Naval Postgraduate School, Monterey, California; and PhD in Management (Accounting) from University of California–Irvine. He previously taught at the University of Arkansas, University of California–Irvine, and University of Alaska.

Dr. Smith has published research in the *Accounting Review, Journal of Information Systems, Journal of Management Accounting Research, Journal of Accounting and Public Policy,* and *International Journal of Accounting Information Systems.* He is a certified public accountant (inactive), certified management accountant, and retired captain in the U.S. Coast Guard.

His research interests include use of financial and nonfinancial measures to assess organizational performance; accounting information systems, enterprise systems, business processes, and business value; design science; and systems dynamics and business process simulation.

Preface

Whether accountants work in public accounting or in industry, they use a variety of technology tools. The International Federation of Accountants (IFAC) describes four roles for accountants with respect to information technology: **(1)** *users* **of technology and information systems, (2)** *managers* **of users of technology and related information systems, (3)** *designers* **of information systems, and (4)** *evaluators* **of information systems.** As users, managers, designers, and evaluators of technology and technology-driven business processes, accountants must understand the organization and how organizational processes generate information important to management. To ensure that processes and systems are documented—and to participate in improvements to processes and systems—accountants must be business analysts.

This textbook aims to provide students with a variety of technology and business analysis concepts and skills. It is intended for use in the first Accounting Information Systems course at both the undergraduate and graduate levels. Ongoing changes in business technology—such as the move to Internet-based systems, Big Data and data analytics, software as a service, and mobile access to enterprise information, as well as increased security and control requirements—make technological skills more important than ever for accounting graduates. This textbook also aims to show how current changes in accounting and technology affect each of these roles. For example, the Sarbanes-Oxley Act affects financial reporting system controls, and XBRL changes system requirements and affects how companies develop and report financial information. We also consider the role of Big Data and data analytics and how they are used in financial accounting, managerial accounting, and auditing. Additionally, we consider both the COBIT and COSO frameworks to describe how organizations deal with risk management. In their roles as managers, designers, and evaluators, accountants must know how those frameworks affect their accounting and related information systems.

The core competencies of the American Institute of Certified Public Accountants (AICPA) emphasize accounting skills over content. This textbook emphasizes examples, problems, and projects through which students can develop the technological skills they need for their accounting careers. It uses real-world companies such as Starbucks, Walmart, Google, and Amazon that students can relate to. It takes a broad view of accounting information systems that emphasizes the accountants' roles in the use, management, design, and evaluation of the systems and the management information that they produce. To assist accounting students in experiencing the benefit of learning information technology/information services (IT/IS) concepts and using IT/IS skills in accounting, we focus on business processes, business requirements, how information technology supports those requirements, and how accountants contribute. In particular, this textbook helps students learn to:

- **Design business processes and represent them with standard documentation tools.** The role of the accounting function has evolved from stewardship and reporting to full partnership, supporting management decisions throughout the organization. As business analysts, accountants must be able to document business processes, identify potential improvements, and design and implement new business processes. Thus, this textbook helps develop business process modeling skills.
- **Design and implement well-structured databases to enable business processes.** Accountants must also understand how business processes generate data and how such data are structured, interrelated, and stored in a database system. To ensure that business processes and the database systems are documented and to participate

in improvements to processes and systems, accountants must understand and be able to model such systems. Thus, this textbook helps develop data modeling and database implementation skills.

- **Query databases to provide insights about the performance of business operations.** Most organizational information resides in databases. To support management decisions throughout the organization, accountants must understand how those data are structured and how to retrieve information to support business management decisions. Thus, this textbook develops skills on the use of Microsoft Access and databases in general. This textbook also develops data analytics tools through the use of Microsoft Excel and Tableau.

- **Evaluate internal control systems and apply business rules to implement controls and mitigate information systems risks.** Recent federal legislation— for example, the Sarbanes-Oxley Act of 2002 and COSO and COBIT guidance— emphasizes the importance of risk mitigation in modern organizations. Internal control systems must constantly evolve to meet a changing risk environment. Accountants are often the internal control experts and must, therefore, understand how internal controls should be implemented in business processes as part of the organization's overall risk mitigation and governance framework. Thus, this textbook presents specific material on internal control and accounting information systems, as well as general information about computer fraud and security. It also describes how to monitor and audit accounting information systems.

AIS 2e Content Updates

General Updates for the 2nd Edition

- Added additional End-of-Chapter Multiple Choice Questions and Problems throughout the text.
- Significantly revised many End-of-Chapter Problems for availability and auto-grading within Connect.
- Revised and added many new Discussion Questions in most chapters.

Chapter by Chapter Updates

Specific chapter changes for *Accounting Information Systems,* 2nd Edition, are as follows:

Chapter 1

- Updated the opening vignette, highlighting the use of **Starbucks** Clover coffee machines.
- Updated real-world references.
- Edited and updated the Progress Check questions.

Chapter 2

- Increased introductory coverage of BPMN.
- Added discussion of flow object types, including gateway and event types.
- Introduced repeating activities.
- Added introduction to data objects, data stores, and associations.

Chapter 3

- Updated discussion of how the multiplicities for associations indicate where foreign keys are posted in relational tables.
- Added discussion of business rules, decision requirements, and decision tables.

Chapter 4

- Updated the section on Using Microsoft Access to Implement a Relational Database. Figures 4.6 through 4.17 were updated using Microsoft Access 2013.
- Updated Appendix A. Figures 4.A1 through 4.A9 were updated using Microsoft Access 2013.

Chapter 5

- Added additional figures related to sales activity models.
- Updated the Chapter 5 Comprehensive Exercise.

Chapter 6

- Updated the Chapter 6 Comprehensive Exercise.

Chapter 7

- Updated BPMN diagrams to include revisions to Chapter 2.

Chapter 8

- Substantially modified the chapter to describe to students how to approach an integrated project.
- Created two new integrated projects with multiple versions to accommodate various class schedules and to allow instructors to rotate projects.
- The first of the two integrated projects is a more challenging project that includes issues related to managing inventory levels and internal inventory transfers. Other topics covered include multiple sales types, including Internet, wholesale, and retail sales, where customers can pay by cash, check, or credit card.
- The second of the two integrated projects is shorter and less challenging and focuses on wholesale sales from multiple distribution centers.

Chapter 9

- This is an all-new chapter emphasizing data analytics.
- Illustrated how data analytics is used to help **Starbucks** pick its store locations.
- Inserted an all-new explanation of how data analytics is used in business and accounting.
- Added an explanation and example of how Audit Data Standards provided by the AICPA are used to facilitate data analytics between a company's financial staff and the external auditors.
- Explained how the DATA Act recently passed by Congress gives firms specific responsibilities to protect privacy and the breach of individual identifying information.
- Illustrated data analytics and data analytics techniques in both Excel and Tableau.

Chapter 10

- Updated the opening vignette, highlighting Kevin Johnson, who has substantial technology leadership as **Starbucks**'s new president and chief operating officer.
- Added an all-new example and inserted an additional figure illustrating a digital marketing dashboard.
- Updated real-world references, particularly of examples of business intelligence.
- Edited and updated Progress Check questions.

Chapter 11

- Updated COSO Internal Control Framework to COSO 2013 by updating the five components and adding the 17 relevant principles of internal controls.
- Added Figure 11.2 to summarize COSO 2013 control components and principles.

Chapter 12

- Updated the opening vignette.
- Revised the contents of computer fraud and abuse as well as vulnerability assessment and management.
- Edited and updated the Progress Check questions.

Chapter 13

- Updated the opening vignette.

Chapter 14

- Added discussion of the IT Governance Institute Val IT Framework.

Chapter 15

- Added an all-new opening vignette, highlighting Gerri Martin-Flickinger as the **Starbucks** chief technology officer.
- Edited and updated Progress Check questions.

Chapter 16

- Updated the opening vignette highlighting technology used at **Walmart**.
- Updated Figure 16.2 with recent information technology project outcomes.

Main Features

Accounting Information Systems, 2nd Edition, focuses on the accountant's role as business analyst in solving business problems by database modeling, database design, and business process modeling.

Chapter Maps

Chapter Maps provide a handy guide at the start of every chapter. These remind students what they have learned in previous chapters, what they can expect to learn in the current chapter, and how the topics will build on each other in chapters to come. This allows them to stay more focused and organized along the way.

A look at this chapter

A look back

A look ahead

Chapter-Opening Vignettes

Do your students sometimes wonder how the course connects with their future? Each chapter opens with a vignette, which sets the stage for the rest of the chapter and encourages students to think of concepts in a business context.

Chapter **Two**

Accountants as Business Analysts

A look at this chapter

As users, managers, designers, and evaluators of technology and technology-driven business processes, accountants must understand the organization and how organizational processes generate information important to management. To ensure that processes and systems are documented—and to participate in improvements to processes and systems—accountants must also be business analysts. This chapter defines business process modeling and describes how it supports the roles of accountants. It explains the potential value of business process modeling. Finally, it describes the types of business process models and introduces basic modeling tools to guide the student's development of modeling skills.

A look back

Chapter 1 discussed the importance of accounting information systems and the role accountants play in those systems. It further described how investments in information technology might improve the ability to manage business processes and create value for the firm.

A look ahead

Chapter 3 introduces data modeling. It describes how data modeling supports the design, implementation, and operation of database systems. It introduces basic modeling tools that will be used throughout the rest of the text.

© AFP/Getty Images

One recent morning, I stopped at a very busy Starbucks in San Francisco. I looked at the line coming out of the door and immediately thought that it would take at least 20 minutes to get my morning coffee. Instead, I was pleasantly surprised at the efficiency of the employees who got me through that line in less than 2 minutes.

I watched closely as the Starbucks partners behind the counter executed the workflow of the process. One partner took my order and relayed my pastry order to another partner behind the pastry case. He also relayed my coffee order to the barista at the other end of the counter. As I moved through the line to the register, my order arrived just as I did, and a fourth partner

30

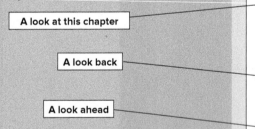

"I believe that the sequence of topics follows a logical pattern by moving from introducing the general concepts of AIS to students to internal controls and a need to automate them, to design of the DB—'backbone' of the IT system—and then to specific accounting cycles, and to general IT-related issues."

—Dmitriy Shaltayev, Christopher Newport University

"I like how it relates many of the concepts to real companies, like Starbucks."

—Linda Wallace, Virginia Tech

Chapter Outline

Each chapter opens with an Outline that provides direction to the students about the topics they can expect to learn throughout the chapter.

Learning Objectives

Learning Objectives are featured at the beginning of each chapter. The objectives provide students with an overview of the concepts they should understand after reading the chapter. These Learning Objectives are repeated in the margin of the text where they apply.

checked the order and took my payment. Within those 2 minutes, they had served at least a dozen other customers, too.

I thought about the number of options they had to deal with, the variety of hot and cold drinks, the pastries and other breakfast items, while also keeping a supply of freshly brewed coffee ready. I was sure that Starbucks had analyzed the process in detail to eliminate waste and enhance their partners' productivity. Then, they had to train all their partners in that process so they could work as one highly synchronized team. Finally, they delivered a hot cup of coffee to a grateful customer on a cool San Francisco morning.

Chapter Outline

Changing Roles of Accountants in Business
Business Process Documentation
Definitions
Purposes of Process Documentation
Value of Business Models
Types of Business Models
Activity Models
Business Process Modeling Notation
Building Blocks for BPMN Diagrams
Example of a Business Process Diagram
Identifying Participants in Business Process Diagrams
Messages in BPMN
Extended Building Blocks for BPMN Diagrams and Modeling Concepts
Subprocesses and Repeating Activities
Data Objects, Datastores, and Associations
Best Practices in Preparing BPMN Diagrams
Appendix A: Flowcharting
Appendix B: Data Flow Diagrams

Learning Objectives

After reading this chapter, you should be able to:

2-1 Describe the roles of the accounting/finance function in business and why those roles require knowledge of technology and business processes.

2-2 Understand the importance of business process documentation.

2-3 Recognize the value of business models.

2-4 Articulate the characteristics of activity models.

2-5 Understand and apply the building blocks for BPMN (activity) diagrams.

2-6 Use pools and lanes to identify process participants.

2-7 Apply message flows to show interactions between pools.

2-8 Understand and apply flow object types.

2-9 Recognize and model repeating activities.

2-10 Understand and apply data objects and datastores to model data created, updated, transferred, and deleted in a process.

31

"Well-written with great examples. Students should like reading this book."

—Marcia Watson, Mississippi State University

Integrated Project

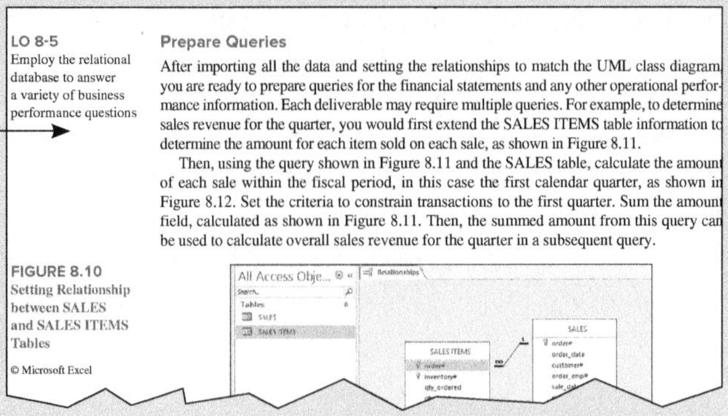

Projects can generate classroom discussion, foster good teamwork, and prepare students for their accounting careers. Chapter 8 provides guidance to students on how to approach a systems project; related material provides information and data for the projects. There are now two different projects, so instructors can select the project level of difficulty to match the time available or the sophistication of their students. Both integrated projects require students to apply the different techniques they have learned in Chapters 5, 6, and 7 to a realistic situation. One project focuses on inventory management in a small business with multiple retail stores and a central warehouse. The second project also involves a small wholesale distribution business with multiple stores but without inventory management complications. Students use Microsoft Access to implement their data models and prepare financial reports in both projects.

LO 8-5
Employ the relational database to answer a variety of business performance questions

Prepare Queries

After importing all the data and setting the relationships to match the UML class diagram, you are ready to prepare queries for the financial statements and any other operational performance information. Each deliverable may require multiple queries. For example, to determine sales revenue for the quarter, you would first extend the SALES ITEMS table information to determine the amount for each item sold on each sale, as shown in Figure 8.11.

Then, using the query shown in Figure 8.11 and the SALES table, calculate the amount of each sale within the fiscal period, in this case the first calendar quarter, as shown in Figure 8.12. Set the criteria to constrain transactions to the first quarter. Sum the amount field, calculated as shown in Figure 8.11. Then, the summed amount from this query can be used to calculate overall sales revenue for the quarter in a subsequent query.

FIGURE 8.10
Setting Relationship between SALES and SALES ITEMS Tables

© Microsoft Excel

"I like comprehensive problems that extend across multiple chapters so students can see how different components of a problem fit together."

—*Janice Benson, University of Wyoming*

Data Analytics

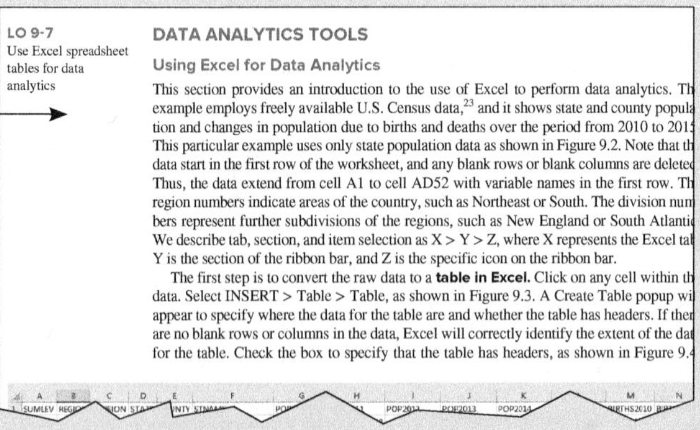

Due to its importance and popularity, we have added an all-new chapter on data analytics (Chapter 9). That chapter introduces the importance and impact of data analytics in the business world and specifically on the accounting profession. Data analytics holds great value to these businesses, whether the data reveal certain patterns in their marketing or advertising, provide insight into seasonal trends, or offer anything else that could be relevant to the businesses' success. However, the value of data analytics is really only as valuable as the insight it provides. We highlight the importance of data analytics in accounting, especially in auditing. The chapter also introduces several data analytics techniques in Excel and Tableau.

LO 9-7
Use Excel spreadsheet tables for data analytics

DATA ANALYTICS TOOLS

Using Excel for Data Analytics

This section provides an introduction to the use of Excel to perform data analytics. The example employs freely available U.S. Census data,[23] and it shows state and county population and changes in population due to births and deaths over the period from 2010 to 2015. This particular example uses only state population data as shown in Figure 9.2. Note that the data start in the first row of the worksheet, and any blank rows or blank columns are deleted. Thus, the data extend from cell A1 to cell AD52 with variable names in the first row. The region numbers indicate areas of the country, such as Northeast or South. The division numbers represent further subdivisions of the regions, such as New England or South Atlantic. We describe tab, section, and item selection as X > Y > Z, where X represents the Excel tab, Y is the section of the ribbon bar, and Z is the specific icon on the ribbon bar.

The first step is to convert the raw data to a **table in Excel.** Click on any cell within the data. Select INSERT > Table > Table, as shown in Figure 9.3. A Create Table popup will appear to specify where the data for the table are and whether the table has headers. If there are no blank rows or columns in the data, Excel will correctly identify the extent of the data for the table. Check the box to specify that the table has headers, as shown in Figure 9.4.

Progress Checks

These self-test questions and problems in the body of the chapter enable the student to determine whether he or she has understood the preceding material and to reinforce that understanding before reading further. Detailed solutions to these questions are found at the end of each chapter.

"I really like the Progress Check box. It is a great tool for students' self assessment."

—Chih-Chen Lee, Northern Illinois University

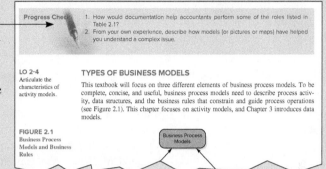

> Progress Check
> 1. How would documentation help accountants perform some of the roles listed in Table 2.1?
> 2. From your own experience, describe how models (or pictures or maps) have helped you understand a complex issue.

LO 2-4
Articulate the characteristics of activity models.

TYPES OF BUSINESS MODELS

This textbook will focus on three different elements of business process models. To be complete, concise, and useful, business process models need to describe process activity, data structures, and the business rules that constrain and guide process operations (see Figure 2.1). This chapter focuses on activity models, and Chapter 3 introduces data models.

FIGURE 2.1
Business Process Models and Business Rules

Business Process Models

Data Modeling and Microsoft Access

Chapter 3 describes how data modeling supports the design, implementation, and operation of database systems. Basic modeling tools are used throughout the rest of the text.

"This textbook would be good when using the database approach. It provides the information needed to develop and use a database without getting into the details of transaction processing (activities, documents, and internal control)."

—Janice Benson, University of Wyoming

Chapter **Three**

Data Modeling

A look at this chapter

Today's accountants must understand how business processes generate data and how those data are structured, interrelated, and stored in a database system. To ensure that business processes and the database systems are documented and to participate in improvements to processes and systems, accountants must understand and be able to model such systems. This chapter describes data modeling. It explains how data models support database-driven systems. It introduces basic data modeling tools to guide the student's development of modeling skills. Finally, it discusses business rules and how the identification of relevant business rules supports both process and data modeling.

A look back

Connect Accounting for *Accounting Information Systems*

The 2nd Edition of *Accounting Information Systems* has a full Connect package, with the following features available for instructors and students.

- **SmartBook**® is the market-leading adaptive study resource that is proven to strengthen memory recall, increase retention, and boost grades. SmartBook, which is powered by LearnSmart, is the first and only adaptive reading experience designed to change the way students read and learn. It creates a personalized reading experience by highlighting the most impactful concepts a student needs to learn at that moment in time. As a student engages with SmartBook, the reading experience continuously adapts by highlighting content based on what the student has mastered or is ready to learn. This ensures that the focus is on the content he or she needs to learn, while simultaneously promoting long-term retention of material. Both students and instructors can use SmartBook's real-time reports to quickly identify the concepts that require more attention from individual students—or the entire class. The end result? Students are more engaged with course content, can better prioritize their time, and come to class ready to participate.
- **Online Assignments.** New to Connect for *Accounting Information Systems,* 2nd Edition, is the addition of all End-of-Chapter Multiple Choice questions as assignable. Additionally, applicable End-of-Chapter Problems from each chapter have been added to Connect in an auto-gradable format. Connect helps students learn more efficiently by providing feedback and practice material when and where they need it. Connect grades homework automatically, and students benefit from the immediate feedback that they receive, particularly on any questions they may have missed.

Example of End-of-Chapter Problem

Required:
Using the Cash table below, show the output for the following SQL query: (**Using the dropdowns, identify which rows and columns would included in the SQL query output shown below. Select "Not included" for rows and columns that would not be included in the output.**)

SELECT Account#, Balance
FROM Cash
WHERE Balance < 50000;

Cash	Included			
	Account #	Type	Bank	Balance
	BA-6	Checking	Boston 5	253
	BA-7	Checking	Shawmut	48,000
	BA-8	Draft	Shawmut	75,000
	BA-9	Checking	Boston5	950

- **Comprehensive Exercises and Integrated Project.** The setup information for the Comprehensive Exercises for Chapters 5 and 6 and the Integrated Project in Chapter 8 have been added to Connect, along with the ability for students to upload their submission files for their instructors to grade. Narrated videos explaining the background, setup, and goals of the Exercises and Project have also been provided.
- **Multiple Choice Quizzes.** The Multiple Choice Quizzes from the Online Learning Center have been revised and can now be assigned to students through Connect for grading.
- **Test Bank.** The Test Bank for each chapter has been updated and significantly expanded for the 2nd Edition to stay current with new and revised chapter material, with all questions available for assignment through Connect. Instructors can also create tests and quizzes from the Test Bank through our TestGen software.
- The Instructor and Student Resources have been updated for the 2nd edition and are available in the Connect Instructor Resources page. Available resources include Instructor Resource and Solutions Manuals, Comprehensive Exercise and Integrated Project setup and solutions files, PowerPoint presentations, Test Bank files, and other ancillary materials. All applicable Student Resources will be available in a convenient file that can be distributed to students for classes either directly, through Connect, or via courseware.

Example of Test Bank Question in Connect

Which of the following is <u>not</u> a best practice in preparing Unified Modeling Language (UML) Class diagrams?

- ◯ Opt for simplicity.
- ◯ Model each process separately.
- ◯ Avoid crossing lines whenever possible.
- ◯ Avoid confusing abbreviations.

Acknowledgments

Throughout the development of this book, we were privileged to have the candid and valuable advice of our contributors, reviewers, and survey and focus group participants. These reviewers instructors provided us with priceless suggestions, feedback, and constructive criticism. The depth and sincerity of their reviews indicate that they are a devoted group of teacher-scholars. The content of the book over various versions and editions was greatly enhanced because of their efforts.

T. S. Amer
Northern Arizona University
Victoria Badura
Chadron State College
James Bay
University of Utah
Tanya Benford
Florida Gulf Coast University
Janice Benson
University of Wyoming
Jennifer Blaskovich
University of Nebraska, Omaha
A. Faye Borthick
Georgia State University
Kristine Brands
Regis University
Linda Bressler
University of Houston
Kimberly Brickler-Ulrich
Lindenwood University
Sandra Cereola
James Madison University
Siew Chan
Nova Southeastern University
Shifei Chung
Rowan University
Kim Church
Oklahoma State University
Ronald Clark
Auburn University
Curtis Clements
Abilene Christian University
Donna Free
Oakland University
Graham Gal
University of Massachusetts, Amherst
Andy Garcia
Bowling Green State University
David Gelb
Seton Hall University
Jan Gillespie
University of Texas

Terry Glandon
University of Texas, El Paso
Severin Grabski
Michigan State University
Gerry Grant
California State University, Fullerton
Rebekah Heath
St. Ambrose University
William Heninger
Brigham Young University
Kenneth Henry
Florida International University
Sarah Hill
Northcentral Technical College
Rani Hoitash
Bentley University
Diane Janvrin
Iowa State University
Nancy Jones
California State University, Chico
Grover Kearns
University of South Florida, St. Petersburg
Kevin Kobelsky
University of Michigan–Dearborn
Joseph Komar
University of St. Thomas
Don Kovacic
California State University, San Marcos
Brenda Lauer
Davenport University
Mark Lawrence
University of North Alabama
Yvette Lazdowski
Plymouth State University
Maria Leach
Auburn University
Chih-Chen Lee
Northern Illinois University
Picheng Lee
Pace University

Acknowledgments **xxi**

Adena LeJeune
Louisiana College
Chan Li
University of Pittsburg
Tina Loraas
Auburn University
Lois Mahoney
Eastern Michigan University
James Mensching
California State University, Chico
Mike Metzcar
Indiana Wesleyan University
Bonnie Morris
West Virginia University
Johnna Murray
University of Missouri, St. Louis
Bruce Neumann
University of Colorado, Denver
Oluwakemi Onwuchekwa
University of Central Florida
Debra Petrizzo
Franklin University
Theresa Phinney
Texas A&M University
Ronald Premuroso
University of Montana
Helen Pruitt
University of Maryland
Jeffrey Pullen
University of Maryland
Austin Reitenga
University of Alabama
Mohd Rujob
Eastern Connecticut State University

Juan Manuel Sanchez
Texas Tech University
Paul San Miguel
Western Michigan University
Arline Savage
Cal Poly, San Luis Obispo
Lloyd Seaton
University of Northern Colorado
Dmitriy Shaltayev
Christopher Newport University
Lewis Shaw
Suffolk University
Robert Slater
University of North Florida
Kathleen Sobieralski
University of Maryland
Eileen Taylor
North Carolina State University
Ryan Teeter
University of Pittsburgh
Barbara Uliss
Metropolitan State University of Denver
Linda Wallace
Virginia Tech
Marcia Watson
Mississippi State University
Mitchell Wenger
The University of Mississippi
Veronda Willis
The University of Texas at Tyler
Darryl Woolley
University of Idaho
Al Chen Yuang-Sung
North Carolina State University

Dedications

To Joe and Mossi White, for being wonderful second parents.

—Vern Richardson

To my students and my family who have inspired and supported me.

—Janie Chang

To my wife, Gayla.

—Rod Smith

Chapter **One**

Accounting Information Systems and Firm Value

A look at this chapter

Information plays a crucial role in today's information age. In this chapter, we discuss the importance of accounting information systems and the role accountants play in those systems. Firms invest in accounting information systems to create business value. In this chapter, we also describe investments in information systems to manage internal and external business processes and how they create value for the firm.

A look ahead

Chapter 2 examines the role of accountants as business analysts. The chapter defines business process modeling and describes how it supports the business analyst role of accountants. It explains the potential value of business process modeling and introduces basic modeling tools to guide the accountant's development of modeling skills.

© Kumar Sriskandan/Alamy

Walking in to Starbucks and ordering a latte, you notice the atmosphere and the quality and variety of its coffees and related offerings. What you may not immediately notice is the accounting information system that supports the recordkeeping, replenishment, financing, etc. To be sure, Starbucks has invested immense resources into planning, designing, and developing a number of accounting information systems to track information needed to run an effective business and to report to its shareholders and regulators (e.g., Internal Revenue Service and Securities and Exchange Commission) on its performance. This accounting information system tracks information as diverse as the number of hours worked each day by each of its 191,000 employees throughout the world to the amount of sales taxes to be paid and remitted to local and national tax authorities at its 22,000 stores in 66 countries.

In addition, through its Clover coffee machines (which track customer preferences through the cloud and also track the expiration dates of milk), Starbucks is always collecting information and making it accessible from headquarters. Many increasingly view Starbucks as a technology company. This chapter focuses on the role accounting information systems play in creating value for a firm such as Starbucks.

Source: *Forbes* Profile, 2015; *Computerworld*, 2014.

Chapter Outline

Introduction

Accountants as Business Analysts

Definition of Accounting Information
   Systems

A Simple Information System

Attributes of Useful Information

Data versus Information

*Discretionary versus Mandatory
   Information*

Role of Accountants in Accounting
   Information Systems

Specific Accounting Roles

*Certifications in Accounting Information
   Systems*

The Value Chain and Accounting
   Information Systems

AIS and Internal Business Processes

AIS and External Business Processes

The Supply Chain

Customer Relationship Management

AIS, Firm Profitability, and Stock Prices

AIS and Firm Profitability

AIS and Stock Prices

Learning Objectives

After reading this chapter, you should be
able to:

1-1   Define an accounting information
      system, and explain characteristics of
      useful information.

1-2   Distinguish among data, information,
      and an information system.

1-3   Distinguish the roles of accountants
      in providing information, and explain
      certifications related to accounting
      information systems.

1-4   Describe how business processes
      affect the firm's value chain.

1-5   Explain how AIS affects firm value.

1-6   Describe how AIS assists the firm's
      internal business processes.

1-7   Assess how AIS facilitates the firm's
      external business processes.

1-8   Assess the impact of AIS on firm
      profitability and stock prices.

INTRODUCTION

Information on business facts, numbers, and other useful indicators for business purposes is all around us. Most firms consider information to be a strategic asset and will use it to develop a competitive advantage to run their business better than their competitors. **Starbucks**, for example, uses information about its customers, suppliers, and competitors to predict how much coffee it will sell and how much coffee it will need to purchase. If the company predicts more customers than it actually has, it will have excess coffee and may incur extra carrying costs of its inventory. If Starbucks underestimates the demand for its products, the store could potentially run out of coffee and miss out on profitable sales. Information is a strategic asset if the firm knows what information it needs, develops systems to collect that information, and uses that information to make critical decisions that will affect performance.

LO 1-1

Define an accounting information system, and explain characteristics of useful information.

ACCOUNTANTS AS BUSINESS ANALYSTS

Firms have access to a tremendous amount of data—for instance, transactional data produced from point-of-sale terminals or bank deposits, consumer behavior data, operational statistics generated throughout a supply chain, and more—that can contain valuable insights to enable decision making. With such data, firms can more easily benchmark activity and compare and contrast results. In that way, firms can determine the most effective way to allocate resources such as talent, capital, and expense dollars (e.g., marketing).[1]

At the same time, however, surveys suggest that 28 percent of senior financial executives say they have little or no information to predict the performance of their firms. Another 54 percent said they had only half the information needed to provide visibility into performance.[2]

Therefore, even with information all around us, it often lacks the needed relevance, clarity, and accuracy. To be sure, as you've learned in your classes to date, accountants keep financial records, prepare financial reports, and perform audits. Because the role of the accountant is to access and attest to the quality of information, accountants may increasingly be considered to be in the best position to serve as a business analyst in looking at the organization as a whole and discussing how best to optimize the overall performance.

Specific questions accountants might be able to address include such business opportunities as whether to outsource a business function to India, promote one electronics product over another based on which will sell best or be most profitable, or structure a warehouse lease in such a way as to minimize current or future taxes.

To address such critical, but diverse, business opportunities, accountants need to decide what information is required, then build an information system to access the necessary information, and finally analyze that information to offer helpful advice to management as input for their decisions.[3]

DEFINITION OF ACCOUNTING INFORMATION SYSTEMS

Of the many information systems that might be used in a firm, one type of information system is used in every firm: an **accounting information system (AIS)**. An AIS is defined as a system that records, processes, summarizes, and reports on business transactions to provide financial and nonfinancial information to facilitate decision making. In addition, an AIS is designed to ensure appropriate levels of internal controls (security measures to

---

[1]B. McCarthy, "A Manual for the Data-Driven Finance Chief," CFO.com (November 6, 2015).

[2]J. Hagel, "Why Accountants Should Own Big Data," *Journal of Accountancy* (November 2013.)

[3]F. Borthick, "Helping Accountants Learn to Get the Information Managers Want: The Role of the Accounting Information Systems Course," *Journal of Information Systems* 10, no. 2 (1996), pp. 75–85.

protect sensitive data) for those transactions. This is the focus of this book. Some might call an AIS just a financial reporting system. Others might include in their AIS a much broader set of data that includes nonfinancial information such as sales and marketing activities or the results of research and development expenditures. Viewed broadly, an AIS collects, processes, and reports information deemed useful in decision making.

The study of AISs lies at the nexus of two traditional disciplines: information systems and accounting. In this book, we will highlight knowledge from both of these disciplines to more fully understand an AIS. While an AIS could take the form of a paper-and-pencil manual bookkeeping system, we will view an AIS in this book as computerized systems.

A Simple Information System

An AIS, just like any system, can be explained using a general systems approach (as in Figure 1.1) with input, storage, processing, and output activities. We cover these activities in subsequent chapters, but the input may come in the form of sales recorded on a **Starbucks** cash register or point-of-sale terminal. Processing those data may take the form of getting the input into storage (such as a database or a data table). Processing might involve querying that database (e.g., using SQL queries) to produce the output in the form of a report for management use. As an example, Starbucks may query its sales database to report how much coffee it sells around Christmas to see if additional sales incentives need to be made to increase sales around Christmas in the future. Whether this report has information that is ultimately useful to management is covered in the next section.

FIGURE 1.1
A Simple Information System

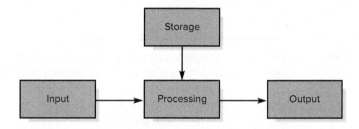

Attributes of Useful Information

To be most useful to decision makers, information from an AIS must be both relevant and reliable and have these attributes:

1. **Relevance**
   a. Predictive value (helps with forecasting the future).
   b. Feedback value (corrects or confirms what had been predicted in the past).
   c. Timeliness (available when needed or in time to have an impact on a decision).
2. **Reliability**
   a. Verifiable (can be confirmed by an independent party).
   b. Representational faithfulness (reports what actually happened).
   c. Neutrality (information is not biased).

Relevance

To be useful, information must be relevant to the decision maker. Information is relevant only if it would affect a business decision. In other words, information is relevant when it helps users predict what will happen in the future (predictive value) or evaluate how past decisions actually worked out (feedback value). It is also relevant if the information is received in time to affect their decisions (timeliness).

Reliability

Information is reliable if users can depend on it to be free from bias and error. Reliable information is verifiable by internal and external parties and faithfully represents the substance of the underlying economic transaction. If **Best Buy** sells a high-definition television for $3,200, it should be recorded and subsequently reported in its sales revenue account as $3,200. Accounting information should not be designed to lead users to accept or reject any specific decision alternative, but rather to offer reliable accounting information that is neutral, or free from bias, to let users make the best decisions.

Sometimes there are trade-offs between information that is relevant and information that is reliable. The best information may be information that only becomes reliable once an audit performed by external auditors is complete. But waiting for an audit to be completed may take so long that it is no longer relevant. The most relevant information may require an estimate of the value of a building, but that estimate might be subject to bias of the building appraiser, which will limit the information's reliability. Management often must make choices and trade off between relevance and reliability of the data.

For certain problems, the best information might include some information that tends to be more reliable (e.g., last period's sales, sales of competitors selling similar products) and other information that tends to be more relevant (estimates, appraisals, predictions gained by running regression models predicting year-ahead sales, etc.) that, in combination, complement each other and give management the necessary information.

AISs exist to provide useful information to decision makers. Considering the attributes of useful information helps AIS designers and users construct a system that delivers useful information.

LO 1-2

Distinguish among data, information, and an information system.

Data versus Information

Hal Varian, **Google**'s chief economist, explains that while data are widely available, "what is scarce is the ability to extract wisdom from them." In that short statement, we learn that data and the information actually needed to make decisions may well have different definitions. **Data** are simply raw facts that describe the characteristics of an event that, in isolation, have little meaning.

Attributes of a simple sale of a U.S. flag at a **Walmart** store in Tempe, Arizona, may include the time and date of sale, bar code number, price, and quantity purchased. However, to be most useful to Walmart, these data must be processed in a meaningful way to provide information useful to Walmart management. Thus, Walmart management would like the information to potentially address such questions as:

Useful Information or Just Data? On September 12, 2001, Walmart sold 88,000 U.S. flags, compared to only 6,400 that same day a year earlier.

- How many flags does Walmart need on hand to prepare for the July 4th holiday each year?
- What is the right price to charge for flags to maximize Walmart's profits?
- Which size of U.S. flag sells best in Tempe, Arizona; Stamford, Connecticut; or Champaign, Illinois? Does it depend on location?
- Do consumers replace flags, or do they last many years and not really need to be replaced?

Data are considered to be an input, whereas information is considered to be the output.

Information is defined as being data organized in a meaningful way to be useful to the user. Thus, data are often processed (e.g., aggregated, sorted, etc.) and then combined with the appropriate context. Decision makers typically require useful information to make decisions. As another example, while the sales prices of a particular toy might be just considered data, subtracting the cost of goods sold from the sales price to compute the net profit would be considered information if the data help a retailer decide whether to carry that particular toy in its inventory. To the extent that computers can process and organize data in a way that is helpful to the decision maker, it is possible that there may be so much information available to actually cause **information overload**, which we define as the difficulty a person faces in understanding a problem and making a decision as a consequence of too much information. Therefore, an AIS must be carefully designed to provide the information that is most useful without overwhelming the user.

The overall transformation from a business need and business event (like each individual sale of a U.S. flag) to the collection of data and information to an ultimate decision is called the **information value chain** and is reflected in Figure 1.2. If Walmart needs to know how many flags it should have at each location (i.e., business need), it will collect transactions involving flag sales (i.e., business event). Then it can take those data and turn them into useful information that might be used to make decisions on flag supply levels at each store. Certainly, the transformation from data to information is a key part of that value chain. Information that is useful (i.e., relevant or reliable) may get to the point of being knowledge and, ultimately, may be helpful in forming the basis for a decision.

FIGURE 1.2
Information Value Chain

Source: Statements on Management Accounting, Institute of Management Accountants, 2008.

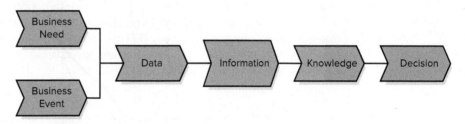

Discretionary versus Mandatory Information

Because you have already taken a few accounting classes, you understand the types of information that are recorded, processed, and subsequently reported for different purposes, including managerial, financial, or tax purposes. Managerial accounting information is generally produced for internal information purposes and would usually be considered to be **discretionary information** because there is no law requiring that it be provided to management. Management simply decides what information it needs to track and builds an information system to track it. For example, management may want an activity-based costing (ABC) system to figure out how overhead costs should be allocated at **Microsoft** to a set of products (like the Microsoft Surface Book as compared to a Microsoft XBox). The value of information equals the difference between the benefits realized from using that information and the costs of producing it. Because discretionary information is not required, management must determine if the benefits of receiving that information are greater than the costs of producing it.

In contrast, much of the financial and tax accounting information is produced for external information purposes such as for investors, banks, financial analysts, bondholders, and the Internal Revenue Service (IRS). This financial and tax accounting information would generally be considered to be **mandatory information**. As mentioned earlier, discretionary information should be produced if the value of the information it provides to management is worth more than the cost to produce it. However, mandatory information is usually produced at the lowest possible cost to comply with the laws of the regulators (e.g., Securities and Exchange Commission, IRS, state banking commission, state tax commission, etc.).

As early as 1989, **Starbucks** installed a costly computer network and hired a specialist in information technology from **McDonald's** Corporation to design a point-of-sale (cash register) system for store managers to use. Every night, stores passed their sales information to the Seattle headquarters, which allowed managers to highlight regional buying trends almost instantly.

An AIS is used to support the mandatory information required by tax returns.
© *Digital Vision/Getty Images RF*

Progress Check

1. Propose useful information that is relevant to a college basketball coach. Also propose useful information that is reliable to a college basketball coach.
2. Give an example of data versus information at a **Walmart** store.
3. Provide two types of discretionary information and two types of mandatory information that might come from an accounting information system.

LO 1-3

Distinguish the roles of accountants in providing information, and explain certifications related to accounting information systems.

ROLE OF ACCOUNTANTS IN ACCOUNTING INFORMATION SYSTEMS

In today's age, technology is a key tool in creating information systems for today's businesses. As a result, accounting and information technology are now more closely linked than ever. As information technology (IT) has gained operational and strategic importance in the business world, the role of accountants, understandably, must adjust as well. The International Federation of Accountants (IFAC) notes:

> IT has grown (and will continue to grow) in importance at such a rapid pace and with such far reaching effects that it can no longer be considered a discipline peripheral to accounting. Rather, professional accounting has merged and developed with IT to such an extent that one can hardly conceive of accounting independent from IT.[4]

Indeed, accountants have a role as business analysts and business partners; that is, they gather information to solve business problems or address business opportunities. They determine what information is relevant in solving business problems, create or extract that information, and then analyze the information to solve the problem. An AIS provides a systematic means for accountants to get needed information and solve a problem. Another illustration of the role of accountants in AIS comes from the Institute of Management Accounting. In this definition, note the role of the accountant in devising planning and performance information systems:

> Management accounting is a profession that involves partnering in management decision making, devising planning and performance management systems, and providing expertise in financial reporting and control to assist management in the formulation and implementation of a firm's strategy.[5]

Specific Accounting Roles

Understanding the design, use, and management of information technology is of vital importance to not only management accountants, but to all of those within the accounting profession. To recognize the needed competencies for accountants with respect to

---

[4]Source: "Information Technology Competencies in the Accounting Profession: AICPA Implementation Strategies for IFAC International Education Guideline No. 11," American Institute of Certified Public Accountants, 1996.

[5]Source: Institute of Management Accountants, *Statements on Management Accounting,* 2008.

information technology, it is important to recognize the potential role of accountants in accounting information systems, including the following:

1. The accountant as *user* of accounting information systems—whether it be inputting journal entries into an accounting system, using a financial spreadsheet to calculate the cost of a product, or using anti-virus software to protect the system, accountants use an AIS.

    - As an example, accountants serving in an audit role should be able to understand how to access their client's AIS and how to use at least one major computer-assisted auditing package (such as Audit Control Language, or ACL), an online or local database system, or a professional research tool.

2. The accountant as *manager* of accounting information systems (e.g., financial manager, controller, CFO).

    - Accountants serving as managers of AISs must be able to plan and coordinate accounting information systems and be able to organize and staff, direct and lead, and monitor and control those information systems.

3. The accountant as *designer* of accounting information systems (e.g., business system design team, producer of financial information, **systems analyst**).

    - Accountants serving in a design capacity must have significant practical exposure as they work to develop a system that will meet the needs of users. Specifically, they need to work with key phases of system analysis and design, such as the preparation of a feasibility analysis; information requirements elicitation and documentation techniques; data file design and documentation techniques; and document, screen, and report design techniques. In particular, accountants must understand business processes and the information requirements of other systems.

4. The accountant as *evaluator* of accounting information systems (e.g., IT auditor, assessor of internal controls, tax advisor, general auditor, consultant)

    - As will be discussed in Chapter 11, the **Sarbanes-Oxley Act of 2002 (SOX)** requires an evaluation of the internal controls in an AIS. As part of that act, and as part of a standard audit, accountants must be able to tailor standard evaluation approaches to an AIS and offer practical recommendations for improvement where appropriate. In addition, the accountant must be able to apply relevant IT tools and techniques to effectively evaluate the system.

In considering the information technology competencies in the accounting profession, the American Institute of Certified Public Accountants (AICPA) and International Federation of Accountants (IFAC) assume that, at a minimum, all accountants will be proficient in the AIS user role and at least one of the other listed roles (e.g., manager, designer, or evaluator). Accountants will be better users, managers, and evaluators of AISs if they understand the design of the system. Thus, throughout the text we touch on all of the roles that accountants have in the firms, but we particularly emphasize skills relevant to the designer role.

Certifications in Accounting Information Systems

In addition to the various roles that accountants play, accountants and related professionals may also seek various certifications to show they are proficient in specific areas of AISs. This will show their competence to specific employers or clients that need some specific services. There are three primary certifications that most directly apply to accounting and information systems (see Figure 1.3).

FIGURE 1.3
Certifications in
Accounting
Information Systems

Name	Certifying Body	Who They Are and What They Do	How to Qualify
Certified Information Systems Auditor (CISA)	Information Systems Audit and Control Association (ISACA) www.isaca.org	The CISA designation identifies those professionals possessing IT audit, control, and security skills. Generally, CISAs will perform IT audits to evaluate the accounting information system's internal control design and effectiveness.	To qualify as a CISA, a candidate must take an examination and obtain specialized work experience.
Certified Information Technology Professional (CITP)	American Institute of Certified Public Accountants (AICPA) www.aicpa.org	The CITP designation identifies accountants (CPAs) with a broad range of technology knowledge and experience. The CITP designation demonstrates the accountant's ability to leverage technology to effectively and efficiently manage information while ensuring the data's reliability, security, accessibility, and relevance. CITPs may help devise a more efficient financial reporting system, help the accounting function go paperless, or consult on how an IT function may transform the business.	A CPA can earn a CITP designation with a combination of business experience, lifelong learning, and an optional exam.
Certified Internal Auditor (CIA)	Institute of Internal Auditors (IIA) http://www.theiia.org/	The CIA designation is the only globally accepted certification for internal auditors and is the standard to demonstrate their competency and professionalism in the internal auditing field.	An individual can earn a CIA designation by having the required education, professional experience, and character references; the individual must also pass the CIA examination.

Progress Check

4. Would an IT auditor be considered to be a user, manager, evaluator, or designer of a client firm's accounting information system?
5. What would be the appropriate designation for someone who wants to be an IT auditor?
6. Let's suppose that **ConocoPhillips** is hiring accountants for an entry-level financial accounting position. Is it reasonable to expect accountants to be proficient in information technology?

LO 1-4
Describe how business processes affect the firm's value chain.

THE VALUE CHAIN AND ACCOUNTING INFORMATION SYSTEMS

Information technology (IT) is increasingly omnipresent! Worldwide spending on IT is expected to exceed \$3.54 trillion in 2016.[6] Clearly, information technology is a huge investment that firms make, and they expect to create value through its use. How IT assists firms to carry out their internal and external business processes and, in turn, creates value is an important topic of this chapter.

A firm makes money by taking the inputs (e.g., raw materials, talented workers, buildings, equipment, etc.) and producing a more valuable output (e.g., iPhones available for

---

[6]"Worldwide IT Spending to Rise 0.6% to \$3.54 Trillion in 2016: Gartner," *The Economic Times,* January 19, 2016.

sale, completed audit report, etc.). Take a university as an example. Universities admit students to the university (as inputs) and use their resources (curriculum, faculty, buildings, computers, etc.) to create a job-ready, educated graduate (the output). Arguably, the university creates value. If it is not creating value in one form or the other, it probably will not continue to survive.

Let's continue the discussion by defining **business value** as all those items, events, and interactions that determine the financial health and/or well-being of the firm. This value may come from suppliers, customers, or employees or even from information systems. Business value does not necessarily need to be determined by stock price or net income. A not-for-profit group like the **International Red Cross** may define business value as how many lives are saved, the amount of blood donated or the number of children that are immunized.

To consider how value is created, we begin by looking at the business processes. A business process is a coordinated, standardized set of activities conducted by both people and equipment to accomplish a specific task, such as invoicing a customer. To evaluate the effectiveness of each of its business processes, a firm can use Michael Porter's value chain analysis. A **value chain** is a chain of business processes for a firm. Products pass through all activities of the chain in order; at each activity, the product is expected to gain some value. It is important not to confuse the concept of the value chain with the actual cost of performing those activities. One way of looking at this is by considering a rough diamond. Although the cutting activity of a diamond may have a very low cost, this cutting activity adds much of the value to the end product because a cut diamond is much more valuable than a rough diamond. And a diamond cut well adds more value than a diamond cut poorly.

The value chain illustrated in Figure 1.4 shows both primary activities and support activities. Primary activities directly provide value to the customer and include the following five activities:

1. **Inbound logistics** are the activities associated with receiving and storing raw materials and other partially completed materials and distributing those materials to manufacturing when and where they are needed.
2. **Operations** are the activities that transform inputs into finished goods and services (e.g., turning wood into furniture for a furniture manufacturer; building a house for a home builder).
3. **Outbound logistics** are the activities that warehouse and distribute the finished goods to the customers.
4. **Marketing and sales activities** identify the needs and wants of customers to help attract them to the firm's products and, thus, buy them.
5. **Service activities** provide the support of customers after the products and services are sold to them (e.g., warranty repairs, parts, instruction manuals, etc.).

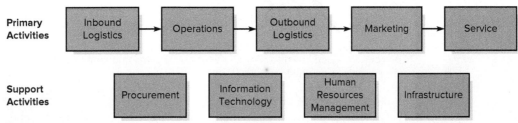

FIGURE 1.4
The Value Chain

These five primary activities are sustained by the following support activities:

1. **Firm infrastructure** activities are all of the activities needed to support the firm, including the CEO and the finance, accounting, and legal departments.
2. **Human resource management** activities include recruiting, hiring, training, and compensating employees.
3. **Technology** activities include all of the technologies necessary to support value-creating activities. These technologies also include research and development to develop new products or determine ways to produce products at a cheaper price.
4. **Procurement** activities involve purchasing inputs such as raw materials, supplies, and equipment.

LO 1-5

Explain how AIS affects firm value.

An AIS can add value to the firm by making each primary activity more effective and efficient. For example, AISs can assist with inbound and outbound logistics. This is done by finding efficiencies and cost savings in logistics (transportation and warehousing costs, etc.) in AISs and geographic information systems to help identify the lowest cost of getting items from one location to another. AISs can make marketing, sales, and service activities more valuable by summarizing data about key customers to help manage and nurture a firm's interactions with its clients.

As an example, **Amazon.com** is one of the best at fostering its interaction with its customers by keeping a record of their past purchases and product searches and using that information to recommend other similar products for its customers to consider (see highlighted circle in Figure 1.5 for an example). As another example, as the loan officers at a bank learn more about the financial products currently being used by its bank's customers through its AIS, they will be able to help identify additional bank products (e.g., insurance, CDs, mutual funds, etc.) to sell to their clients.

As detailed here, AIS can add value to the firm by making each support activity more effective and efficient. An AIS:

- Helps with the firm infrastructure by giving management information relevant to the decision makers.
- May also help provide the internal control structure needed to make sure the information is secure, reliable, and free from error (as discussed in Chapter 11).
- Helps produce external and internal financial reports efficiently and helps decision makers get timely access to the processed information. This may give the information to the decision maker in time to influence the decision.
- Supports the human resources function by assisting employees, who are arguably the most valuable asset of the firm. This assistance includes easy access to payroll information, compensation policies, benefits, tax benefits, and so on.
- Assists procurement by improving the effectiveness and efficiency of the supply chain. This helps ensure that the right product is at the right location at the right time, including receipts of raw material from suppliers to delivery of finished goods to the customers.

Progress Check

7. Consider the value chain for **Ford**. In your opinion, which primary activity is the most critical to creating value for the firm?
8. How does an AIS help **Wayfair** (a popular online furniture and furnishings store) find the right marketing strategy?
9. An AIS adds value to the supporting activities by making access to financial results available on a more timely basis. Why does this matter?

FIGURE 1.5
Amazon.com:
"Inspired by Your
Shopping Trends"

Source: Amazon.com

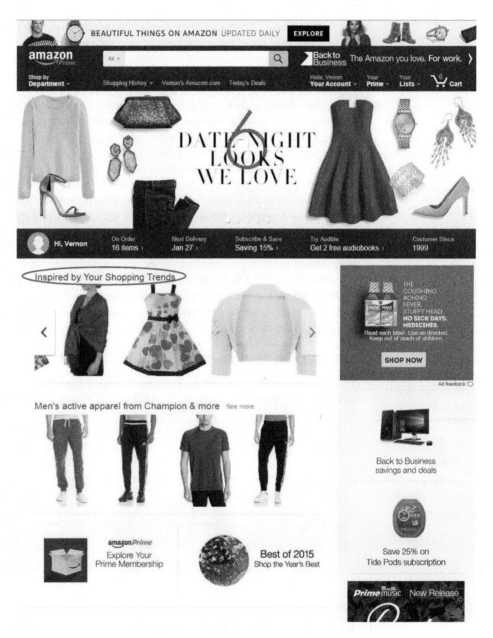

LO 1-6
Describe how AIS
assists the firm's
internal business
processes.

AIS AND INTERNAL BUSINESS PROCESSES

Our discussion now turns to how an AIS can assist the firm with its internal business processes. An AIS within a firm is usually the foundation for an **enterprise system (ES)**—also called an enterprise resource planning (ERP) system. An enterprise system is a centralized database that collects data from throughout the firm. This includes data from orders, customers, sales, inventory, and employees. These data are then accumulated in the centralized database and made available to all enterprise system users, including accounting, manufacturing (or operations), marketing, and human resources. As the data are integrated into one single, centralized database to become useful information, authorized employees throughout the firm (from the CEO all the way to the lowest-paid line worker) have access to the information they need to make a decision. For most firms, the informational benefits of these integrated data include enhanced completeness, transparency, and timeliness of information needed to effectively manage a firm's business activities.

As an example, an enterprise system can automate a business process such as order fulfillment. The enterprise system can take an order from a customer, fill that order, ship it, and then create an invoice to bill the customer. As an example, when a customer service representative receives a customer order into an enterprise system, she has all the information needed to approve and complete the order (e.g., the customer's credit rating and order history from the finance module of the centralized database, the firm's inventory levels to see if the product is available from the warehouse module of the centralized database, and the shipping dock's trucking schedule from the logistics module of the centralized database). Once the order is complete, the enterprise system routes the order to the warehouse and shipping department for order fulfillment and shipping and then to the finance department to make sure the customer is invoiced. During the process, all workers in the various departments can see the same information and update it as needed. As problems arise (e.g., backordered products, returned products, trucker strike, etc.), the enterprise system gives all within the firm the most current information to address these issues.

The enterprise system serves as the backbone of the firm's internal business processes and serves as a connection to the external business processes with external partners as discussed in the next section.

AIS AND EXTERNAL BUSINESS PROCESSES

LO 1-7
Assess how AIS facilitates the firm's external business processes.

Firms do not work in isolation. They are always connected to both their suppliers and customers and their wants and needs. As shown in Figure 1.6, the AIS assists in business integration with external parties such as suppliers and customers. The firm's interaction with the suppliers is generally called *supply chain management,* and the interaction with its customers is generally called *customer relationship management.*

FIGURE 1.6
AIS and External
Business Processes

The Supply Chain

Supply chain refers to the flow of materials, information, payments, and services from raw materials suppliers, through factories and warehouses, all the way to the final customers of the firm's products. A supply chain also includes the firms and processes that create and deliver products, information, and services to the final customers. The supply chain refers to a network of processes that delivers a finished good or service to the final customer. Figure 1.7 reflects the sourcing, manufacturing (making), and delivering to the customer for each member of the supply chain (assuming the **Unilever** product is made in China, sold to **Sam's Club** and convenience stores, and ultimately sold to an end customer). Handling the returns from the firm's customers and to the firm's suppliers also represents a significant process that requires substantial planning.

To make the supply chain function efficiently, supply chain tasks include processes such as purchasing, payment flow, materials handling, production planning and control, logistics and warehousing, inventory control, returns, and distribution and delivery.

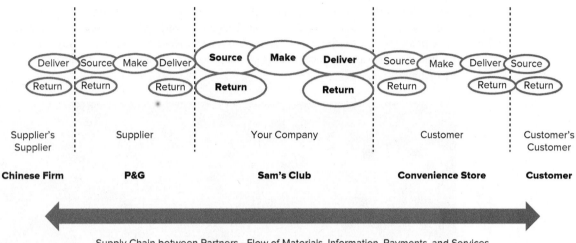

Supply Chain between Partners—Flow of Materials, Information, Payments, and Services

FIGURE 1.7
The Supply Chain

As an illustration, Michael Dell of **Dell Computer** explained one aspect of Dell's use of supply chain management software with suppliers as follows:

> We tell our suppliers exactly what our daily production requirements are so it is not, "Well, every two weeks deliver 5,000 to this warehouse, and we'll put them on the shelf, and then we'll take them off the shelf." It is, "Tomorrow morning we need 8,562, and deliver them to door number seven by 7 am."[7]

The software used to connect the focal firm with its suppliers is generally referred to as **supply chain management (SCM) software**. This software addresses specific segments of the supply chain, especially in manufacturing scheduling, inventory control, and transportation. This SCM software is designed to facilitate decision making and optimize the required levels of inventory to be ordered and held in stock. In the preceding example, Dell might produce expected demand for its products for the next year. As the dates get closer, the estimate is refined so the supplier has a better idea of what exactly will be needed. It is expected that this use of SCM software will optimize inventory and, in turn, will reduce the required amount of raw materials and finished goods inventory the firm will have to hold and thus lower product costs.

A recent study[8] found that firms implementing SCM software are able to reduce the amount of raw materials inventory on hand and reduce selling, general, and administrative expenses. They are also able to increase their gross margins and overall inventory turnover. This suggests that supply chain management systems allow inventory to be optimized to lower the amount of required inventory on hand while not decreasing sales.

Walmart has long been regarded as having one of the best supply chain systems in the world. One aspect of Walmart's supply chain management software is simply communicating the results of its retail sales to its top suppliers. Walmart's Retail Link database is

---

[7]Source: A. A. Thompson, A. J. Strickland and J. Thompson, *Strategic Management: Concepts and Cases,* 11th ed. (New York: McGraw-Hill, 2006).
[8]B. Dehning, V. J. Richardson, and R. W. Zmud, "The Financial Performance Effects of IT-Based Supply Chain Management Systems in Manufacturing Firms," *Journal of Operations Management* 25 (June 2007), pp. 806–24.

one of the world's largest databases and allows many of its suppliers to view real-time sales data of its products for each store. This allows suppliers to assess the demand for their products and to optimize their own level of inventory and related logistics costs. In turn, the cost savings generated from this process are passed on to Walmart itself and its customers.

Walmart uses its supply chain expertise to lower prices and fulfill its motto to "Save Money, Live Better."
© Justin Sullivan/Getty Images

Connection with Practice

One way of measuring the effectiveness of a supply chain is to calculate the fill rate. The fill rate is a calculation of the service level between two parties—generally, a supplier and a customer. The fill rate is a measure of shipping performance usually expressed as a percentage of the total order. The fill rate is often calculated as the value of order lines shipped on the initial order divided by the total value of the order. If the fill rate increases over time, this means the overall service level is improving. Supply chain management software would be expected to improve the fill rate and, in turn, the overall service levels.

Customer Relationship Management

The more a company can learn about its customers, the more likely it will be able to satisfy their needs. **Customer relationship management (CRM) software** is a term that describes the software used to manage and nurture a firm's interactions with its current and potential clients. CRM software often includes the use of database marketing tools to learn more about customers and to develop strong firm-to-customer relationships. CRM software also includes using IT to manage sales and marketing for current sales and customer service and technical support after the sale is done.

As mentioned in the opening vignette of this chapter, a good example of the need for CRM is **Starbucks**. After its quick expansion in the early 2000s, Starbucks felt like it had lost some of the original Starbucks customer coffeehouse experience. This caused a desire within Starbucks to make sure it understood its customers and their coffeehouse needs. Therefore, a recent initiative at Starbucks was implemented to learn more about its customers. The new chief information officer, Stephen Gillett, argues that his most crucial duty is to enhance Starbucks' ability to mine its customer data to help "reignite our passion with our customers." Starbucks uses loyalty cards (Starbucks' Reward cards) and surveys to track its customers' purchases and build profiles of its customers.[9]

As another example, **Royal Bank** (formerly Royal Bank of Canada) considers CRM software to be such an important part of its strategy that the stated objective of the bank is "to capture the full potential of our customer base through the use of customer information to deliver the right solutions in a consistent, professional manner at every point of contact."[10]

Connection with Practice

Salesforce.com is a popular vendor of CRM software. Note the explanation of CRM on the home page of its website:

Build more meaningful and lasting relationships with your customers—better understand their wants and needs, identify new opportunities to help, and address any problems faster with an overview of every customer interaction.

Source: Accessed January 26, 2016, www.salesforce.com/what-is-salesforce/?d=70130000000mA5n&internal=true

Progress Check

10. Give an example of how supply chain management software might work for **General Motors**. What type of information does General Motors need to share with its suppliers?
11. Using CRM techniques, what information could universities gather about their current and prospective customers, the students? What information might be most useful to them in recruiting future students?

LO 1-8
Assess the impact of AIS on firm profitability and stock prices.

AIS, FIRM PROFITABILITY, AND STOCK PRICES

Throughout this chapter, we have tried to make the case that AIS facilitates value-creating activities. This section presents a direct test of whether an investment in AIS, in fact, creates value by considering whether an AIS investment led to more profits or higher market value.

AIS and Firm Profitability

One way to consider how AIS creates value is to look at an income statement. Accountants understand that to make more profits, a firm either needs to increase revenues or decrease expenses (or both!). Figure 1.8 illustrates how AIS affects the income statement, making the case for how an AIS may increase profitability.

In an academic study,[11] a positive association was found between the level of the firm's annual IT investment and its subsequent accounting earnings (as measured by return on

[9]T. Wallgum, "Starbucks' Next-Generation CIO: Young, Fast and in Control," *CIO Magazine*, January 2009, www.cio.com/article/474127/Starbucks_Next_Generation_CIO_Young_Fast_and_In_Control?page=3&taxonomyId=3123.
[10]"CRM Case Study: The Analytics That Power CRM at Royal Bank (of Canada)," www.mindbranch.com.
[11]K. Kobelsky, V. J. Richardson, R. Smith, and R. W. Zmud, "Determinants and Consequences of Firm Information Technology Budgets," *The Accounting Review* 83 (July 2008), pp. 957–96.

assets and return on sales), suggesting that IT investment does create value. In a completely different study,[12] researchers found both an improvement in profitability as well as stock returns around the implementation of supply chain information systems.

FIGURE 1.8
The Potential Effect of AIS on an Income Statement

Income Statement	Effect of AIS on Income Statement
Revenues	Customer relationship management (CRM) techniques could attract new customers, generating additional sales revenue.
Less: Cost of Goods Sold	Supply chain management (SCM) software allows firms to carry the right inventory and have it in the right place at the right time. This, in turn, will lower obsolescence as well as logistics and procurement costs.
Gross Margin	The gross margin will change as the result of changes in revenues or cost of goods sold due to the effects of AIS.
Less: Selling, General, and Administrative Expenses (SG&A)	An efficient enterprise system can significantly lower the cost of support processes included in sales, general, and administrative expenses.
Less: Interest Expense	SCM software allows the firm to carry less inventory. Less inventory leaves less assets to finance and may possibly reduce debt and its related interest.
Net Income	All combined, a well-designed and well-functioning AIS with investments in enterprise systems, SCM, and/or CRM may be expected to improve net income.

AIS and Stock Prices

Every time a firm makes an investment, it expects a return of its original investment as well as a return on that investment. This is the case for AIS investments as well. When an investment is announced by a public firm, stock market participants assess whether the investment will pay off or not, either by enhancing revenues or reducing expenses or some combination of both. If the stock market participants believe the future cash flows from the investment will increase for the firm, the stock price of that firm is expected to increase. If the stock market participants believe the future cash flows from the investment will decrease for that firm, the stock price is expected to fall.

An academic study[13] divided up announcements of 315 firms making new AIS investments. The study broke these announcements into three groups, depending on what strategic role the technology was expected to fill within the firm. If AIS investments simply replace human labor to automate business processes, they are defined as automate AIS investments. The automate process will typically digitize (i.e., put in a digital form) the business processes. Once digitized, this information can be automatically and easily summarized in a usable form (i.e., reports, etc.) for management use (defined as the IT strategic role of informate-up) or in a usable form to employees across the firm (defined as IT strategic role of informate-down). IT can also change the basis of competition and redefine business and industry processes (defined as the IT strategic role of transform). As an example, **FedEx**, which allows its customers to track their own packages on the web, changed the basis of competition for the express transportation industry by fundamentally redefining business processes and relationships.

[12]K. B. Hendricks, V. R. Singhal, and J. K. Stratman, "The Impact of Enterprise Systems on Corporate Performance: A Study of ERP, SCM and CRM System Implementations," *Journal of Operations Management* 25, no. 1 (January 2007), pp. 65–82.

[13]B. Dehning, V. J. Richardson, and R. W. Zmud, "The Value Relevance of Announcements of Transformational Information Technology Investments," *MIS Quarterly* 27, no. 4 (2003), pp. 637–56.

Using strategic role as a way to group the IT investments, the lowest strategic role for technology is to automate manual processes. The highest strategic role for technology is transform, with informate-up and informate-down having a medium strategic role. Here is a summary of these strategic roles:

- **Automate**—replace human labor in automating business processes.
- **Informate-up**—provide information about business activities to senior management.
- **Informate-down**—provide information about business activities to employees across the firm.
- **Transform**—fundamentally redefine business processes and relationships.

Figure 1.9 shows how the stock market responded (adjusted for level of risk and overall market returns) on the day the AIS investment was announced. This analysis assumes there were no other significant news events at the firm on the same day as the AIS investment announcement. On average, the 172 "automate" AIS investments increased firm market value by 0.05 percent and the 95 "informate" AIS investments increased firm market value by 0.40 percent. On average, the "transform" AIS investments increased firm market value by 1.51 percent. The authors found that those 48 AIS investments that transformed the business processes and changed the way business is done had the greatest impact on firm value. Automate and informate investments do have an impact, but they are substantially smaller than the value-enhancing impact of transform investments.

FIGURE 1.9
Stock Market
Reaction to AIS
Investments

Stock Market Increase around AIS Investment Announcements

AIS Investment Strategic Role

Automate	Informate*	Transform
0.05%	0.40%	1.51%

*Informate-up and Informate-down are consolidated in a single strategic role: Informate.

Progress Check

12. How does the use of supply chain management software reduce the cost of goods sold for a retailer like **Target**?
13. Many hospitals and doctor's offices are beginning to digitize the medical records of their patients. Would this be an example of an automate, informate, or transform IT strategic role?

Summary

Information plays a crucial role in the information age.

- Accountants play a critical role in recording, processing, and reporting financial information for decision making and control. An accounting information system (AIS) is defined as an information system that records, processes, and reports on transactions to provide financial information for decision making and control.
- The accounting profession (including the IFAC and the AICPA) recommends that accountants develop proficiency in at least two areas of information systems: as a user and as a manager, designer, or evaluator of information systems. Accountants often seek certification in information systems to show their level of proficiency to both prospective employers and clients.
- Firms invest in accounting information systems to create value. The value chain illustrates how, during each primary activity, the product should gain some value. An AIS serves an important role in providing value in each primary and supporting activity.

- An AIS creates value by managing internal and external business processes. Enterprise systems, sometimes called ERP or back-office systems, generally manage transactions within the firm. Supply chain management software is used to manage transactions and communications with suppliers. Customer relationship management software is used to manage and nurture the relationship with current and potential customers.
- An AIS generally helps make business processes more efficient and effective. A well-designed and well-functioning AIS can be expected to create value by increasing revenues and reducing expenses.

Key Words

accounting information system (AIS) (4)   A system that records, processes, and reports on transactions to provide financial and nonfinancial information to make decisions and have appropriate levels of internal controls for those transactions.

automate (19)   The use of technology to replace human labor in automating business processes.

business value (11)   Items, events, and interactions that determine the financial health and well-being of the firm.

Certified Information Systems Auditor (CISA) (10)   The CISA designation identifies those professionals possessing IT audit, control, and security skills. Generally, CISAs will perform IT audits to evaluate the accounting information system's internal control design and effectiveness.

Certified Information Technology Professional (CITP) (10)   The CITP designation identifies accountants (CPAs) with a broad range of technology knowledge and experience.

Certified Internal Auditor (CIA) (10)   The CIA designation is the certification for internal auditors and is the standard to demonstrate competency and professionalism in the internal auditing field.

customer relationship management (CRM) software (16)   Software used to manage and nurture a firm's interactions with its current and potential clients. CRM software often includes the use of database marketing tools to learn more about the customers and to develop strong firm-to-customer relationships.

data (6)   Raw facts or statistics that, absent a context, may have little meaning.

discretionary information (7)   Information that is generated according to one's own judgment.

enterprise system (ES) (13)   A centralized database that collects data from throughout the firm. Commercialized information system that integrates and automates business processes across a firm's value chain located within and across organizations.

firm infrastructure (12)   Activities needed to support the firm, including the CEO and the finance, accounting, and legal departments.

human resource management (12)   Activities include recruiting, hiring, training, and compensating employees.

inbound logistics (11)   Activities associated with receiving and storing raw materials and other partially completed materials and distributing those materials to manufacturing when and where they are needed.

informate-down (19)   The use of computer technology to provide information about business activities to employees across the firm.

informate-up (19)   The use of computer technology to provide information about business activities to senior management.

information (6)   Data organized in a meaningful way to the user.

information overload (6)   The difficulty a person faces in understanding a problem and making a decision as a consequence of too much information.

information value chain (7)   The overall transformation from a business need and business event to the collection of data and information to an ultimate decision.

mandatory information (7)   Information that is required to be generated or provided by law or regulation.

marketing and sales activities (*11*)   Activities that identify the needs and wants of their customers to help attract them to the firm's products and buy them.

operations (*11*)   Activities that transform inputs into finished goods and services.

outbound logistics (*11*)   Activities that warehouse and distribute the finished goods to the customers.

procurement (*12*)   Activities that involve purchasing inputs such as raw materials, supplies, and equipment.

relevance (*5*)   Information that is capable of making a difference in a decision.

reliability (*5*)   Information that is free from bias and error.

Sarbanes-Oxley Act of 2002 (SOX) (*9*)   A federal law in the United States that set new and enhanced standards for all U.S. public companies, management, and public accounting firms; a response to business scandals such as Enron, WorldCom, and Tyco International. It requires public companies registered with the SEC and their auditors to annually assess and report on the design and effectiveness of internal control over financial reporting.

service activities (*11*)   Activities that provide the support of customers after the products and services are sold to them (e.g., warranty repairs, parts, instruction manuals, etc.).

supply chain (*14*)   The flow of materials, information, payments, and services from raw materials suppliers, through factories and warehouses, all the way to the final customers of the firm's products.

supply chain management (SCM) software (*15*)   Software that connects the focal firm with its suppliers. It generally addresses segments of the supply chain, including manufacturing, inventory control, and transportation.

systems analyst (*9*)   Person responsible for both determining the information needs of the business and designing a system to meet those needs.

technology (*12*)   Supports value-creating activities in the value chain. These technologies also include research and development to develop new products or determine ways to produce products at a cheaper price.

transform (*19*)   The use of computer technology to fundamentally redefine business processes and relationships.

value chain (*11*)   A chain of critical business processes at a company that creates value.

Answers to Progress Checks

1. Useful relevant information may include the number of times an opposing player goes to his left, makes a spin move, or shoots a three pointer instead of passing the ball. Receiving this relevant information in a timely manner may help the team prepare for its upcoming basketball games. An example of useful reliable information might include the information collected and verified by an independent official keeping the score and statistics of a basketball game. This information might include the score of the game, the shooting percentages, the numbers of blocks and steals by each team and player, the type of defense they used, whether players shoot with the left or right hand, the number of assists and turnovers, etc. Having an unbiased source of information allows the coach to use the information received without having to worry about whether the information is biased.

2. Data at **Walmart** might be any random factoid without context. An example might be that one store in the United States had sales of $1.2 million yesterday. It is only when put in context that the data become useful. If we know that the store is in Lawrence, Kansas, and that on the same date, a year earlier, the store had sales of $0.8 million, the data become information.

3. Two types of discretionary information include the cost of manufacturing each **Apple** iPad or the type of pastry that sells best with hot chocolate at **Starbucks**. Two types of mandatory information might be the amount of sales taxes collected and remitted to the state tax collector or the number of common shares of stock outstanding reported to the Securities and Exchange Commission.

4. Generally, an IT auditor would be considered to be an evaluator of a client firm's accounting information system. In general, an IT auditor will assess the accounting information system to ensure the audit risk (the risk of reaching an incorrect conclusion based on the audit findings) will be limited to an acceptable level.

5. The Certified Information Systems Auditor (CISA) designation would be the most appropriate credential for an IT auditor. In some cases, the Certified Information Technology Professional (CITP) designation would also be an appropriate credential.

6. Most, if not all, entry-level financial accounting positions would expect some reasonable level of proficiency as a user of accounting information systems, such as the ability to use a basic accounting/bookkeeping package (e.g., QuickBooks, Peachtree, Microsoft Excel, Microsoft Windows, etc.) However, the International Federation of Accountants suggests accountants have proficiency not only as a user but also as an evaluator, manager, or designer of an accounting information system. Some of that desirable proficiency will be gained in this textbook, so read carefully!

7. Clearly, all portions of the value chain have to be working well for **Ford** to be successful and create value for the firm and its shareholders. A case could be made for any and all of the primary activities. I will argue that marketing and sales are the most important because, to be successful, companies need to completely understand and then meet their customers' needs.

8. **Wayfair** is a popular online site for furniture and home furnishings. An AIS may help Wayfair find the right marketing strategy by figuring out where to advertise Wayfair's product offerings (e.g., banner ads, referral pages, Facebook ads, e-mails, etc.) to its customers. AIS may also help Wayfair figure out which products sell best and which products have the biggest profit margins to know which products to push.

9. An AIS can add value to the firm by providing financial results in time to make a difference to the decision maker. As an example, if the firm finds out quickly that one of its products is too expensive to manufacture, the firm may choose to discontinue the product or choose a cheaper way to manufacture it. If that financial information is not received until weeks or months later, then the firm will have lost profits.

10. Let's suppose that **General Motors** will decide how many Chevrolet Corvettes to produce at each plant. Once General Motors knows how many it will likely produce, the supply chain management software can immediately compute the specific parts needed and share this information with its suppliers. The suppliers can then plan and begin production of the parts they provide. For example, if General Motors plans to produce 50,000 Corvettes at its Kansas City assembly plant, the tire suppliers can plan on producing and delivering 200,000 tires to meet those needs.

11. Universities are increasingly using CRM techniques to catalog information about their students from overall trends about the new millennials (who prefer more choices, experiential learning, flexibility, etc.) to archiving individual inquiries (i.e., e-mail, Snapchat, Instagram, Facebook, Twitter, etc.) by each prospective student. Students generally don't like to be treated as one among the masses, so any information that might target a specific student need or interest would be particularly useful to recruiters.

12. Supply chain software can help reduce procurement, logistics, and inventory-carrying costs for **Target**. If the whole supply chain has a better idea of the final customer's demand of the product, it will reduce the need to carry more inventory than is needed or to miss customer sales by not having enough product on hand. This, in turn, will reduce procurement, logistics, and inventory-carrying costs.

13. Digitizing medical records is an example of the automate IT strategic role.

![Mc Graw Hill Education] **connect**

Multiple Choice Questions

1. Accounting information systems: **LO 1-1**
   a. are always computerized.
   b. report only financial information.
   c. are an information system that records, processes, and reports on transactions to provide financial and nonfinancial information for decision making and control.
   d. require a CITP designation to understand.

2. Which of the following is *not* a characteristic of useful information? **LO 1-1**
   a. Predictive value
   b. Timeliness
   c. Verifiable
   d. Expensive to generate

3. Which of the following is considered to be mandatory information required by a regulatory body? **LO 1-2**
   a. U.S. tax return
   b. The cost to produce a textbook
   c. The number of U.S. flags that are sold on July 4
   d. The cost to build an all-new Starbucks restaurant in Shanghai, China

4. The correct order of effects in the value chain is: **LO 1-4**
   a. Inbound logistics → Operations → Service.
   b. Inbound logistics → Outbound logistics → Marketing and Sales.
   c. Inbound logistics → Operations → Outbound logistics.
   d. Inbound logistics → Operations → Marketing and Sales.

5. What designation would be most appropriate for those professionals possessing IT audit, control, and security skills? **LO 1-3**
   a. Certified Internal Auditor (CIA)
   b. Certified Public Accountant (CPA)
   c. Certified Information Technology Professional (CITP)
   d. Certified Information Systems Auditor (CISA)

6. A supply chain: **LO 1-7**
   a. supplies bicycle chains.
   b. refers to the flow of materials, information, payments, and services.
   c. is similar in function and purpose to the value chain.
   d. does not apply to a service firm like an accounting firm.

7. Customer relationship management software does *not* include information about: **LO 1-7**
   a. current customers.
   b. prospective customers.
   c. former customers.
   d. current suppliers.

8. IT strategic roles of AIS investments are classified as: **LO 1-8**
   a. automate, informate, transform.
   b. value creation, value destruction, value neutral.
   c. digitize, report, transform.
   d. automate, digitize, transport.

9. According to a recent study, the IT strategic role that has the greatest impact on shareholder value is: LO 1-8

    a. informate.

    b. digitize.

    c. automate.

    d. transform.

10. The income statement account most likely affected by an AIS investment in supply chain management software would be: LO 1-8

    a. revenues.

    b. cost of goods sold.

    c. selling, general, and administrative expenses.

    d. unearned revenue.

11. The balance sheet account most likely to be affected by supply chain management software would be: LO 1-7

    a. Owner's Equity.

    b. Inventory.

    c. Short-term Marketable Securities.

    d. Property, Plant, and Equipment.

12. Customer relationship management software would be most likely to affect which income statement account? LO 1-7

    a. Selling, General, and Administrative Expenses

    b. Interest Expense

    c. Revenues

    d. Cost of Goods Sold

13. Enterprise systems would generally be considered to be an: LO 1-6, LO 1-7

    a. internal business process.

    b. external business process.

    c. interior business process.

    d. exterior business process.

14. A systems analyst would generally be considered to fill which role with respect to accounting information systems? LO 1-3

    a. User

    b. Manager

    c. Designer

    d. Evaluator

15. Which of these represents the proper transformation from data to decision according to the information value chain? LO 1-2

    a. Data → Information → Knowledge → Decision

    b. Data → Knowledge → Information → Decision

    c. Data → Business Event → Information → Decision

    d. Data → Analysis → Information → Decision

Discussion Questions

1. Brainstorm a list of discretionary information that might be an output of an accounting information system and be needed by **Starbucks**. Prioritize which items might be most important, and provide support. **LO 1-2**

2. Explain the information value chain. How do business events turn into data, then into information, and then into knowledge? Give an example starting with the business event of the purchase of a CD at **Best Buy** all the way to useful information for the CEO and other decision makers. **LO 1-2**

3. Give three examples of types of discretionary information at your college or university, and explain how the benefits of receiving that information outweigh the costs. **LO 1-2**

4. After an NBA basketball game, a box score is produced detailing the number of points scored, assists made, and rebounds retrieved (among other statistics). Using the characteristics of useful information discussed at the beginning of the chapter, please explain how this box score meets (or does not meet) the characteristics of useful information. **LO 1-2**

5. Some would argue that the role of accounting is simply as an information provider. Will a computer ultimately completely take over the job of the accountant? As part of your explanation, explain how the role of accountants in information systems continues to evolve. **LO 1-3**

6. How do you become a Certified Information Technology Professional (CITP)? What do they do on a daily basis? **LO 1-3**

7. Explain the value chain for an appliance manufacturer, particularly the primary activities. Which activities are most crucial for value creation (in other words, which activities would you want to make sure are the most effective)? Rank the five value chain–enhancing activities in importance for an appliance manufacturer. **LO 1-4**

8. Which value chain–supporting activities would be most important to support a health insurance provider's primary activities? How about the most important primary activities for a university? **LO 1-4**

9. List and explain three ways that an AIS can add value to the firm. **LO 1-5**

10. Where does new-product development fit in the value chain for a pharmaceutical company? Where does new-product development for a car manufacturer fit in the value chain? **LO 1-4**

11. An enterprise system is a centralized database that collects and distributes information throughout the firm. What type of financial information would be useful for both the marketing and manufacturing operations? **LO 1-6**

12. Customer relationship management software is used to manage and nurture a firm's interactions with its current and potential clients. What information would **Boeing** want about its current and potential airplane customers? Why is this so critical? **LO 1-7**

Problems

⊠connect   1. An article suggests:

> A monumental change is emerging in accounting: the movement away from the decades-old method of periodic financial statement reporting and its lengthy closing process, and toward issuing financial statements on a real-time, updated basis . . . real-time financial reporting provides financial information on a daily basis. Current technology allows for financial events to be identified, measured, recorded, and reported electronically, with no paper documentation.[14]

Indeed, many corporations are pressing their finance and accounting departments for more timely financial information and ad hoc analysis. Would a shift toward real-time financial statements make the financial information more useful or less useful? More or less relevant? More or less reliable? **LO 1-1**

[14] "Real-Time Accounting," *The CPA Journal,* April 2005.

2. Consider the following bar chart of how accounting professionals' activities have changed over time. Comment on how information technology affects the role of accountants. In what respect is this a positive trend or a negative trend? What will this bar chart look like in 2020? LO 1-3

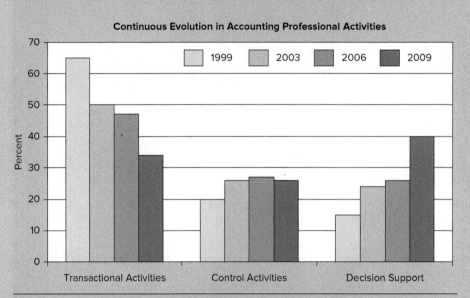

Continuous Evolution in Accounting Professional Activities

Source: *The Agile CFO: A Study of 900 CFOs Worldwide,* IBM, 2006.

connect 3. Match the value chain activity in the left column with the scenario in the right column: LO 1-4

1.	Service activities	A.	Surveys for prospective customers
2.	Inbound logistics	B.	Warranty work
3.	Marketing and sales activities	C.	Assembly line
4.	Firm infrastructure	D.	Delivery to the firm's customer
5.	Human resource management	E.	New-product development
6.	Technology	F.	Receiving dock for raw materials
7.	Procurement	G.	CEO and CFO
8.	Outbound logistics	H.	Buying (sourcing) raw materials
9.	Operations	I.	Worker recruitment

connect 4. Match the value chain activity in the left column with the scenario in the right column. LO 1-4

1.	Customer call center	A.	Operations
2.	Supply schedules	B.	Inbound logistics
3.	Order taking	C.	Procurement
4.	Accounting department	D.	Firm infrastructure
5.	Staff training	E.	Human resource management
6.	Research and development	F.	Technology
7.	Verifying quality of raw materials	G.	Service activities
8.	Distribution center	H.	Outbound logistics
9.	Manufacturing	I.	Marketing and sales activities

5. **John Deere**'s $4 billion commercial and consumer equipment division implemented supply chain management software and reduced its inventory by $500 million. As sales continued to grow, the company has been able to keep its inventory growth flat. How did the supply chain management software implementation allow John Deere to reduce inventory on hand? How did this allow the company to save money? Which income statement accounts (e.g., revenue, cost of goods sold, SG&A expenses, interest expense, etc.) would this affect? **LO 1-7**

6. **Dell Computer** used customer relationship management software called IdeaStorm to collect customer feedback. This customer feedback led the company to build select consumer notebooks and desktops pre-installed with the Linux platform. Dell also decided to continue offering Windows 10 as a pre-installed operating system option in response to customer requests. Where does this fit in the value chain? How will this help Dell create value? **LO 1-7**

connect 7. **Ingersoll Rand** operates as a manufacturer in four segments: Air Conditioning Systems and Services, Climate Control Technologies, Industrial Technologies, and Security Technologies. It installed an Oracle enterprise system, a supply chain system, and a customer relationship management system. The company boasts the following results.[15]

   - Decreased direct product costs by 11 percent.
   - Increased labor productivity by 16 percent.
   - Increased inventory turns by four times.
   - Decreased order processing time by 90 percent and decreased implementation time by 40 percent.
   - Ensured minimal business disruption.
   - Streamlined three customer centers to one.

   Take each of these results and explain how the three systems (enterprise system, supply chain system, and customer relationship management system) affected these financial results and created value for the firm. **LO 1-8**

connect 8. Using the accompanying explanations of each IT strategic role, suggest the appropriate IT strategic role (automate, informate, or transform) for the following types of IT investments. Depending on your interpretation, it is possible that some of the IT investments could include two IT strategic roles. **LO 1-8**

   a. Digital health records

   b. Google Maps that recommend hotels and restaurants along a trip path

   c. Customer relationship management software

   d. Supply chain management software

   e. Enterprise systems

   f. Airline flight reservations systems

   g. PayPal (www.paypal.com)

   h. Amazon.com product recommendation on your homepage

   i. eBay

   j. Course and teacher evaluations conducted online for the first time (instead of on paper)

   k. Payroll produced by computer

[15]Source: http://www.ediguys.net/pages/SCIS/ingersoll-rand-siebel-casestudy.pdf

IT Strategic Roles[16]

Automate IT Strategic Role

- Replace human labor by automating business processes.
- Virtually no IT-driven transformation efforts.
- IT providing enhancements to existing processes or practices.

Informate-Up/-Down IT Strategic Role

- Provide new data/information to empower management, employees, or customers.
- An intermediate level of IT-driven transformation efforts.
- Gain clearer picture of cause-and-effect relationships, greater understanding of operating environment.

Transform IT Strategic Role

- Fundamentally alter traditional ways of doing business by redefining business capabilities and/or (internal or external) business processes and relationships.
- Strategic acquisition to acquire new capabilities or to enter a new marketplace.
- Use of IT to dramatically change how tasks are carried out recognized as being important in enabling firm to operate in different markets, serve different customers, and gain considerable competitive advantage by doing things differently.

connect

9. Information systems have impact on financial results. Using Figure 1-8 as a guide, which system is most likely to impact the following line items on an income statement. The systems to consider are enterprise systems, supply chain systems, and customer relationship management systems. **LO 1-8**

Income Statement Item	System
Revenues	
Cost of goods sold	
Sales, general, and administrative expenses	
Interest expense	
Net Income	

connect

10. Accountants have four potential roles in accounting information systems: user, manager, designer, and evaluator. Match the specific accounting role to the activity performed. **LO 1-8**

1. Controller meeting with the systems analyst to ensure accounting information system is able to accurately capture information to meet regulatory requirements
2. Cost accountant gathering data for factory overhead allocations from the accounting information system
3. IT auditor testing the system to assess the internal controls of the accounting information system
4. CFO plans staffing to effectively direct and lead accounting information system

[16]B. Dehning, V. J. Richardson, and R. W. Zmud, "The Value Relevance of Announcements of Transformational Information Technology Investments," *MIS Quarterly* 27, no. 4 (2003), pp. 637–56.

connect 11. In 2013, Frey and Osborne[17] wrote a compelling article suggesting that up to 47 percent of total US employment is at risk due to computerization. The chart below suggests the probability that each occupation will lead to job losses in the next 20 years. **LO 1-8**

Selected Occupation	Probability of Job Loss
Tax preparers	0.99
Accountants and auditors	0.94
Retail salespersons	0.92
Sheet metal workers	0.82
Economists	0.43
Plumbers	0.35
Commercial drivers	0.18
Police	0.10
Chemical engineers	0.02
Preschool teachers	0.007
Physician and surgeon	0.004

1. Given these predictions, which jobs are most likely to be replaced by computerization? Those that primarily have tasks that automate, informate, or transform?

2. Noticing the high probability of predicted job loss in the accounting and auditing area, are those job losses expected to be due to automate, informate, or transform?

3. As accountants become business partners in giving critical information to management for decision making, are those tasks automate, informate, or transform?

4. Is the use of data analytics by accountants an example of automate, informate, or transform?

[17]C. B. Frey and M. A. Osborne, "The Future of Employment: How Susceptible Are Jobs to Computerisation?" (Oxford Martin School, University of Oxford, September 17, 2013), www.oxfordmartin.ox.ac.uk/downloads/academic/The_Future_of_Employment.pdf.

Chapter **Two**

Accountants as Business Analysts

A look at this chapter

As users, managers, designers, and evaluators of technology and technology-driven business processes, accountants must understand the organization and how organizational processes generate information important to management. To ensure that processes and systems are documented—and to participate in improvements to processes and systems—accountants must also be business analysts. This chapter defines business process modeling and describes how it supports the roles of accountants. It explains the potential value of business process modeling. Finally, it describes the types of business process models and introduces basic modeling tools to guide the student's development of modeling skills.

A look back

Chapter 1 discussed the importance of accounting information systems and the role accountants play in those systems. It further described how investments in information technology might improve the ability to manage business processes and create value for the firm.

A look ahead

Chapter 3 introduces data modeling. It describes how data modeling supports the design, implementation, and operation of database systems. It introduces basic modeling tools that will be used throughout the rest of the text.

© AFP/Getty Images

One recent morning, I stopped at a very busy **Starbucks** in San Francisco. I looked at the line coming out of the door and immediately thought that it would take at least 20 minutes to get my morning coffee. Instead, I was pleasantly surprised at the efficiency of the employees who got me through that line in less than 2 minutes.

I watched closely as the Starbucks partners behind the counter executed the workflow of the process. One partner took my order and relayed my pastry order to another partner behind the pastry case. He also relayed my coffee order to the barista at the other end of the counter. As I moved through the line to the register, my order arrived just as I did, and a fourth partner checked the order and took my payment. Within those 2 minutes, they had served at least a dozen other customers, too.

I thought about the number of options they had to deal with, the variety of hot and cold drinks, the pastries and other breakfast items, while also keeping a supply of freshly brewed coffee ready. I was sure that Starbucks had analyzed the process in detail to eliminate waste and enhance their partners' productivity. Then, they had to train all their partners in that process so they could work as one highly synchronized team. Finally, they delivered a hot cup of coffee to a grateful customer on a cool San Francisco morning.

Chapter Outline

Changing Roles of Accountants in Business

Business Process Documentation

Definitions

Purposes of Process Documentation

Value of Business Models

Types of Business Models

Activity Models

Business Process Modeling Notation

Building Blocks for BPMN Diagrams

Example of a Business Process Diagram

Identifying Participants in Business Process Diagrams

Messages in BPMN

Extended Building Blocks for BPMN Diagrams and Modeling Concepts

Subprocesses and Repeating Activities

Data Objects, Datastores, and Associations

Best Practices in Preparing BPMN Diagrams

Appendix A: Flowcharting

Appendix B: Data Flow Diagrams

Learning Objectives

After reading this chapter, you should be able to:

2-1   Describe the roles of the accounting/finance function in business and why those roles require knowledge of technology and business processes.

2-2   Understand the importance of business process documentation.

2-3   Recognize the value of business models.

2-4   Articulate the characteristics of activity models.

2-5   Understand and apply the building blocks for BPMN (activity) diagrams.

2-6   Use pools and lanes to identify process participants.

2-7   Apply message flows to show interactions between pools.

2-8   Understand and apply flow object types.

2-9   Recognize and model repeating activities.

2-10 Understand and apply data objects and datastores to model data created, updated, transferred, and deleted in a process.

32   Chapter 2   *Accountants as Business Analysts*

LO 2-1
Describe the roles of
the accounting/finance
function in business
and why those roles
require knowledge
of technology and
business processes.

CHANGING ROLES OF ACCOUNTANTS IN BUSINESS

Over the past 15 years, a number of studies have highlighted the changing role of the accountant in business. Rapid changes in the global marketplace substantially affect the accounting profession. In the past, accountants typically focused on stewardship and reporting functions; they kept financial records, prepared financial reports, and performed audits. Now, they face the challenge of helping the enterprise to optimize its processes (financial, administrative, and operational) to achieve the competitive performance levels and maximize shareholder value.

Rapid changes in technology such as business intelligence (BI) and enterprise resource planning (ERP) systems have increased the availability of data throughout the organization. However, technology alone will not ensure good decision making. To be fully effective, the information produced by the technology must support the information requirements of the business's decision makers. Consequently, accountants are involved in supporting evidence-based decision making throughout the business. Although they continue to face the challenge of conducting their core transaction processing and reporting more efficiently, accountants must also act as business partners involved in a host of business management activities— including strategic planning, process improvement, and compliance management—to produce better management information for both internal and external stakeholders. Table 2.1 summarizes the traditional stewardship and reporting and accounting management roles, as well as the increasingly important business management support roles.

To perform all the roles described in Table 2.1 and be valuable business partners, accountants must first understand the business, as well as the various ways that the business

TABLE 2.1
Roles of the
Accounting/Finance
Function in Business

Stewardship and Reporting	Accounting/Finance Operations	Business Management Support
Regulatory compliance	Finance and accounting processes (procure to pay, order to cash, record to report, payroll and treasury)	Management information
Tax returns	Financial close—completing period-end accounts	Planning, budgeting, and forecasting
Stakeholder assurance	Financial consolidation, reporting, and analysis	Performance measurement, reporting, and analysis
Investor relations	Providing comprehensive management information	Performance management
Raising capital and loans	People management	Risk management—from strategic to operational, including fraud risk
Board reports	Using IT to make finance and accounting processes more efficient and effective	Investment appraisal
Statutory reporting		Cost management
		Supply chain management
		Value-based management
		Project management
		Change management
		Capital structure and dividend policy
		Strategic planning
		Professional expertise (e.g., merger and acquisition or tax)

Source: Based on *Improving Decision Making in Organisations: The Opportunity to Transform Finance* (London: CIMA, 2007), Figure 3.

collects data and summarizes and communicates business information. They must understand how the business delivers value to its customers, interacts with other businesses, and meets requirements for good corporate citizenship. They must also understand the risks that the business faces and the internal controls in place to mitigate those risks. Finally, they must understand how accounting information systems collect, summarize, and report business process information. This highlights the need for good documentation of business processes and business systems. To ensure that processes and systems are documented—and to participate in improvements to business processes and systems—accountants must also be business analysts.

BUSINESS PROCESS DOCUMENTATION

LO 2-2
Understand the importance of business process documentation.

Definitions

Before we describe how business analysis and business process modeling can support accountants' roles, we first present some definitions.

- **Business process**: A defined sequence of business activities that use resources to transform specific inputs into specific outputs to achieve a business goal. A business process is constrained by business rules.
- **Business analysis**: The process of defining business process requirements and evaluating potential improvements. Business analysis involves ascertaining, documenting, and communicating information about current and future business processes using business process modeling and related tools.
- **Business model**: A simple, abstract representation of one or more business processes.[1] A business model is typically a graphical depiction of the essential business process information.
- **Documentation**: Explains how business processes and business systems work. Documentation is "a tool for information transmission and communication. The type and extent of documentation will depend on the nature of the organization's products and processes."[2]

Purposes of Documentation

Documentation includes business process models, business rules, user manuals, training manuals, product specifications, software manuals, schedules, organization charts, strategic plans, and similar materials that describe the operation, constraints on, and objectives of business processes and systems. Although documentation has always been important for accounting information systems, the Sarbanes-Oxley Act of 2002 made documentation essential for businesses. That act requires managers to assess and attest to the business's internal control structure and procedures. The U.S. Securities and Exchange Commission (SEC) rules require "management to annually evaluate whether ICFR (internal control of financial reporting) is effective at providing reasonable assurance and to disclose its assessment to investors. Management is responsible for maintaining evidential matter, including documentation, to provide reasonable support for its assessment. This evidence will also allow a third party, such as the company's external auditor, to consider the work performed by management."[3] The act also requires external auditors to audit management's assessment of the effectiveness of internal controls and express an opinion on the

---

[1]In other contexts, the term "business model" is often used to describe the plan by which a company generates revenue.

[2]ISO 9001: 2008, International Standards Organization.

[3]SEC Interpretive Guidance 33-8810, issued June 27, 2007.

Documentation supports audits of business processes.

© Keith Brofsky/Getty Images

company's internal control over financial reporting.[4] Thus, documentation is necessary for internal audit to support management's assertions as well as external auditors to evaluate management's assertions on internal control over financial reporting.

In addition to Sarbanes-Oxley compliance requirements, documentation is important for the following reasons:

- *Training.* User guides, employee manuals, and operating instructions help employees learn how business processes and systems operate.
- *Describing current processes and systems.* Documentation provides an official description of how business processes and systems, including AIS, work. Thus, documentation supports internal and external audit requirements; establishes accountability; and standardizes communications within the business and between the business and its customers, suppliers, and other stakeholders.
- *Auditing.* Documentation provides audit trails, which can assist auditors in determining the effectiveness of internal controls.
- *Accountability.* Documentation includes checklists, delegations of authority, and similar assignments of responsibility. Thus, documentation would specify who is authorized to approve orders or sign checks, for example.
- *Standardized interactions.* Documentation clearly describes the inputs and outputs of business processes and systems and thus provides a common language for all parties that interact with the process or system.
- *Facilitating process improvement.* Because it describes the way processes currently work, documentation is also the basis for determining what should be changed. Well-managed businesses regularly review all processes with a view to continuous improvement in four major areas:

1. Effectiveness: Are the outputs of the process obtained as expected?
2. Efficiency: Can the same outputs be produced with fewer inputs and resources?
3. Internal control: Are the internal controls working?
4. Compliance to various statutes and policies: Does the process comply with constantly changing local, state, federal, and international laws and regulations?

LO 2-3
Recognize the value of business models.

Value of Business Models

Imagine a map of a city like Los Angeles, California, or even a small city like Fayetteville, Arkansas. How many words would it take to provide the same information as the map? Undoubtedly, the graphical representation (map) presents the information more concisely and perhaps more clearly than a written description. Business processes and systems can also be difficult to describe concisely using words alone. Thus, business models allow us to depict the important features of business processes and systems clearly and concisely.

Organizational change—including mergers, acquisitions, outsourcing, offshoring, product innovation, and continuous process improvement—and other business transformations are common. Change, however, can be expensive and risky. Careful planning is necessary to implement change in a way that minimizes those costs and risks. This is where business models create value. Business models provide communication, training,

[4]See Public Company Accounting Oversight Board (PCAOB) Auditing Standard No. 5, *An Audit of Internal Control over Financial Reporting That Is Integrated with an Audit of Financial Statements.*

analysis, and persuasion tools that are particularly suited for planning business transformations. Business models allow managers to assess what needs to be changed and plan how to make the change. In particular, business models create value in the following ways.

- *Managing complexity.* Models are simpler than the processes and systems they depict, but they incorporate the essential elements.
- *Eliciting requirements.* Models offer a communications tool that can be used to interview involved parties and discuss the impact of possible changes.
- *Reconciling viewpoints.* Models can combine various local views into one integrated view. Some models can be used to simulate potential outcomes from a change to better assess the impact of the change.
- *Specifying requirements.* Models can be the basis for documentation of the changed process or system. Additionally, some models can be used to generate working software directly.
- *Managing compliance.* Models can be used to identify legal and regulatory requirements and how those requirements affect business processes. When new laws are passed, the models quickly show where changes must be made to comply.
- *Supporting training.* Models can support training of employees on how to implement new business processes.
- *Managing and reusing knowledge.* Models support knowledge management, the practice of systematically capturing individuals' knowledge and making it available where needed throughout the organization. Business models can convert tacit knowledge, found only in people's heads, to explicit knowledge that can be taught to others.

Progress Check

1. How would documentation help accountants perform some of the roles listed in Table 2.1?
2. From your own experience, describe how models (or pictures or maps) have helped you understand a complex issue.

LO 2-4
Articulate the characteristics of activity models.

TYPES OF BUSINESS MODELS

This textbook will focus on three different elements of business process models. To be complete, concise, and useful, business process models need to describe process activity, data structures, and the business rules that constrain and guide process operations (see Figure 2.1). This chapter focuses on activity models, and Chapter 3 introduces data models.

FIGURE 2.1
Business Process Models and Business Rules

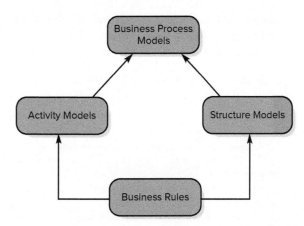

ACTIVITY MODELS

Activity models describe the sequence of workflow in a business process or processes. While the purpose of structure models is to create a blueprint for the development of a relational database to support the collection, aggregation, and communication of process information, the purpose of activity models is to represent the sequential flow and control logic of a set of related activities. They are tools for planning, documenting, discussing, and implementing systems; however, they also facilitate the use of those systems once implemented. Furthermore, they are important tools for analyzing and improving business processes.

Activity models, such as flowcharts, have been used to analyze business processes and design changes since well before 1920.[5] As technology changed, designers developed a variety of activity models, such as data flow diagrams, business process maps, and IDEF0 functional modeling method,[6] to document and analyze business process workflow.

Regardless of the specific modeling notation, workflow models must be able to describe:

1. Events that start, change, or stop flow in the process.
2. Activities and tasks within the process.
3. The sequence of flow between tasks.
4. Decision points that affect the flow.
5. Division of activity depending on organizational roles.

LO 2-5

Understand and apply the building blocks for BPMN (activity) diagrams.

Business Process Modeling Notation

For this textbook, we employ **business process modeling notation (BPMN)** for activity models, although the concepts discussed also apply to other modeling notation, such as UML activity diagrams and data flow diagrams.[7] The Object Management Group (OMG) also maintains the specifications for BPMN. The original specification for BPMN was issued in 2004. Since then, BPMN has been widely adopted because it was specifically designed for process modeling in a way that can be understood by businesspeople rather than software engineers (in contrast with UML activity diagrams). Additionally, there are free or inexpensive software products that support modeling and subsequent simulation of the process. The International Standards Organization (ISO) has adopted a specification for BPMN identical to OMG BPMN 2.0.1.

Good BPMN models have the following important characteristics:

1. They are correct. They do not violate BPMN standards.
2. They are clear. They describe the logic of a business process unambiguously, although they may not present the details of how individual tasks are performed.
3. They are complete. They show how the process starts, all the significant ends, and all important communications with relevant external parties.
4. They are consistent. Given the same facts about the process logic, all modelers should create similar models of the process.

Basic Building Blocks for BPMN Diagrams

Events include start, intermediate, and end events. Basic events are modeled as small circles, as shown in Figure 2.2. Start events have a single thin line circle. End events have

---

[5]D. J. Couger, "Evolution of Business System Analysis Techniques," *Computing Surveys* 5, no. 3 (1973), pp. 167–98. The article describes the use of flowcharts for industrial engineering by Frederick W. Taylor and others prior to 1920.

[6]See Federal Information Processing Standards Publication 183, www.idef.com.

[7]Data flow diagrams encompass elements of both activity and structure models, but they are primarily used to depict the sequence of data flows related to activities in a business process.

a single thick line circle. Intermediate events have a double thin line circle. Intermediate events affect the flow of a process, but do not start or end the process. Icons placed in events are used to further define event categories, such as message, timer, or error events.

Activities represent specific steps in the business process. Basic activities are modeled as rounded rectangles, as shown in Figure 2.2. Each activity is described with a short verb phrase placed within the rectangle (e.g., process credit card payment or bill customer). An activity can depict a single action or some logical combination of actions depending on the required level of detail to achieve the objectives of the business process analysis.

Sequence flows are represented by arrows to indicate the progression of activity within the process, as shown in Figure 2.2. The diagram should show the sequence of activity from left to right and top to bottom.

Gateways show process branching and merging as the result of decisions. Basic gateways are depicted as diamonds. Usually, gateways appear as pairs on the diagram. The first gateway shows the branching, and the second gateway shows merging of the process branches.

Annotations allow the modeler to add additional descriptive information to the model. Annotations are modeled with text inside a bracket connected to other model symbols with a dashed line.

FIGURE 2.2
Basic Elements of Business Process Diagrams

Element	Description	Symbol
Events	Events are things that happen; they affect the flow of the business process when they occur. For example, a start event begins a process, an intermediate event may change the flow, and an end event signals the end of the process.	start intermediate end
Activities	Activities are where the work takes place; they can represent processes, subprocesses, or tasks depending on the diagram's level of detail.	Activity
Sequence Flows	An arrow shows the normal sequence flow—i.e., the order of activities—in a business process diagram.	Sequence Flow ⟶
Gateways	Gateways control the branching and merging of flow paths in the business process.	Gateway
Annotations	Text annotations allow the analyst to add descriptive information to the diagram.	text annotation

Example of a Business Process Diagram

Figure 2.3 illustrates a simple business process activity diagram showing the checkout process at a retail store. In this process, the customer presents items for checkout. The clerk scans items and identifies payment method. Then, the process branches depending on the nature of payment. The payment is accepted, and the process branches merge.

The clerk bags the items for the customer, and the process ends. Note that the start event can be labeled to explain the start event, and the gateway branches can be labeled to show the purpose of the branches (handling cash or credit payment in this case).

FIGURE 2.3
Sample Business Process Diagram

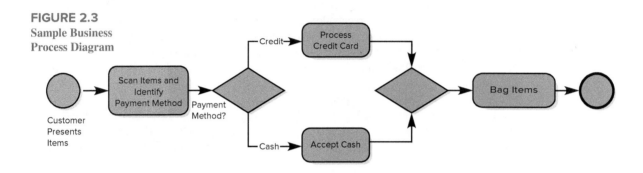

Figure 2.3 also demonstrates some other features of BPMN models. First, the models are usually presented left to right or top to bottom. All processes start with a start event and end with an end event, although there may be more than one end event. The flow of the process is shown by the sequence flow arrows. The sequence flows following the branching gateway are labeled to describe the circumstances under which the process would follow that specific flow. Each step in the process, each task, is named to describe the nature of the task. Tasks are named with a verb and an object, such as *bag items* and *accept cash*. The branching gateway represents an important question that affects the subsequent flow; in this case, the gateway questions the payment method. However, the gateway is not a decision. The information to answer the question is determined in the task labeled "Scan Items and Identify Payment Method." The second gateway shows that the two paths merge and the flow then continues. In this model, the second, merging, gateway is optional. Later, you will see models where the merging gateway is not optional.

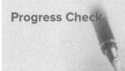

Progress Check   3. Draw a business process model (using BPMN) of a drive-through window at a fast-food restaurant. What starts the process? What ends the process? What are the important steps? Are there any decision points that would require gateways?

LO 2-6
Use pools and lanes to identify process participants.

Identifying Participants in Business Process Diagrams

It is often important to identify who performs which activity in a business process. A participant is an actor or person that performs activities and interacts with other participants in a process. Participants include people, systems, organizations, and machines. Participants can also be identified by the role of the actor in the process. BPMN provides notation to identify both the organizations and the departments or individual actors participating in a process. The organization is identified by a **pool** and the department is identified by **lanes** within the pool, as shown in Figure 2.4. Every diagram contains at least one pool, but if there is only one pool, the pool may be presented without a boundary. Activities can be assigned to only one participant, and thus may appear in only one pool or lanes.

Let's examine Figure 2.4 more closely. You should note that regardless of the number of lanes in the pool, there is still one start event per pool and at least one end event.

FIGURE 2.4
Pools and lanes to
Identify Participants

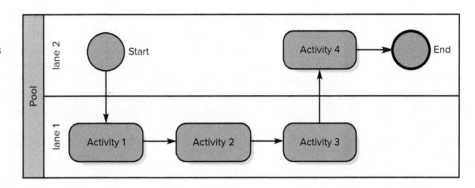

Each task is located in only one lane. Tasks may not span lanes. In other words, one task cannot be performed by two departments. The sequence must flow continuously from the start event to each end event, but the sequence flows can cross lane boundaries. Sequence flows, however, do not extend beyond one pool.

LO 2-7

Apply message flows
to show interactions
between pools.

Messages in BPMN

BPMN represents exchanges between two participants (pools) in the same process as message flows. For example, in a sales process with a customer pool and a store pool, the customer order would be represented as a message flow. The activities within a pool are organized by sequence flow, but the interactions between pools are represented as **message flows.** A message flow is shown as a dashed arrow with a small circle at the starting end, as shown in Figure 2.5.

FIGURE 2.5
Message Flow
Symbol

Figure 2.6 provides a simple example of message flows between two pools. One pool represents a patient and the other pool represents the doctor's office. The patient becomes ill and calls the doctor's office for an appointment. The doctor's office receives the request and assigns the appointment. Each pool has a start event and in the case one event. The sequence flows are continuous from the start events to the end events and do not cross pool

FIGURE 2.6
Message Flow
Example

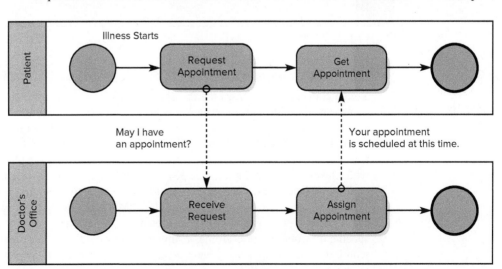

boundaries. The message flows are between pools and not within pools. While the nature of each message flow is pretty clear in this model, it is good practice to label the message flows. As models become more refined, it is sometimes necessary to define the specific content of each message flow to aid the implementation of the process.

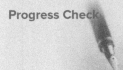

Progress Check

4. Using Figure 2.6 as a guide, draw a simple model of a customer interacting with **Amazon.com**'s website to purchase an item. Assume the customer is an Amazon Prime™ member and can buy an item with 1-click (i.e., Amazon already has the credit card information). Use two pools and the associated message flows.

Usually, modelers are not very interested in activities in the external pool. So, if we are modeling the doctor's office process in Figure 2.6, we might not care about the activities in the patient's pool. Yet, we remain concerned about the message flows between the pools. So, we can make the patient's pool opaque, hiding the activities, but still showing the message flows. Figure 2.7 shows the opaque patient's pool. Note that the message flows now attach to the edge of the patient's pool.

FIGURE 2.7
Message Flow to Edge of Pool

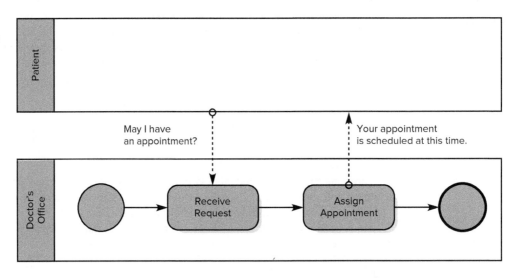

LO 2-8
Understand and apply flow object types.

Extended Building Blocks for BPMN Diagrams and Modeling Concepts

Token concept. BPMN uses the theoretical concept of a token flowing through the process to understand how various elements interact. A start event generates a token that must then be able to flow through the process until it reaches an end event, which consumes the token. In most cases, tokens only travel along sequence flows and pass through process flow objects. Process flow object behavior can be defined by how that element interacts with a token as it flows through the process. A token does not traverse message flows.

Flow object types. Flow objects include events, activities, and gateways. Sequence flows only connect to flow objects. Within BPMN, each flow object can be further characterized by type. To show the type of element, BPMN includes a type icon within the specific flow object. For example, a "timer" event would show the event with a clock face icon inside, and a "message" event would show the event with an envelope icon inside. Within this text, we will focus on the types that are widely used.

Gateway types. Figure 2.8 shows three common gateway types. Exclusive gateways pass the token along the path established by the gateway conditions. Inclusive gateways can create additional tokens depending on the number of paths taken after the branching gateway. Parallel gateways also create additional tokens for each path leaving the gateway. The merging gateways synchronize the process. For inclusive and parallel gateways, the merging gateways delay the flow until all tokens for that instance arrive, then one token proceeds along the exiting sequence flow.

FIGURE 2.8
Gateway Types

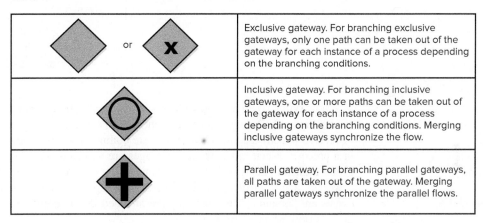

	Exclusive gateway. For branching exclusive gateways, only one path can be taken out of the gateway for each instance of a process depending on the branching conditions.
	Inclusive gateway. For branching inclusive gateways, one or more paths can be taken out of the gateway for each instance of a process depending on the branching conditions. Merging inclusive gateways synchronize the flow.
	Parallel gateway. For branching parallel gateways, all paths are taken out of the gateway. Merging parallel gateways synchronize the parallel flows.

Consider the process of planning a trip. Figure 2.9 shows an example of an exclusive gateway where the trip will involve either traveling by air or traveling by car. In Figure 2.10 an inclusive gateway indicates that the planned trip could involve either traveling by air or traveling by car or both. In Figure 2.11 a parallel gateway indicates that the trip will involve air travel, car travel, and hotel stays.

FIGURE 2.9
Exclusive Gateway Example Where the Trip Involves Air Travel or Car Travel but Not Both

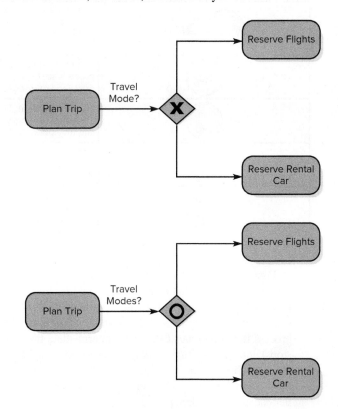

FIGURE 2.10
Inclusive Gateway Example Where the Trip May Involve Either Air Travel, Car Travel, or Both

FIGURE 2.11
Parallel Gateway
Example Where the
Trip Involves Air
Travel, Car Travel,
and Hotel Stays

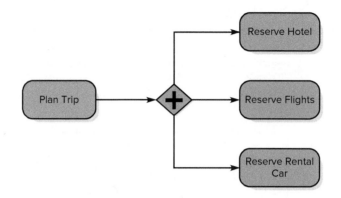

Event types. The basic flow objects include start events, intermediate events, and end events. Figure 2.12 shows common event types. First, message events either create (throw) or receive (catch) messages. Messages are communications from individual participants in a process. When modeled, the messages are shown as message flows. Second, timer events indicate a delay until a specific time and/or date or a specific cycle (such as 8 hours, 2 weeks). Third, error events indicate an interruption to the process. Intermediate error events are "boundary" events; they are attached to an activity and indicate an alternate process flow when an error occurs.

FIGURE 2.12
Event Types

✉ (circle)	Start message (catching) event. This is used to begin a process based on an incoming message, such as a sales order. Start events can only receive (catch) messages and not send (throw) them.
✉ ✉ (white and black envelope circles)	Intermediate message events. The white envelope is the catching event and the black envelope is the throwing event. These indicate that the process sends a message to or receives a message from an external participant.
✉ (bold circle, black envelope)	End message (throwing) event. This indicates that the process sends a message when it ends. End events can only send messages and not receive them.
🕐 (clock circle)	Start timer event. This is used to indicate a process that starts at a particular time or date, such as creating monthly budgets.
🕐 (double-circle clock)	Intermediate timer event. This indicates a delay in the process flow until a specific time or date or for a specified period.
⚡ (double-circle lightning)	Intermediate error event. This is a boundary event, discussed in more detail below, to indicate the alternate process flow when an error occurs in an activity.

Figure 2.13 shows a generic example using message events. The process starts with a start message event that receives (catches) the "Request" message from the external participant. The process proceeds to the "Evaluate Request" task, and then the intermediate message event sends (throws) the "Evaluation" message flow to the external participant. The process flow continues to the next intermediate message event, where it waits (the token stops) until the external participant responds with the "Confirm" message flow. When the event catches the message, the sequence flow continues to the "Do Something" task and then the process ends. The end message event throws a message to the external participant that the process is done.

FIGURE 2.13
Message Events
Example

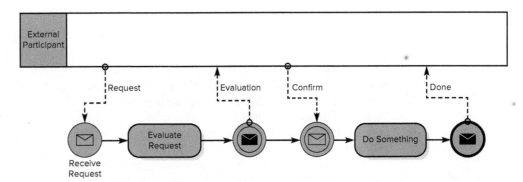

Figure 2.14 shows an example using timer events and a boundary intermediate error event. The start timer begins the process two weeks before the birthday to be celebrated. The "Plan Party" task has an intermediate error event attached to its boundary (a boundary event). Specifically, this is an example of an interrupting boundary event that affects process flow when an error occurs in the Plan Party task. If an error occurs, then the process flows to the "Cancel Party" task and then ends. However, if the Plan Party task completes successfully, the process flows to the intermediate timer event and then waits two weeks (the token waits to proceed). After two weeks, the process continues to the "Hold Party" task and then ends.

FIGURE 2.14
Timer and Error
Events Example

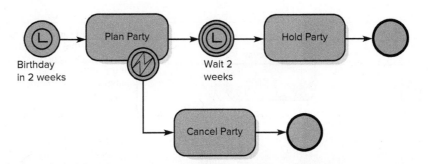

In later chapters, we will discuss other types of boundary events, both interrupting and noninterrupting. Note that you could also model the process shown in Figure 2.14 using a task to test whether the plans are good and then using a gateway to branch to the Cancel Party task if the plans fail. The use of the error boundary event provides a clear and more concise way to show the error.

Task types. Finally, BPMN offers different task types, but task types are used less often than gateway and error types. There are tasks to send and receive messages. These would be modeled with envelope icons (white for receiving, black for sending) in the upper left corner of the task rectangle. These tasks correspond to catching and throwing message events, and in most cases, the message events are preferred. Normally, you would use the send and receive tasks when you need to attach boundary events to the task as you can't do that with events. Modelers are often tempted to use the send and receive tasks to forward work to the next task in the process. This is unnecessary because the sequence flow implies that the work is forwarded. So, send and receive tasks are only related to message flows. Next, there are business rules tasks. In a business rules task, one or more business rules are applied in order to produce a result or make a decision. There are several other task types, such as user, script, manual, service, etc., and users can define their own tasks. In most cases, there is little need to use other than the general abstract task type (without any type icon). In this textbook, we will not use task types.

LO 2-9

Recognize and model repeating activities.

Subprocesses and Repeating Activities

Activities are the place where work takes place in BPMN diagrams. An activity can represent a process, subprocess, or task. So far, we've focused on tasks, but sometimes it is helpful to show a higher level of abstraction. In other words, we might want to lump several related tasks together into a subprocess. Figure 2.15 shows how subprocesses are modeled. Subprocesses can be used to show processes that are reused in several other processes. They are a useful modeling tool when the modeler doesn't want to add unnecessary detail to a diagram, especially when that detail will be presented in another model.

Sometimes, we want to show that the same task is performed multiple times. In this case, we can show the task as looping. Looping tasks repeat until a condition is satisfied. This has the same effect as using a gateway that sends the process back to the task if the condition is not satisfied. When the number of times that a task will repeat is known in advance, we can use a multi-instance task. A parallel multi-instance task is performed several times by different actors at the same time. A sequential multi-instance task is performed several times by the same actor in sequence. Think about taking a test. Each student takes the test at the same time, so this would be an example of a parallel multi-instance task. Then, the instructor grades the tests sequentially, so this would be an example of a sequential multi-instance task.

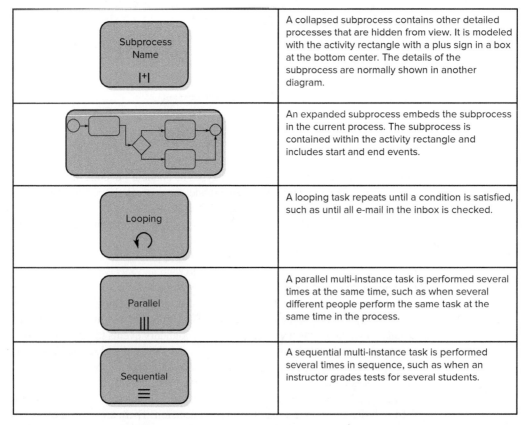

Subprocess Name |+|	A collapsed subprocess contains other detailed processes that are hidden from view. It is modeled with the activity rectangle with a plus sign in a box at the bottom center. The details of the subprocess are normally shown in another diagram.
(expanded subprocess diagram)	An expanded subprocess embeds the subprocess in the current process. The subprocess is contained within the activity rectangle and includes start and end events.
Looping ↺	A looping task repeats until a condition is satisfied, such as until all e-mail in the inbox is checked.
Parallel |||	A parallel multi-instance task is performed several times at the same time, such as when several different people perform the same task at the same time in the process.
Sequential ≡	A sequential multi-instance task is performed several times in sequence, such as when an instructor grades tests for several students.

FIGURE 2.15

Subprocesses and Repeating Activities

LO 2-10
Understand and apply data objects and datastores to model data created, updated, transferred, and deleted in a process.

Data Objects, Datastores, and Associations

Processes create, update, transfer, and delete data in various forms. Sometimes the data management is implicit. At other times, it is important to explicitly model where data are created or used. The two main BPMN elements used to model data are the data object and the datastore, as shown in Figure 2.16. Data objects are modeled with document icons. Datastores are modeled with a disk icon. Associations are dotted lines that show the movement of data between the data objects and datastores and activities. Associations may use arrowheads to show the direction of data flow.

FIGURE 2.16
Data Objects, Datastores, and Associations

	A data object. This element represents data that are only available for the duration of a process.
Datastore	A datastore. This element represents data that are available across processes.
- - - - - - - - - - ->	An association connecting a data object/store to an activity. The arrowhead shows the direction of data flow when necessary.

Figure 2.17 shows alternative examples of one simple process with a data object. The process starts and the actor buys concert tickets. Time passes until the date of the concert and then the actor attends the concert using the tickets. The same data object, tickets, can be repeated in the process as necessary to avoid confusion. In our simple example, the first alternative seems to make more sense, since it is clear that one ticket data object is created and then used. If it is necessary for other processes to access the stored ticket information, then tickets should be modeled as a datastore.

FIGURE 2.17
Examples of Process Using Data Objects

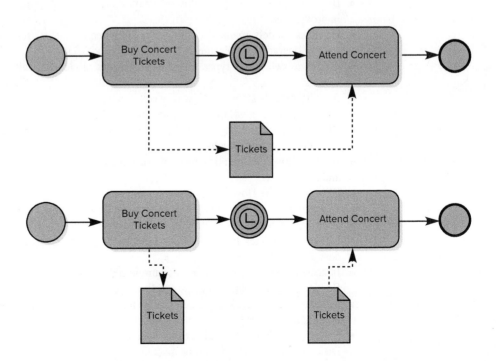

Best Practices in Preparing BPMN Diagrams

The primary objective of process activity modeling is to describe the important steps in a business process clearly, concisely, and accurately. Diagrams are tools to aid in planning, documenting, discussing, implementing, and using systems. Here are some modeling best practices that can enhance the use of models for these purposes.

1. Focus on one business process at a time.
2. Clearly identify the events that start and end the process.
3. Include essential elements, but avoid distracting detail.
4. Think about a token flowing from the start event through the process to the end event; the flow of the token should be clear for all paths through the process.
5. Label activities clearly with a verb and an object (e.g., pay invoice).
6. Model iteratively, getting feedback to improve accuracy and clarity.
7. Use message flows to show interactions between process participants. Remember that tokens do not flow across message flows.
8. Each pool must have a start and at least one end.
9. Make the external participant's pool opaque, hiding the elements in that pool, when the external participants activities are not important for the model. When the pool is opaque, attach the message flow arrows to the edge of the pool.
10. Use sequence flows within pools and not between pools.

Summary

Information plays a crucial role in the information age.

- Accountants' roles in business are evolving rapidly.
- Accountants are increasingly involved in business management support.
- Business process documentation is essential for training, describing current processes and systems to support internal and external audits, establishing accountability, and communicating among employees and various stakeholders.
- Business process documentation provides a starting point for business process improvement.
- Business models manage complexity, elicit requirements, reconcile viewpoints, and specify operating requirements for business processes.
- There are two major types of business process models: activity models and structure models.
- Activity models show the flow of work in a business process.
- BPMN provides a notation for specifying workflow.
- BPMN notation includes flow objects: events, activities, sequence flows, and gateways that allow process branching.
- BPMN allows the identification of participants in a process through the use of pools and swimlanes.
- BPMN message flows document exchanges between pools.
- External pools may be opaque with message flows attached to the edge of the pool.
- The token concept is a method to understand sequence flow within a process.
- BPMN establishes types for flow objects, i.e., events, gateways, and tasks, to help describe specific uses.
- Intermediate error events are an example of boundary events that interrupt the normal flow of a process when an error condition occurs.
- Timer events are used to indicate events that occur at a specific time or date or cause the process to wait for a specific period of time.
- Subprocesses represent collections of tasks.
- Data objects and datastores allow modeling of process information processing requirements.

Key Words

activities (37)   In business process modeling, activities represent specific steps in a business process.

activity models (36)   Models that describe the sequence of workflow in a business process or processes.

annotations (37)   Model elements that allow the modeler to add additional descriptive information to the model. Annotations are modeled with text inside a bracket connected to other model symbols with a dashed line.

business analysis (33)   The process of defining business process requirements and evaluating potential improvements. Business analysis involves ascertaining, documenting, and communicating information about current and future business processes using business process modeling and related tools.

business model (33)   A simple, abstract representation of one or more business processes. A business model is typically a graphical depiction of the essential business process information.

business process (33)   A defined sequence of business activities that use resources to transform specific inputs into specific outputs to achieve a business goal.

business process modeling notation (BPMN) (36)   A standard for the description of activity models.

data flow diagram (DFD) (52)   Another type of activity model that graphically shows the flow of data through a system and also incorporates elements of structure models.

documentation (33)   An information transmission and communication tool that explains how business processes and business systems work.

events (36)   Important occurrences that affect the flow of activities in a business process. BPMN includes symbols to define start, intermediate, and end events.

flowcharts (47)   Visualizations of a process activity; they are activity models much like models using BPMN.

gateways (37)   Show process branching and merging as the result of decisions. Basic gateways are depicted as diamonds. Usually, gateways appear as pairs on the diagram. The first gateway shows the branching, and the second gateway shows merging of the process branches.

lanes (or swimlanes) (38)   BPMN symbols that provide subdivisions of pools to show, for example, functional responsibilities within an organization.

message flows (39)   BPMN represents exchanges between two participants (pools) in the same process as message flows, which are modeled as dashed arrows.

pools (38)   BPMN symbols used to identify participants, actors, or persons that perform activities and interact with other participants in a process.

process maps (48)   Simplified flowcharts that use a basic set of symbols to represent a business process activity.

sequence flows (37)   BPMN symbols that show the normal sequence of activities in a business process. Sequence flows are modeled as solid arrows, with the arrowhead showing the direction of process flow.

Appendix A

Flowcharting

WHAT IS A FLOWCHART?

Like business process models, **flowcharts** are visualizations of a process activity. Flowcharts have been widely used since they were first introduced in the 1920s. Modern techniques such as UML activity diagrams and BPMN are extensions of flowcharts. Flowcharts are useful tools for systems development, process documentation, and understanding internal controls. Three types of flowcharts are often used by accountants. These three types typically differ in the level of detail modeled.

1. *Systems flowcharts* provide an overall view of a system, including the inputs, activities, and outputs of the process.
2. *Process maps* use the basic set of flowchart symbols to provide a representation of the steps within a business process. **Process maps** are conceptually similar to business process diagrams created with BPMN.
3. *Document flowcharts* present the flow of documents through an entity, often describing the areas within the entity with responsibility for particular tasks.

BASIC BUILDING BLOCKS FOR FLOWCHARTS

The basic flowchart symbols shown in Figure 2.A1 are similar to, and serve the same basic functions as, the BPMN symbols for activity models.

- *Start/End.* Each flowchart should show the flow of process activities from one start to one or more logical ends. The start and end steps are drawn as ovals.
- *Tasks/Activities.* Tasks or activities represent specific steps in the business process. Basic activities are modeled as rectangles. Each activity is described with a short verb phrase placed within the rectangle (e.g., process credit card payment or bill customer). An activity can depict a single action or some logical combination of actions depending on the required level of detail to achieve the objectives of the business process analysis.
- *Sequence Flows.* Sequence flows are represented by arrows to indicate the progression of activity within the process. The diagram should show the sequence of activity from left to right and top to bottom.
- *Decisions.* Decisions are modeled as diamonds with multiple exits (sequence flows) based on the result of decisions.

FIGURE 2.A1
Basic Elements of
Flowcharts

Element	Description	Symbol
Start/End	The Start/End steps indicate the beginning and ending of the process flow.	Start
Tasks/Activities	Tasks/Activities are the steps that describe the work; they can represent individual tasks or collections of tasks depending on the diagram's level of detail.	Task/Activity
Sequence Flows	An arrow shows the normal direction of flow—i.e., the order of activities—in a diagram.	Sequence Flow →
Decisions	Decision diamonds portray the nature of the decision and the exit options.	Decision

EXAMPLE OF BUSINESS PROCESS FLOWCHART

Figure 2.A2 shows a simple business process activity diagram depicting the checkout process at a retail store. In this process, the customer presents items for checkout. The clerk scans items and identifies payment method. Then the process branches depending on the nature of payment. The payment is accepted, and the process branches merge. The clerk

FIGURE 2.A2
Sample Business
Process Flowchart

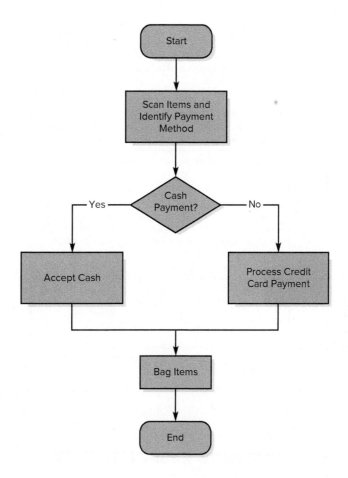

bags the items for the customer, and the process ends. Note that the start event can be labeled to explain the start event, and the gateway branches can be labeled to show the purpose of the branches (handling cash or credit payment in this case).

ADDITIONAL FLOWCHART SYMBOLS

The additional symbols shown in Figure 2.A3 are also widely used to depict specific operations within flowcharts. While none of these symbols are necessary for system flowcharts, they are often used in document flowcharts to differentiate manual and system operations and the media used in the process.

Element	Description	Symbol
Input/Output; Journal/ Ledger	The parallelogram is a generalized symbol for input or output when the medium is not specified.	In/Out
Input/Output of Document(s) or Report(s)	The document symbol indicates hard-copy documents or reports coming into or going out of the process.	One Document / Multiple

FIGURE 2.A3
Additional Flowchart Symbols

(continued)

Element	Description	Symbol
Online Keying	This symbol indicates data entry using online devices such as a computer or a handheld device.	
Storage Offline	This symbol indicates storage, typically of documents, not accessible by computer. File-ordering sequence is indicated as follows: N = numerically, A = alphabetically, D = by date.	N
Magnetic Disc Storage	This symbol includes database (online) storage accessible by computer.	
Manual Task/Activity	This symbol indicates a manual task. If the flowchart differentiates between manual and computer operations, the basic task/activity symbol shown in Figure 2.A1 then shows a computer operation.	Manual Task
On/Off Page Connectors	This symbol indicates data entry using online devices such as a computer or a handheld device.	On Page / Off Page
Annotation	This symbol is to add descriptive comments or explanatory notes to clarify the process.	

FIGURE 2.A3
(continued)

SHOWING RESPONSIBILITY

Deployment flowcharts show both the sequence of steps in a process as well as the organizational responsibility for each step. Like business process models (BPMN), deployment flowcharts use swimlanes to represent different organizational units or functions. These flowcharts are particularly useful in identifying the multiple handoffs between organization units in a process. These handoffs can be sources of problems, and making these steps clear can help identify those problems. Additionally, deployment flowcharts are useful in documenting processes for activities such as employee training. The flowchart in Figure 2.A4 illustrates swimlanes and responsibilities.

SHOWING OPPORTUNITY

Opportunity flowcharts highlight opportunities for improvement by, for example, separating value-added from cost-added activities within a process. Opportunity flowcharts use swimlanes to separate the activities that add value from those that add to the costs of the process, such as the costs of redoing work, waiting for information, waiting for parts, or correcting problems in general. Value-added activities are those that are essential to producing the process's product or service given the current state of technology, even if the process runs perfectly every time. Cost-added-only activities are those related to checking for defects, reworking, or supplying missing information.

For example, Figure 2.A5 shows the simple process of printing out and turning in an assignment document. If the process went as expected, we would select the printer, print the document, and turn in the assignment. The example assumes that, in some cases, the printer can be out of paper, which requires adding more paper before proceeding, or that the print cartridges could be out of ink, which requires replacing the cartridges and reprinting the document.

FIGURE 2.A4
Flowchart with
Swimlanes Showing
Responsibility

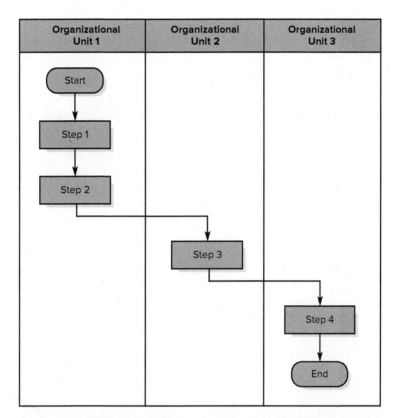

FIGURE 2.A5
Opportunity Flowchart
Example of a
Document Printing
Process

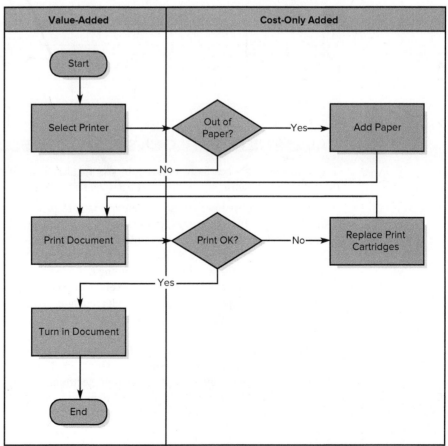

Appendix B

Data Flow Diagrams

WHAT IS A DATA FLOW DIAGRAM (DFD)?

A **data flow diagram (DFD)** represents graphically the flow of data through a system, such as one or more business processes. Data flow diagrams are often used to perform structured systems analysis and design, whereby a system is described at increasing levels of detail to facilitate new systems design. DFDs use a limited set of symbols (see Figure 2.B1) and are easily read and understood. Unlike most flowcharts, DFDs specifically represent the datastores—that is, the system files affected by or supporting the process—as well as the data that flow to and from the datastores. DFDs have no start and end symbols, which is also unlike flowcharts and BPMN business process diagrams. Instead, data flow diagrams present the external sources of—or destinations for—the data.

FIGURE 2.B1
Basic Elements of
Data Flow Diagrams

Element	Description	Symbol
Process	The activities within a system that use or generate data (e.g., Receive customer order).	Process
Data Source or Destination	The entities that interact with the system (e.g., customers, employees, or bank).	Source/ Destination
Datastores	This symbol describes the physical or electronic data storage.	Datastore
Data Flows	This symbol shows the flow of data (e.g., an order coming from a customer); data flows are named to indicate the data content.	data flow 1

BASIC BUILDING BLOCKS FOR DATA FLOW DIAGRAMS

The following describes basic building blocks for data flow diagrams. The structure of these diagrams is substantially different from the structure of BPMN activity models.

- *Processes* are activities that use or generate data. Depending on the software tools used to draw DFDs, processes may be represented with circles or rectangles with rounded corners. As with BPMN diagrams and flowcharts, processes are given names using short verb phrases (e.g., receive customer order). A process must have at least one or more data flows coming in and going out.
- *Terminators* are external entities that are either sources or destinations for data. Terminators are typically represented with rectangles. Examples of terminators are customers, suppliers, or other entities external to the particular system being represented.
- *Datastores* represent the physical or electronic repositories of data within the system. Datastores are typically represented as rectangles with one or both ends open.
- *Data flows* represent the flow of physical or electronic data through the system. These are represented by arrows that show the direction of data flow.

EXAMPLE OF A DFD

Figure 2.B2 shows a simple example of a DFD showing the checkout process at a retail store. In this process, the customer (external source) presents items for checkout. The system includes scanning and bagging the items and accepting payment while updating sales and inventory records.

FIGURE 2.B2

Sample Level 0 DFD of Customer Checkout System

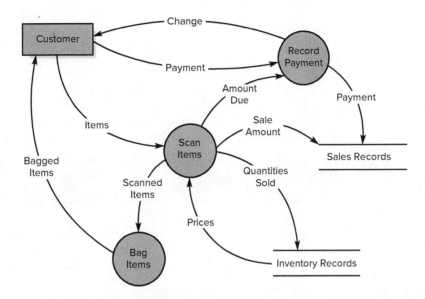

NESTING OR EXPLODING DFDs

DFDs describe a system at increasing levels of detail to facilitate new systems design. The context diagram shows the entire system as one process and identifies all relevant external sources and destinations for data, as well as the type of data coming from or going to those external entities. Then, subsequent models showing increasing detail would be identified as level 0, level 1, and level 2. Each process in a DFD is designated by the level and the number of the process. In Figure 2.B2, for example, assuming that is the level 0 diagram, then *Scan Items* could be designated process 1.0. If any subprocesses of *Scan Items* are subsequently modeled, those would be designated 1.1, 1.2, and so on.

BEST PRACTICES FOR DFDs

There are several best practices to ensure that DFDs provide useful descriptions of systems. Similar to flowcharts and BPMN diagrams, DFDs are a communications tool. Thus, the names given to processes, datastores, data flows, and external entities are important. The names should be clear to the system users. With regard to modeling specific elements of the diagram, modelers should remember that processes do not spontaneously generate or absorb data. Processes only modify data; therefore, all processes should have at least one data flow coming in and going out, and the data flow out of a process should be different than the data flow in. Datastores support the system's processing requirements, so every datastore should be connected to at least one process in the system. Finally, systems are developed to respond to inputs from external entities or to deliver information to external entities, so every external entity must be connected to at least one data flow.

USING DFDs FOR SYSTEM DOCUMENTATION

To form complete documentation for a system, the business analyst would augment the DFDs with additional information. For example, the analyst would define each datastore completely, specifying the fields, data types, data limits, and formats. The analyst would also define each element of a data flow in terms of the specific fields that it contains. Plus, the analyst would describe the business rules or logic for each process and confirm those with the process owners.

Answers to Progress Check

1. Documentation is important to almost all accounting/finance functions listed.

2. The answer depends on the student, but all of us have used maps. Many of us have assembled a product from **IKEA**. Most of us have installed software on our computers.

3. Here's a simple business process model (without pools and swimlanes) for a fast-food drive-through:

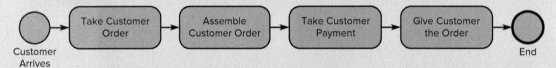

4. Here is one possible example of a process model using pools and message flows to show a customer interacting with **Amazon.com**'s website to purchase an item.

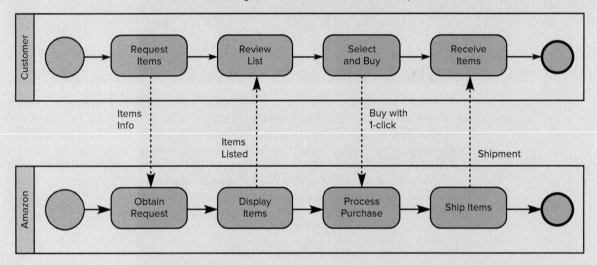

Mc Graw Hill Education **connect**

Multiple Choice Questions

1. Which of the following is not a role of the accounting function in business? **LO 2-1**

   a. Financial close

   b. Regulatory compliance

   c. Project management

   d. Using IT to make finance and accounting processes more efficient

   e. All of the above are roles of the accounting function.

2. Which of the following is not an example of business process documentation? **LO 2-2**
    a. Business process models
    b. Training manuals
    c. Organization charts
    d. Internal audit
    e. All of the above are examples of business process documentation.

3. Which of the following is not a purpose of business process documentation? **LO 2-2**
    a. Facilitating process improvement
    b. Specifying accountability
    c. Training
    d. Supporting internal audit
    e. All of the above are purposes of business process documentation.

4. Which of the following best describes the value of business models? **LO 2-3**
    a. A communication tool   d. A tool for managing complexity
    b. A planning tool   e. All of the above
    c. A process improvement tool

5. Which of the following describes how participants in a process are identified in BPMN? **LO 2-6**
    a. Message flows   d. Gateways
    b. Swimlanes   e. Both b and c
    c. Pools   f. Both a and d

6. Which of the following symbols is used to represent a gateway in BPMN? **LO 2-5**

    a.    c.

    b.    d.

7. Which of the following symbols is used to represent sequence flow in BPMN? **LO 2-5**

    a.    c.

    b.    d.

8. Which of the following statements about BPMN is not true? **LO 2-5**
    a. Arrows represent sequence flows.
    b. The BPMN specification is maintained by the Object Management Group (OMG).
    c. Events are modeled with a circle symbol.
    d. Annotations allow the modeler to add descriptive text.
    e. All of the above are true.

9. Which of the following describe characteristics of good BPMN models? **LO 2-5**
    a. They are clear.   d. They are correct.
    b. They are complete.   e. All of the above
    c. They are consistent.

10. Which of the following statements about sequence flows is not true? **LO 2-5**
    a. Sequence flows are continuous from the start event through activities and gateways, if any, to an end event in a pool.
    b. Sequence flows may not cross pool boundaries.
    c. Sequence flows may not cross lane boundaries.
    d. Tokens move along sequence flows.
    e. None of the above

11. Which of the following best describes message flows? **LO 2-7**
    a. Message flows are continuous within each pool.
    b. Message flows are modeled with solid arrows.
    c. Message flows represent exchanges between pools.
    d. Message flows may not cross pool boundaries.
    e. Message flows may not cross lane boundaries.

12. Which of the following is not true about the token concept? **LO 2-8**
    a. The token concept is a theoretical concept that describes process flow.
    b. The start event generates a token.
    c. The end event consumes the token.
    d. Tokens do not traverse message flows.
    e. All of the above are true

13. Which of the following is not a flow object? **LO 2-8**
    a. Gateways
    b. Message events
    c. Activities
    d. Message flows
    e. Timer events

14. Which of the following best describes an exclusive gateway? **LO 2-8**
    a. The only gateway in a BPMN diagram
    b. A gateway that does not connect to message flows
    c. A gateway with only one exit path per instance of a process
    d. A gateway where all exit paths are taken for each instance of a process
    e. None of the above

15. Which of the following best describes an inclusive gateway? **LO 2-8**
    a. The gateway that is shared among two pools
    b. A gateway with one or more exit paths per instance of a process
    c. A gateway with only one exit path per instance of a process
    d. A gateway where all exit paths are taken for each instance of a process
    e. None of the above

16. Which of the following is true about start events? **LO 2-8**
    a. A start event can catch a message.
    b. A start event cannot be a timer event.
    c. A start event can throw a message.
    d. A start event cannot be a message event.
    e. None of the above is true.

17. Which of the following is true about end events? **LO 2-8**
    a. An end event can catch a message.
    b. An end event can throw a message.

    c. An end event can be a timer event.

    d. An end event can be shared among pools.

    e. None of the above is true.

18. Which is the following is true about intermediate timer events? **LO 2-8**

    a. The process delays until a specific date or time.

    b. The process delays for a specific period of time, e.g., 1 day.

    c. The process delays for an unspecified amount of time.

    d. The process delays until a message is received.

    e. Both a and b are true.

19. Which of the following best describes an intermediate error event? **LO 2-8**

    a. It is a boundary event attached to the boundary of an activity.

    b. It indicates alternate sequence flow begins when an error occurs.

    c. It is modeled with a leaning Z or flash sign.

    d. All of the above describe intermediate error events.

    e. None of the above describes intermediate error events.

20. Which of the following best describes a looping task? **LO 2-9**

    a. The task repeats until a condition is satisfied.

    b. A looping task only repeats twice.

    c. A looping task is modeled as a subprocess.

    d. A looping task happens multiple times in parallel.

    e. None of the above

21. Which of the following best describes a data object? **LO 2-10**

    a. It is modeled with a document icon.

    b. It represents data that are only available for the duration of the process.

    c. It is linked to tasks with data associations.

    d. It is different from a datastore.

    e. All of the above describe data objects.

22. Which of the following are true with respect to data associations? **LO 2-10**

    a. It is modeled as a dotted arrow.

    b. The association arrowhead shows the direction of data flow.

    c. Tokens flow across data associations.

    d. Gateways can be used to show optional data updates.

    e. Both a and b are true.

Discussion Questions

1. Do you think that your accounting education has prepared you for all roles of an accountant in business (see Table 2.1)? Which roles do you feel best prepared for? Which roles do you feel least prepared for? Why? **LO 2-1**

2. Choose one of the Accounting/Finance Operations roles in Table 2.1. How could a BPMN activity model help an accountant better understand that role? **LO 2-1**

3. Compare BPMN activity diagrams with flowcharts and DFDs. What is different? What is the same? When would one notation be better or worse than another? **LO 2-1, LO 2-4**

4. Consider the Stewardship and Reporting role of accountants shown in Table 2.1. What information would you need to collect and use to manage the regulatory compliance function? **LO 2-3, LO 2-4**

5. Assume that your company has BPMN diagrams of all their main processes. How could they use this information? **LO 2-5**

6. Describe some situations that might lead you to conclude that a BPMN diagram is not complete. LO 2-6

7. Each activity/task can only be assigned to one pool or lane. Why is that an important rule? LO 2-5, LO 2-8

8. Describe situations where you would use exclusive, inclusive, and parallel gateways? LO 2-8

9. Your process waits until you receive a response from your customer. What kind of flow object would you use to show this? LO 2-8

10. Give some examples of processes that would start with a timer event based on your experience. LO 2-4

Problems

connect

1. Consider the following narrative describing the process of filling a customer's order at a **Starbucks** branch:

> A Starbucks customer entered the drive-through lane and stopped to review the menu. He then ordered a Venti coffee of the day and a blueberry muffin from the barista. The barista recorded the order in the cash register. While the customer drove to the window, the barista filled a Venti cup with coffee, put a lid on it, and retrieved the muffin from the pastry case and placed it in a bag. The barista handed the bag with the muffin and the hot coffee to the customer. The customer has an option to pay with cash, credit card, or Starbucks gift card. The customer paid with a gift card. The barista recorded the payment and returned the card along with the receipt to the customer.

Use BPMN to model Starbucks' process of taking a customer order using the following independent assumptions:

a. No additional assumptions. Identify the start and end events and the tasks that the barista performs. Include any gateways whenever there are alternative tasks. LO 2-5

b. The barista prepares each item in the order before delivering the order to the customer. Model the process to include a looping task. LO 2-5, LO 2-9

c. The coffee needs time to brew and isn't immediately available. The barista asks the customer if he wants to wait. If the customer waits, 5 minutes will pass, and then the coffee can be prepared. Model the process to include an intermediate error event and a intermediate timer event. LO 2-5, LO 2-8

d. The manager wants to see the interaction between the barista and the customer. Model the process with two pools, message flows, and intermediate message events to show that interaction. LO 2-5, LO 2-6, LO 2-7

connect

2. Consider the following narrative describing the process of going to class:

> Larry awoke to his alarm clock buzz. He got up and dressed for the day. Then, he ate a hearty breakfast of oatmeal, toast, orange juice, and coffee. He grabbed his books and prepared to leave for school. Before he left home, he checked the weather. If it looked like rain, he put on a jacket and took his umbrella, and he drove to school. If it looked sunny, he left his jacket and umbrella at home and walked to school. If he drove to school, he parked his car and walked to class. If he walked to school, he went straight to class.

Use BPMN to model Larry's process of going to class using the following independent assumptions:

a. No additional assumptions. Identify the start and end events and the tasks Larry performs, including any gateways whenever there is a decision to be made. LO 2-5

b. Larry arrives at school early. Use an intermediate timer event to show the delay between arriving at school and going to class. LO 2-5, LO 2-8

c. Larry doesn't own a car. If it is raining, he texts his friend Jazmin for a ride. She texts back whether she's available or not, and Larry either rides with her or walks to school in the rain. LO 2-5

connect   3. Consider the following narrative describing the process of planning a vacation:

Yannis is planning a trip to Hawaii with a friend. They first decide when they want to go and how much they can afford to spend. Then, they make their flight and hotel reservations. They wait until the scheduled departure. They travel to Hawaii and stay in the hotel. They enjoy a number of tourist activities. When their time in Hawaii is done, they fly home.

Use BPMN to model the process using the following independent assumptions:

a. When in Hawaii, they enjoy a number of tourist activities. Include a looping task to show this. **LO 2-5, LO 2-9**

b. There is a possibility that the hotel room and/or flights aren't within their budget. If reservations are too expensive, they will try different dates. If reservations are still too expensive, they will cancel their trip. Use a collapsed subprocess and an intermediate error event to model these assumptions. **LO 2-5, LO 2-8**

connect   4. Consider the following narrative describing the process of preparing an income tax return:

Each year before April 15, you file your income taxes. You collect multiple W-2 and 1099 documents. You prepare your tax return and double-check it for accuracy. You file your forms.

Use BPMN to model the process using the following independent assumptions. Use inclusive gateways to model simultaneous events.

a. When you prepare your tax return, you download multiple forms from the IRS website. You fill out the forms, double-check your work, and then print them out. If you owe money, you write a check. You mail your tax return along with the check if you owe money. If you are getting a refund, you wait to receive your refund by check and deposit your refund in your bank account. **LO 2-8**

b. When you prepare your tax return, you use cloud-based tax software. You answer the questions and the tax software prepares the tax return for you. Once you've double-checked your work, you enter your checking account details and file your return electronically. If you owe money, the IRS will automatically deduct the amount from your checking account in 7 days. If you are getting a refund, the IRS will deposit the refund directly into your checking account. **LO 2-8**

connect   5. Consider the following narrative describing the process of registering a car with the DMV:

Heide lives in California and it is time to renew her automobile registration. The California DMV sends her a renewal form and indicates that she needs a smog check for her automobile. She takes her car to the smog check station. She completes the smog check. If the smog check is successful, she can then go to the DMV website and renew her registration, paying with a credit card. Two weeks later she receives a new registration form and tags for her license plates. She puts the registration in the glove box of her car and places the tags on her license plates.

Use BPMN to model this process using the following independent assumptions:

a. No additional assumptions. Use a messaging start event to begin the process. **LO 2-8**

b. If the car fails the smog check, Heide must schedule maintenance service with her dealer. She completes the service and returns for a new smog check. If the car passes, she can complete the renewal process. **LO 2-8**

c. Heide uses the renewal form information at the smog check station. The smog check station provides a smog check certificate that Heide submits along with the renewal form to update her registration on the DMV website. She places the new registration document in her car. Use data objects to represent these documents. **LO 2-8, LO 2-10**

Additional problems are available in connect only.

Chapter **Three**

Data Modeling

A look at this chapter

Today's accountants must understand how business processes generate data and how those data are structured, interrelated, and stored in a database system. To ensure that business processes and the database systems are documented and to participate in improvements to processes and systems, accountants must understand and be able to model such systems. This chapter describes data modeling. It explains how data models support database-driven systems. It introduces basic data modeling tools to guide the student's development of modeling skills. Finally, it discusses business rules and how the identification of relevant business rules supports both process and data modeling.

A look back

Chapter 2 described the roles of accountants as users, managers, designers, and evaluators of technology and technology-driven business processes. To perform in those roles, accountants need to ensure that processes and systems are documented—and to participate in improvements to processes and systems. Thus, accountants must be business analysts. The chapter continued to introduce types of business process models as well as the potential value of business process modeling.

A look ahead

In the next several chapters, we use business process and data models to examine sales, acquisition, conversion, and related management processes.

© Purestock/SuperStock

Recently, Starbucks replaced a variety of systems with Oracle's application suite. According to Karen Metro, vice president of global business system solutions for Starbucks, "Many of our systems had grown up in silos and were loosely connected, and we were having a hard time keeping them upgraded or getting the functionality we needed out of those systems. Accenture came in to help us review the state of the environment and put together a global program to deploy standardized business processes and systems around the world." About 200 people from both Accenture and Starbucks worked full time for 3 years on the project. The software was first implemented in Europe, then North America, and finally China. Starbucks expects a variety of performance benefits, including improved margins. In particular, the software will help Starbucks understand where its money is spent and "leverage that with our suppliers around the world."

Source: Information provided by Accenture case study posted on its website, www.accenture.com, 2009.

Chapter Outline

Structure Models

Unified Modeling Language Class Diagrams

Building Blocks for UML Class Diagrams

Best Practices in Preparing Class Diagrams

UML Class Models for Relational Database Design

Decision Requirements and Business Rules

Business Rules and Decision Tables

Appendix A: Entity-Relationship Diagrams

Learning Objectives

After reading this chapter, you should be able to:

3-1   Understand the purpose of structure models.

3-2   Understand and apply the building blocks for UML class (structure) diagrams.

3-3   Describe multiplicities for a UML class diagram.

3-4   Understand how to implement a relational database from a UML class diagram.

3-5   Understand process decision requirements and how business rules support process decisions.

3-6   Describe business rules and the various forms of rules.

LO 3-1
Understand the
purpose of structure
models.

STRUCTURE MODELS

Structure models describe the data and information structures inherent in a business process or processes. The primary purpose of these models is to create a blueprint for the development of a relational database to support the collection, aggregation, and communication of process information. They are tools for planning, documenting, discussing, and implementing databases; however, they also facilitate the use of databases after they are implemented.

For more than 50 years, **data models** have been used to represent the conceptual contents of databases to communicate with the users of those databases. For example, Charles Bachman developed data structure diagrams, also known as Bachman diagrams, in the 1960s. Using similar notation, Peter Chen developed entity-relationship modeling in 1976 to describe the entities (e.g., people, things, and events) and the relationships among entities in databases. Since then, a number of others have offered a variety of notations to describe the elements of databases, but the concepts in all variations are similar.

A model of logical database structures must be able to describe:

1. The entities or things in the domain of interest.
2. The relationships among those things.
3. The cardinalities that describe how many instances of one entity can be related to another.
4. The attributes or characteristics of the entities and relationships.

Unified Modeling Language Class Diagrams

This textbook employs the Unified Modeling Language (UML) class diagram notation for structure models, although the concepts also apply to other notation standards, such as entity-relationship modeling. The Object Management Group is a not-for-profit consortium of computer industry members that maintains and publishes the specification for the UML. **Class diagrams** are one type of diagram within UML and are similar in many ways to entity-relationship diagrams. They describe the logical structure of a database system.

LO 3-2
Understand and apply
the building blocks for
UML class (structure)
diagrams.

Building Blocks for UML Class Diagrams

Classes

A **class** is any separately identifiable collection of things (objects) about which the organization wants to collect and store information. Classes can represent organization resources (e.g., trucks, machines, buildings, cash, investments), persons (e.g., customers, employees), events (e.g., sales, purchases, cash disbursements, cash receipts), and conceptual structures (e.g., accounts, product categories, budgets). Classes are typically implemented as tables in a relational database, where individual instances of objects are represented as rows in the table.

Each class is represented by a rectangle with three compartments, as shown in Figure 3.1. The top compartment shows the name of the class. The middle compartment shows the attributes (data elements) shared by all instances in the class. The bottom compartment describes operations that each instance in the class can perform. The attribute and operation compartments are optional. In this text, we will typically omit the attribute and operations compartments and use the class symbol with only the name of class when depicting classes.

**Cash disbursements represent events in a class. The class
symbol would be name only such as bank account.**
© *Image Source/Getty Images*

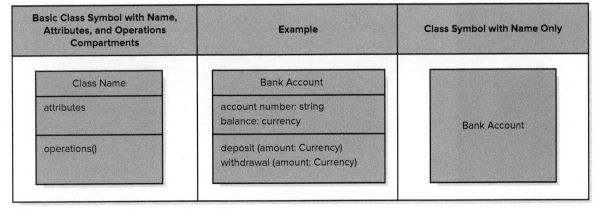

Basic Class Symbol with Name, Attributes, and Operations Compartments	Example	Class Symbol with Name Only

FIGURE 3.1
Class Notation

Associations

An **association** depicts the relationship between two classes. For example, customers (class) *participate* in sales (class); professors (class) *teach* courses (class); employees (class) *work for* organizations (class). It allows navigation between instances in one class and instances of another class, such as linking customer information to a particular sale. A generic association is drawn as a line connecting two classes. When the business purpose of the association is not clear, the association can be named by placing the text name on the line, as shown in Figure 3.2. Association names are verbs or verb phrases that indicate why instances of one class relate to instances of another class.

FIGURE 3.2
Classes with
Associations

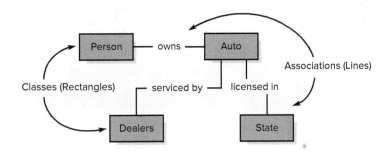

LO 3-3
Describe multiplicities for a UML class diagram.

Multiplicities

Multiplicities describe the minimum and maximum number of times instances in one class can be associated with instances in another class. Multiplicities for a class are represented by a pair of numbers placed on the opposite side of the association. In a binary association, there would then be two sets of multiplicities. Minimum values can be 0 or 1. The minimum values of multiplicities indicate whether participation in the relationship is optional (0) or mandatory (1). The maximum values can be 1 or many (*). In Figure 3.3, for example, it is optional for a person to own an automobile, but it is mandatory that each auto be owned by a person (assuming the auto class represents registered automobiles). The maximum values for a pair of multiplicities for a single association describe the nature of the relationship between classes: one-to-one, one-to-many, or many-to-many. In Figure 3.3, for example, a person could own many autos, so this is a one-to-many relationship.

FIGURE 3.3
Multiplicities
Each Person owns a minimum of 0 and a maximum of many Autos. Each Auto is owned by a minimum of 1 and a maximum of 1 Person.

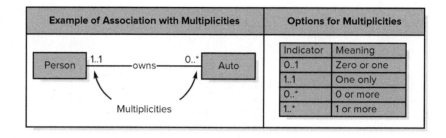

Attributes

Attributes are data elements that describe the instances in a class. Figure 3.4 lists the attribute names for the classes in a domain of interest (related to taking orders from customers) and identifies primary and foreign keys. The full specification of attributes would also include data type, default value (if any), **constraints** on the value (such as minimum and maximum possible values), and other descriptive information.

Primary Keys.   A **primary key (PK)** is an attribute or combination of attributes that uniquely identifies each instance in a class or row in a table. Primary keys can be modeled as part of the attribute list for each class on the UML class diagram; often, however, they are defined in the supporting documentation, such as the table listing shown in Figure 3.4, especially when using class symbols that only show the class name, as shown earlier in Figure 3.2. The primary key is a unique identifier for each instance in the class. For example, the "State" class in Figure 3.2 collectively defines all the states. Each state is an instance in that class, and each state would be identified by a unique primary key, such as the abbreviations AR, CA, WA, and so on.

FIGURE 3.4
List of Tables with Attribute Names

Customers	[Customer_Number (PK), Customer_Name, Customer_City, Customer_State, Customer_Zip, Customer_Phone]
Orders	[Order_Number (PK), Order_Date, Delivery_Date, Order_Amount, Shipping_Cost, Customer_Number (FK)]
Order_Items	[Order_Number + Product_Number (PK), Quantity_Ordered, Price]
Inventory	[Product_Number (PK), Product_Description, Quantity_on_Hand (QOH), Unit_of_Issue, Current_List_Price, Standard_Cost]

There are often several candidates for the primary key of a class or database table. There are several important criteria that guide the selection of appropriate primary keys:

- The primary key must uniquely identify each instance of the class (or row of the table). Consequently, the designer should avoid anything that could be duplicated, such as names.
- The primary key cannot be null (blank) under any circumstances. For this reason, the designer should avoid using attributes for the primary key that are potentially unavailable for any instance of the class; for example, not everyone has a Social Security number.
- The primary key cannot change over time.
- The primary key should be controlled by the organization that assigns it. When the assigning organization does not control the primary key values, it becomes difficult to ensure uniqueness. For example, names are not good primary keys.
- A primary key with sequential values makes it easier to recognize gaps in the data.
- All else equal, shorter primary key values are better than longer ones because shorter keys ease data entry, indexing, and retrieval.

Foreign Keys. A **foreign key (FK)** is an attribute or combination of attributes that allows tables to be linked together. A foreign key is linked *to the primary key of another table* to support a defined association. In Figure 3.3, for example, the Auto class would include a foreign key to match the primary key for the Person class to support the Owns association. In the table attribute listing shown in Figure 3.4, the primary key of the Customers Table is Customer_Number. The foreign key Customer_Number in the Orders Table allows rows in the Orders Table to be linked to corresponding rows in the Customers Table.

Progress Check

1. Consider students enrolled in courses taught by professors. Draw a simple class diagram with associations that describes the registration process. *Hint:* Include courses, students, and professors.
2. Add multiplicities to your diagram. Can a student be enrolled in many courses? Can a course have many students enrolled?
3. Create a listing of the tables with attributes. What are the primary keys? What attributes do you think go with each table definition?

Other Relationships

The generic relationship between two classes is modeled as an *association*, as described earlier. However, UML includes modeling notation for other types of relationships: **generalization** (or inheritance), **aggregation,** and **composition,** as shown in Figure 3.5. These special-purpose relationship notations should be used when they clarify relationships in a particular model, but they can also be modeled using associations.

Other Useful UML Class Model Notation

UML is semantically rich; it provides notation that accommodates a wide variety of modeling situations. We have outlined the basic notation that should allow you to build most

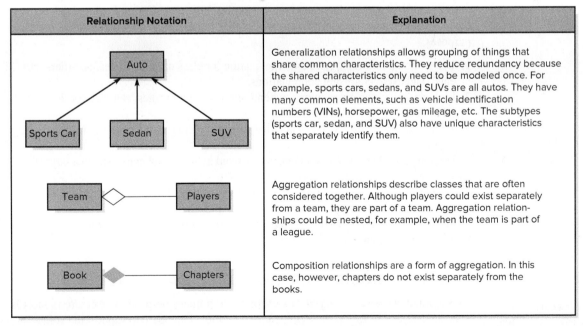

Relationship Notation	Explanation
Auto / Sports Car / Sedan / SUV	Generalization relationships allows grouping of things that share common characteristics. They reduce redundancy because the shared characteristics only need to be modeled once. For example, sports cars, sedans, and SUVs are all autos. They have many common elements, such as vehicle identification numbers (VINs), horsepower, gas mileage, etc. The subtypes (sports car, sedan, and SUV) also have unique characteristics that separately identify them.
Team — Players	Aggregation relationships describe classes that are often considered together. Although players could exist separately from a team, they are part of a team. Aggregation relationships could be nested, for example, when the team is part of a league.
Book — Chapters	Composition relationships are a form of aggregation. In this case, however, chapters do not exist separately from the books.

FIGURE 3.5
UML Notation for Other Relationships

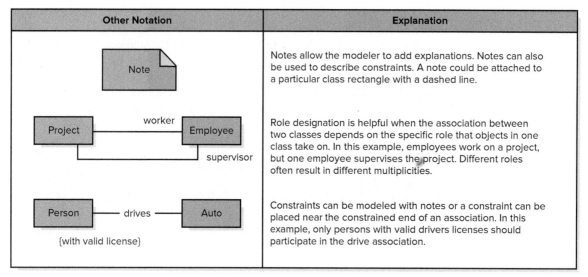

Other Notation	Explanation
Note	Notes allow the modeler to add explanations. Notes can also be used to describe constraints. A note could be attached to a particular class rectangle with a dashed line.
Project — worker — Employee — supervisor	Role designation is helpful when the association between two classes depends on the specific role that objects in one class take on. In this example, employees work on a project, but one employee supervises the project. Different roles often result in different multiplicities.
Person — drives — Auto {with valid license}	Constraints can be modeled with notes or a constraint can be placed near the constrained end of an association. In this example, only persons with valid drivers licenses should participate in the drive association.

FIGURE 3.6
Other Useful Class Diagram Notations

business process structural models. However, there are three other UML class model notations that can be particularly useful for modeling business processes from an accounting viewpoint. These three notations are described in Figure 3.6.

Best Practices in Preparing Class Diagrams

The primary objective of a class diagram is to describe the important elements of a domain of interest clearly, concisely, and accurately. As noted previously, class diagrams are tools to aid in planning, documenting, discussing, implementing, and using database systems. Here are some modeling best practices that can enhance the use of models for these purposes.

1. Use common terminology in the organization for class names (e.g., sales, orders, clients), and avoid confusing abbreviations.
2. Link classes on the diagram only when there is a clear business purpose for the relationship.
3. Avoid crossing lines where possible because that increases the potential for misreading the diagram.
4. Use consistently sized class rectangles to avoid an unwanted emphasis on a larger symbol.
5. Avoid running association lines close together because they may be hard to follow.
6. Opt for simplicity; show only what you need to show.
7. Focus first on the accuracy of the content, then address appearance.
8. Use notes to explain more complex situations.

UML CLASS MODELS FOR RELATIONAL DATABASE DESIGN

LO 3-4
Understand how to implement a relational database from a UML class diagram.

As we noted at the beginning of this chapter, the primary purpose of structure models is to create a blueprint for the development of a relational database to support the collection, aggregation, and communication of process information. They are tools for planning, documenting, discussing, and implementing databases. This section describes basic processes

FIGURE 3.7
Mapping Classes
to Tables

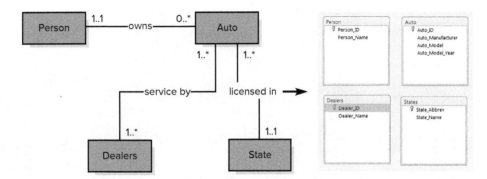

for mapping a UML class diagram to a relational database schema, which defines the tables, fields, relationships, keys, etc., in the database.[1]

1. *Map classes to tables.* The first step is to map the classes to tables. In Figure 3.7, for example, the UML class diagram (shown earlier in Figure 3.2 without multiplicities) would map to four tables in the relational database. Each instance of the class maps to a row in the corresponding table.

2. *Map class attributes to table fields and assign primary keys.* Map the attributes for each class to fields in the corresponding relational table. If the primary keys have not been designated, determine an appropriate primary key for each relational table. In the example shown in Figure 3.7, the primary keys for the tables are indicated by **Microsoft** Access's primary key symbol, a gold key icon.

3. *Map associations to foreign keys.* Each association in Figure 3.7, except the "serviced by" association between Dealers and Auto, will be implemented by adding foreign keys. The maximum multiplicities on each side of an association determine the foreign key placement. The figure indicates that one person owns a maximum of many autos. This is an example of a one-to-many relationship that will be implemented with a foreign key. A one-to-one relationship occurs when the maximum multiplicity on each side of the association is 1, and, in general, one-to-one relationships will also be implemented with a foreign key.

   a. There is a rule of thumb that can help identify where the foreign key is placed. Remember that each association is implemented in your database with a foreign key or a linking table, as described later. Assume a one-to-many relationship—that is, a relationship where the maximum multiplicity on one side of the association is 1 and the maximum multiplicity on the other side is many. The foreign key is posted toward the "many" side of the association. In other words, the primary key for the class on the 1 side of the association is posted as a foreign key for the class on the "*" side of the association. Thus, in Figure 3.7 the primary key for Person is posted in Auto as a foreign key, and the primary key of State is also posted in Auto as a foreign key. Table 3.1 provides general rules for posting foreign keys based on the type of association between two classes.

   b. The minimum multiplicities are often determined by the timing of entries to both tables involved in one association. If an entry in one table must match an entry in the other table, then the minimum is 1. If an entry in one table can occur without an entry in the other table, then the minimum is 0. In Figure 3.7, we've assumed that each auto is owned by one person, and you can't have any auto listed in the Auto table without a corresponding owner in the Person table. Thus, the minimum

---

[1]Schemas can also define other database requirements, such as levels of access, but this section focuses on designing the basic elements.

TABLE 3.1
Posting Foreign Keys[a]

[a] The foreign key is the primary key of the related table; however, foreign keys may be assigned different names if it improves understanding.

[b] Foreign keys can be posted in either table, but the minimum multiplicity of 0 indicates an optional association for that table and a general rule provides the most efficient option for posting the foreign key.

Multiplicity for A	Multiplicity for B	Relationship Type	General Rules for Posting Foreign Keys
0..1	0..1	One-to-one[b]	Post foreign key in either A or B but not both
0..1	1..1	One-to-one	Post foreign key in A
0..1	0..*	One-to-many	Post foreign key in B
0..1	1..*	One-to-many	Post foreign key in B
1..1	0..1	One-to-one	Post foreign key in B
1..1	1..1	One-to-one	Post foreign key in either A or B but not both
1..1	0..*	One-to-many	Post foreign key in B
1..1	1..*	One-to-many	Post foreign key in B
0..*	0..1	One-to-many	Post foreign key in A
0..*	1..1	One-to-many	Post foreign key in A
0..*	0..*	Many-to-many	Create linking table
0..*	1..*	Many-to-many	Create linking table
1..*	0..1	One-to-many	Post foreign key in A
1..*	1..1	One-to-many	Post foreign key in A
1..*	0..*	Many-to-many	Create linking table
1..*	1..*	Many-to-many	Create linking table

multiplicity next to Person is 1. Conversely, an individual in the Person table may or may not own an auto. If the individual did not own an auto, there would be no matching auto in the Auto table. In this case, the matching entry is optional and the minimum multiplicity next to Auto is 0. Note that the minimum is 0 even if some individuals own autos. As long as our requirements indicate that some individual may not own an auto, the minimum is 0.

4. *Create new tables to implement many-to-many relationships.* A many-to-many relationship is when the maximum multiplicity is * on both ends of the association, regardless of the minimum multiplicities. In this situation, the database designer creates a new table to implement the association. The default primary key for the new table is the combination of the two primary keys for the associated tables. In Figure 3.7, for example, each Auto can be serviced by many Dealers, and each Dealer can service many Autos. Thus, the "serviced by" association is implemented by creating a new table with a primary key that includes both Auto_ID and the Dealer_ID (called a concatenated or composite key), as shown in Figure 3.8.

FIGURE 3.8
Implementing a
Many-to-Many
Relationship
In theory, every
relationship type can
be implemented with a
linking table as shown
in this figure.

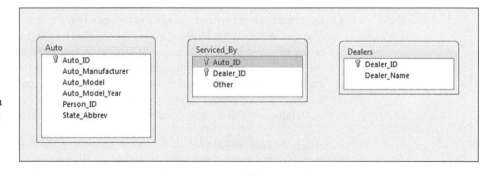

FIGURE 3.9
Mapping Class
Diagram Associations
to Relationships

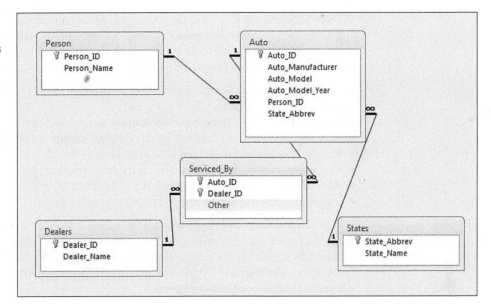

5. *Implement relationships among tables.* Create relationships among the relational tables to match the associations shown on the class diagram. After the foreign keys are posted and the linking tables created for the many-to-many relationships, the database designer can implement the relationships, as shown in Figure 3.9. Note that each half of the composite primary key for the Serviced_By table acts as a foreign key: Auto_ID in the Serviced_By table links to Auto_ID in the Auto table and Dealer_ID in Serviced_By table links to Dealer_ID in the Dealers table.

The set of relational tables shown in Figure 3.9 then implements the class diagram shown in Figure 3.4. In other words, the class diagram is the blueprint from which the database is built. Just as inadequate plans result in substandard buildings, an incomplete or erroneous class diagram will result in an ineffective database. It is easier to change the blueprint than change the building, and it is easier to change the class diagram (and ensure that it is correct) than to change the database.

LO 3-5

Understand process
decision requirements
and how business
rules support process
decisions.

DECISION REQUIREMENTS AND BUSINESS RULES

In addition to the process activities described in Chapter 2 and the information structures introduced in this chapter, analysts also need to focus on the process decision-making requirements. Then, business rules can be developed to support those decision-making requirements. Recognizing the importance of decision making in business processes, the Object Management Group recently issued version 1.0 of its standard for Decision Model and Notation (DMN).

Decision modeling involves four basic steps that are performed iteratively:

1. Identify decisions required in the process.
2. Describe and document these decisions and how they impact the business objectives for the process.
3. Specify decision requirements in terms of the information and knowledge required to make the decision.
4. Decompose and refine the requirements, determining where existing business rules apply and where new business rules need to be developed.

Once decisions are identified, the analyst can focus on identifying the decision logic—that is, the business rules—required to make the decision as well as the contextual input data that would be available to decision makers. Operational decisions depend on the business process but can be categorized into several general types as follows:

- Eligibility or approval—is this individual or organization eligible for this product or service?
- Validation—is this claim valid for processing?
- Calculation—what is the correct discount for this product/service for this customer?
- Risk—what is the risk of relying on this supplier's promised delivery date?
- Fraud—how likely is this claim to be fraudulent?
- Opportunity—which of these options is the best opportunity?
- Assignment—to whom should this issue be assigned?
- Targeting—how should we respond to this person?

Consider the simple example shown in Figure 3.7. Persons own automobiles that are licensed in states and serviced by dealers. What decisions might be involved in processing this information? Is this person eligible to own this auto? Is this license request valid? Is this auto under warranty? Once each decision is identified, the corresponding business rules must be developed and documented.

Business Rules and Decision Tables

LO 3-6
Describe business rules and the various forms of rules.

Business rules support decision making in business processes. They standardize and constrain process action. A **business rule** is a succinct statement of a constraint on a business process. It is the logic that guides the behavior of the business in specific situations. Business rules are typically written in text, not modeled; however, they influence the structure and flow of models. Business rules establish multiplicities in class models, and they set criteria for branching in activity models.

Rule: Credit card payments are allowed if the card is MasterCard.
© Thomas Trutschel/Photothek via Getty Images

There are several forms for business rules. To put these in context, let's consider a simple example of customer payments at a restaurant. Suppose the restaurant accepts cash or credit card payments as long as the credit card is American Express. Additionally, the restaurant only accepts payments in U.S. dollars, not foreign currency, and it does not accept checks. These payment constraints involve the following rule forms:

- *Obligatory.* This rule form states what should occur: Payment should be made in U.S. dollars.
- *Prohibited.* This rule form states what should not occur: No payments by check.
- *Allowed.* This rule form states what is allowed under what conditions: Credit card payments are allowed if the card is American Express.

Rules are stated in short sentences, as described earlier. In an attempt to formalize the statement of rules, the Object Management Group published a standard, titled "Semantics of Business Vocabulary and Business Rules" (SBVR), in 2008.[2] SBVR sets standards for stating business rules using natural language. The standard describes operative business rules, such as the three forms just described: obligatory, prohibited, and allowed. It also describes similar structural rules that describe fundamental characteristics—such as, "It is

[2]For further information on SBVR, see www.omg.org/spec/SBVR/1.0/.

necessary that each sale be made to a customer"—rather than operating policy rules that are stated in terms of preferred outcomes.

Rules must be enforceable. So, there must be related enforcement-level information that describes how to deal with potential violations. Enforcement levels include strict enforcement, pre-override, and post-override. If a rule is strictly enforced, violations are not authorized. If a rule is subject to pre-override, violations are allowed if authorized in advance. If a rule is subject to post-override, violations are allowed if authorized after the violation. When rules are subject to override, there should also be a statement of who can authorize a violation. Additionally, certain rules can be considered guidelines, which are generally followed but not enforced. The enforcement level can vary for different parts of the organization.

Rules are valuable because they make modeling business processes easier. They limit the number of options to those allowed by business policy. The rules for a business process establish systems requirements when acquiring new technology. However, rules can also inhibit process improvements because they can be tied to outdated technology. Thus, a close examination of business rules—and the business reasons for them—can reveal unnecessary constraints. In most situations, however, business rules are not stated formally; they are implicit. The process analysis should, therefore, elicit important business rules.

Decision tables combine multiple business rules to support likely circumstances requiring a decision. A decision table consists of a name, a set of inputs, a set of outputs, and a set of rules. The rules associate the inputs to the decision outputs at that point in the process. Figure 3.10 presents a sample decision table where three rules are shown as rows in the table. The table name is *Discounts*. The columns *Customer Type* and *Size of Order* are the inputs to the decision. The *Discount to Offer* is the output of the decision. The number column could be indexed to identify the process, decision, and rule, but in this case it simply numbers the three rule options.

FIGURE 3.10
Sample Decision Table

Discounts			
Number	**Customer Type**	**Size of Order**	**Discount to Offer**
1	Business	<10	10%
2	Business	>=10	15%
3	Individual	All	5%

Summary

- Structure models, such as UML class models, describe the information structures of one or more business processes.
- Structure models allow communication about database design.
- Structure models support the design, implementation, and use of databases.
- The building blocks for UML class diagrams include classes, associations, multiplicities, and attributes.
- Attributes for each class include the primary key, foreign keys, and other attributes describing characteristics of the class.
- Primary keys uniquely define each instance of a class (and each row in a relational database table).
- Foreign keys allow tables to be linked together.
- Foreign keys are primary keys of other tables posted in the current table to allow linking.
- Other class diagram relationships include generalizations, aggregations, and compositions.
- Associations model the business purpose of a relationship between two classes, such as the role that members of one class have with respect to the other class.

- UML class models can be used to create tables by mapping classes to tables, mapping class attributes to table fields, mapping associations to foreign keys depending on the multiplicities of the association, and creating new tables to implement many-to-many relationships.
- Analysts must understand process decision requirements to truly understand how the process should perform.
- Business rules and decision tables establish business policies and constrain business processes.

Key Words

aggregation relationship (65)   A special-purpose UML notation representing the relationship between two classes that are often considered together, such as when a sports league is made up of a collection of teams.

association (63)   UML symbol that depicts the relationship between two classes; it is modeled as a solid line that connects two classes in a model.

attributes (64, 73)   Data elements that describe instances in a class, very much like fields in a database table; characteristics, properties, or adjectives that describe each class.

business rule (70)   Succinct statements of constraints on business processes; they provide the logic that guides the behavior of the business in specific situations.

cardinalities (74)   *See* multiplicities.

class (62)   Any separately identifiable collection of things (objects) about which the organization wants to collect and store information. Classes can represent organization resources (e.g., trucks, machines, buildings, cash, investments), persons (e.g., customers, employees), events (e.g., sales, purchases, cash disbursements, cash receipts), and conceptual structures (e.g., accounts, product categories, budgets). Classes are typically implemented as tables in a relational database, where individual instances of the class are represented as rows in the table.

class diagrams (62)   Structure models prepared using UML notation.

composition relationship (65)   A special-purpose UML notation representing the relationship between two classes that are often considered together, similar to aggregation relationships, except in composition relationships, one class cannot exist without the other, such as a book and the chapters that compose the book.

constraints (64)   Optional or mandatory guidance about how a process should perform in certain situations.

data models (62)   A graphic representation of the conceptual contents of databases; data models support communication about database contents between users and designers of the database.

entities (73)   The people, things, and events in the domain of interest; in UML notation, entities are modeled as classes.

foreign key (FK) (65)   Attribute that allows database tables to be linked together; foreign keys are the primary keys of other tables placed in the current table to support the link between the two tables.

generalization relationship (65)   A special-purpose UML symbol that supports grouping of things that share common characteristics; it reduces redundancy because the shared characteristics need only be modeled once.

multiplicities (63)   UML symbols that describe the minimum and maximum number of times an instance of one class can be associated with instances of another class for a specific association between those two classes; they indicate whether the two classes are part of one-to-one, one-to-many, or many-to-many relationships.

primary key (PK) (64)   An attribute or a combination of attributes that uniquely identifies an instance of a class in a data model or a specific row in a table.

relationship (73)   The business purpose for the association between two classes or two database tables; *see* association.

structure model (62)   A conceptual depiction of a database, such as a UML class model or an entity-relationship model.

Appendix A

Entity-Relationship Diagrams

WHAT IS AN ENTITY-RELATIONSHIP DIAGRAM?

An entity-relationship diagram (ERD) represents graphically the logical data structure of a system, such as a database supporting one or more business processes. ERDs were originally proposed in a 1976 paper[3] by Peter Chen as a tool to capture the conceptual design (schema) of a relational database system, and ERD modeling techniques have evolved over time. Fundamentally, ERDs and UML class models are equivalent tools for modeling data structures.

BASIC BUILDING BLOCKS OF ERDS

Not surprisingly, the basic building blocks of ERDs include entities and relationships. Each entity has attributes that describe its characteristics. Entities correspond to tables in a relational database where the attributes are the fields in the table. Each relationship indicates a business purpose for connecting two or more entities. Relationships correspond to the links between tables. Cardinalities (i.e., multiplicities) define how one entity links to another. See Figure 3.A1.

FIGURE 3A.1

Basic Elements of Entity-Relationship Diagrams

Element	Description	Symbol
Entity	Separately and uniquely identifiable things of interest in a system.	Entity
Relationship	Associations between two entities reflecting a business purpose (Chen's notation).	Relationship
Relationship with Cardinalities	Associations between two entities reflecting a business purpose (information engineering style), where the ends indicate the cardinalities.	

Entities represent separately and uniquely identifiable things of interest in a system, for example, customers, employees, sales, inventory, and cash receipts. Entities are modeled as rectangles. Entities correspond to classes in UML class models.

Relationships represent associations between entities, for example, customers (entity) *participate in* (relationship) sales (entity). Relationships are modeled as diamonds. Relationships correspond to associations in UML class models.

Attributes are characteristics of entities; for example, customer attributes could include name, address, city, state, zip code, and credit limit. Attributes correspond to fields in a relational table, so the selection of attributes for an entity should reflect efficient table design, as discussed within Chapter 3.

[3] P. P. Chen, "The Entity-Relationship Model: Toward a Unified View of Data," *ACM Transactions on Database Systems* 1 (1976), pp. 9–36.

Cardinalities describe the nature of the relationship between two entities; they describe how many instances of an entity relate to one instance of another entity—for example, each *customer* may *participate in* many *sales*. Cardinalities correspond to multiplicities in UML class diagrams.

ERD EXAMPLE USING CHEN'S NOTATION

Figure 3.A2 shows a simple ERD using min-max cardinality notation. The two entities are Singers and Songs. The relationship between the two entities shows that we are modeling the singers that recorded the songs. This example uses min-max notation to describe the cardinalities. The cardinalities next to the Singers entity indicate the minimum (0) and maximum (N) number of songs that each singer recorded. The cardinalities next to the Songs entity indicate the minimum (1) and maximum (1) number of singers that recorded each song.

FIGURE 3.A2
ERD Example Using
Chen's Notation

ERD EXAMPLE USING INFORMATION ENGINEERING NOTATION

Figure 3.A3 shows the same example as Figure 3.A2 using information engineering notation. Again, the two entities are Singers and Songs. In this case, however, the purpose of the relationship between the two entities is not as clearly identified. The "crow's feet" markings on the relationship line indicate the cardinalities. The cardinality notation next to the Singers entity indicates there is one singer for each song. Note that a double line symbol (—++—) is sometimes used to indicate one and only one (mandatory). The cardinality notation next to the Songs entity indicates a singer can record many songs (optional). Thus, there may be singers in the database who did not record any songs, but each song must be recorded by one singer.

FIGURE 3.A3
ERD Example
Using Information
Engineering Notation

CARDINALITY OPTIONS

In general, there are four options for each cardinality. The minimum can be zero (the relationship is optional) and the maximum can be either one or many, or the minimum can be one (the relationship is mandatory) and the maximum can again be either one or many. Considering the cardinalities at each end of the relationship between two entities (entity A and entity B), there are three basic types of relationships (see Figure 3.A4):

- *One-to-one (1:1).* One instance of entity A is related only to one instance of entity B. For example, each sale earns one cash receipt.
- *One-to-many (1:N).* One instance of entity A is related to many instances of entity B (or vice versa). For example, a customer participates in many sales.
- *Many-to-many (M:N).* Many instances of entity A are related to each instance of entity B and many instances of entity B are related to entity A. For example, a sale can include many inventory items, and each inventory item could be sold on many sales.

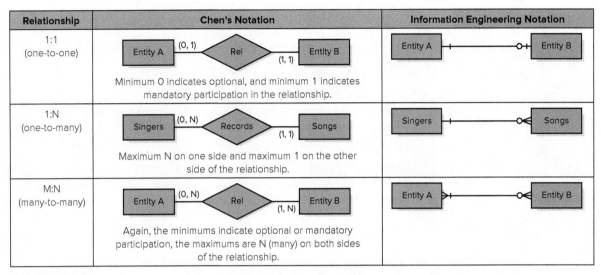

FIGURE 3.A4
Examples of Cardinality Options Using Both Chen's Notation and Information Engineering Notation

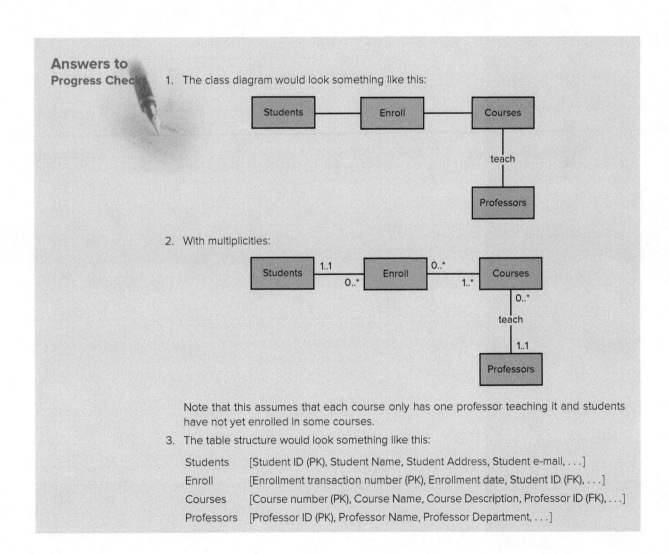

Answers to Progress Checks

1. The class diagram would look something like this:

2. With multiplicities:

Note that this assumes that each course only has one professor teaching it and students have not yet enrolled in some courses.

3. The table structure would look something like this:

Students   [Student ID (PK), Student Name, Student Address, Student e-mail, . . .]

Enroll   [Enrollment transaction number (PK), Enrollment date, Student ID (FK), . . .]

Courses   [Course number (PK), Course Name, Course Description, Professor ID (FK), . . .]

Professors   [Professor ID (PK), Professor Name, Professor Department, . . .]

![Mc Graw Hill Education] connect®

Multiple Choice Questions

1. Which of the following is not an objective of a structure model? **LO 3-1**
   a. Designate things of interest in the business domain.
   b. Describe characteristics of things of interest in the business domain.
   c. Support relational database design.
   d. Describe the sequence of activities.
   e. All of the above are objectives of structure models.

2. Which of the following symbols is used to represent a class in a UML class diagram? **LO 3-2**

   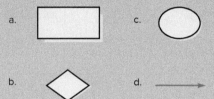

3. Which of the following statements concerning this class diagram with multiplicities is not true? **LO 3-2, LO 3-3**

   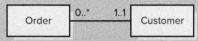

   a. An order can involve only one customer.
   b. A customer can place only one order.
   c. A customer can place many orders.
   d. A customer may not have ordered yet.
   e. All of the above are true.

4. Which of the following statements is true about the following class diagram? **LO 3-2, LO 3-3**

   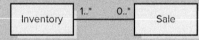

   a. A sale can involve zero inventory items.
   b. A sale can involve one inventory item.
   c. A sale can involve many inventory items.
   d. A and C are true.
   e. B and C are true.

5. Which of the following is an example of an *obligatory* business rule? **LO 3-6**
   a. Customers must provide a valid credit card number.
   b. Customers must enter a shipping address.
   c. Customers may not enter a post office box as a shipping address.
   d. Customers may use Visa or MasterCard.
   e. Both a and b are obligatory business rules.

6. Which of the following is not an enforcement level for a business rule? **LO 3-6**
   a. Strict enforcement
   b. Optional enforcement
   c. Pre-override enforcement
   d. Post-override enforcement
   e. Guideline

7. Contrast the UML class diagrams with the entity-relationship diagrams shown in Appendix A. Which of the following pairs are not equivalent? **LO 3-1, LO 3-2, LO 3-3**

    a. Class and Entity
    b. Class and Relationship
    c. Association and Relationship
    d. Multiplicity and Cardinality
    e. All of these are equivalent.

8. Which of the following best describes the meaning of this diagram? **LO 3-2, LO 3-3**

    a. Each sale can result in many subsequent cash receipts.
    b. Each cash receipt can apply to many sales.
    c. All sales must have cash receipts.
    d. Each sale can result in only one cash receipt.
    e. None of the above

9. Which of the following best describes the meaning of this entity-relationship diagram? **LO 3-2, LO 3-3**

    a. Every student is enrolled in many classes.
    b. Every class must have at least one student enrolled.
    c. Every student must be enrolled in at least one class.
    d. No students are enrolled in any classes.
    e. None of the above

10. Which of the following best describes the meaning of this UML class diagram? **LO 3-2, LO 3-3**

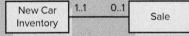

    a. Each new car can be sold once.
    b. A sale can involve multiple new cars.
    c. Each new car can be sold multiple times.
    d. No new cars are in inventory.
    e. None of the above

Refer to this diagram to answer questions 11 through 20.

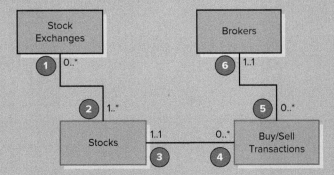

11. Which of the following best describes the meaning of the multiplicities next to the number 1 in the preceding diagram? **LO 3-2, LO 3-3**

    a. Stocks are traded in only one exchange.

    b. Stocks are traded in at least one exchange.

    c. Stocks are traded in a minimum of zero exchanges.

    d. Stocks are traded in a maximum of many exchanges.

    e. Both c and d are correct.

12. Which of the following best describes the meaning of the multiplicities next to the number 2 in the preceding diagram? **LO 3-2, LO 3-3**

    a. Each exchange trades at least one stock.

    b. Each exchange trades only one stock.

    c. Each exchange trades a minimum of zero stocks.

    d. Each exchange trades a maximum of many stocks.

    e. Both a and d are correct.

13. Which of the following is true to implement the Stock Exchanges and Stocks classes and the association between them in the preceding UML class diagram in a database? **LO 3-2, LO 3-3, LO 3-4**

    a. The primary key of Stocks is a foreign key in Stock Exchanges.

    b. The primary key of Stock Exchanges is a foreign key in Stocks.

    c. The association between Stocks and Stock Exchanges is implemented as a linking table.

    d. Both a and b are true.

    e. None of these is true.

14. Which of the following best describes the meaning of the multiplicities next to the number 3 in the preceding diagram? **LO 3-2, LO 3-3**

    a. Each transaction involves at least one stock.

    b. Each transaction involves only one stock.

    c. Each transaction involves a minimum of zero stocks.

    d. Each transaction involves a maximum of many stocks.

    e. Both a and b are correct.

15. Which of the following best describes the meaning of the multiplicities next to the number 4 in the preceding diagram? **LO 3-2, LO 3-3**

    a. Each stock is bought/sold at least once.

    b. Each stock is bought/sold only once.

    c. Each stock is bought/sold a maximum of many times.

    d. Each stock is bought/sold a minimum of many times.

    e. Both a and c are correct.

16. Which of the following is true to implement the Buy/Sell Transactions and Stocks classes and the association between them in the preceding UML class diagram in a database? **LO 3-2, LO 3-3, LO 3-4**

    a. The primary key of Stocks is a foreign key in Buy/Sell Transactions.

    b. The primary key of Buy/Sell Transactions is a foreign key in Stocks.

    c. The association between Stocks and Buy/Sell Transactions is implemented as a linking table.

    d. Both a and b are true.

    e. None of these is true.

17. Which of the following best describes the meaning of the multiplicities next to the number 5 in the preceding diagram? **LO 3-2, LO 3-3**

    a. Each Broker is involved in one Buy/Sell Transaction.

    b. Each Broker is involved in many Buy/Sell Transactions.

    c. Each Broker is involved in a minimum of one Buy/Sell Transaction.

    d. Each Broker is involved in a minimum of zero Buy/Sell Transactions.

    e. Both b and d are correct.

18. Which of the following best describes the meaning of the multiplicities next to the number 6 in the preceding diagram? **LO 3-2, LO 3-3**

    a. Each Buy/Sell Transaction involves one Broker.

    b. Each Buy/Sell Transaction involves many Brokers.

    c. Each Buy/Sell Transaction involves a minimum of zero Brokers.

    d. Each Buy/Sell Transaction involves a maximum of many Brokers.

    e. Both a and d are correct.

19. Which of the following is true to implement the Buy/Sell Transactions and Brokers classes and the association between them in the preceding UML class diagram in a database? **LO 3-2, LO 3-3, LO 3-4**

    a. The primary key of Brokers is a foreign key in Buy/Sell Transactions.

    b. The primary key of Buy/Sell Transactions is a foreign key in Brokers.

    c. The association between Brokers and Buy/Sell Transactions is implemented as a linking table.

    d. Both a and b are true.

    e. None of these is true.

20. Which of the following is true to implement the Stock Exchanges and Brokers classes in the preceding UML class diagram in a database? **LO 3-2, LO 3-3, LO 3-4**

    a. The primary key of Brokers is a foreign key in Stock Exchanges.

    b. The primary key of Stock Exchanges is a foreign key in Brokers.

    c. The association between Brokers and Stock Exchanges is implemented as a linking table.

    d. Both a and b are true.

    e. None of these is true.

21. Which of the following is not a general category of operational decision? **LO 3-5**

    a. Eligibility

    b. Accumulation

    c. Validation

    d. Risk

    e. Opportunity

22. Which of the following is not a basic step in modeling process decision requirements? **LO 3-5**

    a. Identify process steps.

    b. Document decisions and how they impact business objectives.

    c. Decompose and refine requirements.

    d. Specify decision information and knowledge requirements.

    e. Identify required decisions.

Discussion Questions

1. Consider the following one-to-one association between classes. You are mapping the diagram to a set of relational tables. Where would you post the foreign key? Why would you post it there? LO 3-1, LO 3-2, LO 3-3, LO 3-4

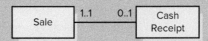

2. Consider the sale and cash receipt classes shown in Discussion Question 1. What kind of business is this (in terms of its payment requirements from customers)? How would the multiplicities change if the business (e.g., a used car dealer) accepted multiple payments over time? LO 3-1, LO 3-3

3. Consider the following model and corresponding relational tables. Describe the meaning of the diagram in words. Assume that Students are identified by Student ID Number and Courses are identified by Course Number. List the relational tables that would implement the diagram (you may make assumptions about the nonidentifying fields in the tables). LO 3-1, LO 3-2, LO 3-3, LO 3-4

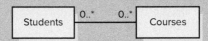

4. How would the following model look if you used a composition relationship? Which is more descriptive? *Hint:* Consider a composition relationship. LO 3-1, LO 3-2

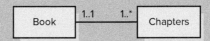

5. Consider the diagram in Discussion Question 4. Identify some examples of classes that would be modeled with a compostion model. Identify some examples of classes that would be modeled with an aggregation relationship model. LO 3-1, LO 3-2

6. Think about the process you went through to enroll in this class. What business rules do you think applied to the enrollment process? Are all of these rules written? Why or why not? LO 3-5, LO 3-6

7. Think about the last time that you purchased something over the Internet. What did the checkout page look like? What categories of operational decisions do you think were made by the website operator. What business rules applied? LO 3-5, LO 3-6

8. Compare the UML class diagram shown in Figure 3.3 with the entity-relationship diagram shown in Figure 3.A2. Describe the differences and the similarities. LO 3-1, LO 3-2

9. In your college career, you may have attended several universities. Draw a simple UML class diagram or an entity-relationship diagram showing your relationship with those universities. Now add the multiplicities or cardinalities. Would the multiplicities/cardinalities be different if the diagram was drawn from the university's perspective rather than your perspective? Why or why not? LO 3-1, LO 3-2, LO 3-3

10. Describe some real-world examples of (a) one-to-one relationships, (b) one-to-many relationships, and (c) many-to-many relationships. Which do you think is most common? Which does a relational database handle most easily? LO 3-3, LO 3-4

Problems

connect

1. Identify the classes and associations in the following narrative, and draw a class diagram with multiplicities: LO 3-2, LO 3-3

   Dr. Franklin runs a small medical clinic specializing in family practice. She has many patients. When the patients visit the clinic, she may perform several tests to diagnose their conditions. She bills the patient one amount for the visit plus additional amounts for each test.

■ **connect** 2. Identify the classes and associations in the following narrative, and draw a class diagram with multiplicities: **LO 3-2, LO 3-3**

> Paige runs a small frozen yogurt shop. She buys several flavors of frozen yogurt mix from her yogurt supplier. She buys plastic cups in several sizes from another supplier. She buys cones from a third supplier. She counts yogurt and cones as inventory, but she treats the cups as an operating expense and doesn't track any cup inventory.

■ **connect** 3. Write out a set of relational tables that correspond to the class diagram that you prepared for Problem 1. Identify primary and foreign keys. **LO 3-4**

■ **connect** 4. Write out a set of relational tables that correspond to the class diagram that you prepared for Problem 2. Identify primary and foreign keys. **LO 3-4**

■ **connect** 5. Develop a UML class diagram with classes, associations, and multiplicities based on the following narrative: **LO 3-2, LO 3-3**

> The Multnomah County Library provides a variety of services to citizens of the county. First, the library offers a number of traditional books and movies that may be checked out by patrons. Each patron may check out up to 5 books and 2 movies at one time. The library also offers several computers for patron use. The library tracks computer use sessions. Each patron may use the computer for up to 30 minutes per session. The library also maintains a number of small meeting rooms that patrons may reserve for classes or events during normal operating hours. Although library services are offered to all county citizens, each patron must obtain a library card to check out books, use the computers, or reserve a room.

■ **connect** 6. Use the UML class diagram you created for Problem 5 to create an Access database for the library. Make up at least three fields for each table, including one field that will be the primary key. **LO 3-4**

Additional problems are available in connect only.

Chapter **Four**

Relational Databases and Enterprise Systems

A look at this chapter

Databases serve as a means of organizing information. We focus on relational databases that store information in tables. We explore relational database principles, including primary and foreign keys, basic requirements of database design, and data retrieval using Structured Query Language (SQL). We also explain enterprise systems (or ERP systems) using a relational database system and their relevance to the organization.

A look back

Chapter 3 described data modeling, explaining how data models support database-driven systems. It introduced basic data modeling tools to guide the student's development of modeling skills. The chapter also provided a discussion of business rules and how identifying relevant business rules supports both process and data modeling.

A look ahead

Chapters 5 through 8 use data models to describe business processes such as sales to cash collection, procurement to pay, and product conversion.

© Tim Boyle/Getty Images

As **Starbucks'** main competitor in the northeast United States, **Dunkin' Donuts** looks to use relational database technology to help determine who ends up on the corner of your block first!

To help it win this race, Dunkin' Donuts is using a new system that helps it more quickly close deals with its new franchisees. Franchisees apply to run a Dunkin' Donuts franchise, pay the franchise fee after the approval process, and then pay royalties on each dollar of sales thereafter. Dunkin' Donuts' management uses the system to manage information about these potential franchisees, including the status of each potential deal and the status of the franchisee financing. This is particularly important in the competition against Starbucks, which doesn't franchise its stores, so its growth isn't delayed by issues with finding suitable franchise operators and getting them signed up to sell coffee in a timely fashion.

Dunkin' Donuts' managers use this dashboard-type system to get a geographic view of regions where deals are stalling; it then has the ability to drill down to see which specific item is slowing down the process. It can identify potential deals in locations that are too close in proximity. Key metrics the company is tracking and monitoring include the average cycle time to complete a franchise deal and the expected size of those deals.

Source: *Informationweek*, 2007, www.informationweek.com/news/global-cio/showArticle.jhtml?articleID=199001001; www.betheboss.ca/franchise_news_april_2007%5Cdunkin-donuts-crm161.cfm.

Chapter Outline

Introduction
Definitions for Databases
Fundamentals of Relational Databases
Entities and Attributes
Keys and Relationships
Basic Requirements of Tables
Using Microsoft Access to Implement a Relational Database
Introduction to Microsoft Access
Steve's Stylin' Sunglasses
A Data Model and Attributes for Steve's Stylin' Sunglasses' Sales Process
Multiplicities in Steve's Stylin' Sunglasses' Data Model
Using Access to Implement a Simple Database for Steve's Stylin' Sunglasses
Structured Query Language (SQL)
Enterprise Systems
Challenges of Enterprise System Implementation
Enterprise Systems Computing in the Cloud
Appendix A: Creating a Form for Data Entry and Display

Learning Objectives

After reading this chapter, you should be able to:

4-1 Describe the advantages of relational databases.

4-2 Explain basic relational database principles.

4-3 Describe how to query using Structured Query Language (SQL).

4-4 Understand the purpose and basic framework for an enterprise system.

4-5 Assess how cloud computing facilitates enterprise systems.

INTRODUCTION

A **database** is a collection of related data for various uses. Databases used in a business setting often maintain information about various types of objects (e.g., raw materials inventory), events (e.g., sales transactions), people (e.g., customers), and places (e.g., retail store). In databases today, three types of data models are used: the hierarchical model, the network model, and the relational model.

Hierarchical data models were widely used in mainframe database management systems. Hierarchical data models organize data into a tree-like structure that allows repeating information using defined parent/child relationships. One example of a tree-like structure is financial statements, where a financial statement element (parent) can be decomposed into finer elements (child). More specifically, assets (parent) can be decomposed into current assets (child 1) and noncurrent assets (child 2). Current assets (parent) could be further decomposed into cash and cash equivalents (child 3), accounts receivable (child 4), and inventory (child 5). You can see how the hierarchical relationships define the relationships among the data elements associated with a balance sheet in a tree-like structure. In a hierarchical data model, data elements are related to each other using a notation known as 1:N mapping (one parent: more than one child), also known as one-to-many relationships.

A **network data model** is a flexible model representing objects and their relationships. The network model allows each record to have multiple parent and child records or M:N mapping, also known as many-to-many relationships. These form a lattice structure (often looking like a big net) connecting parent and child records together.

The **relational data model** is a data model that stores information in the form of related two-dimensional tables. It allows designers and users to identify relationships at the time the database is created or much later whenever new informational requirements from the data model are desired. While hierarchical and network data models require relationships to be formed at the database creation, relational data models can be made up as needed.

Relational data models are the dominant data model form in use today, likely because they offer many advantages over other data models, including:

1. *Flexibility and scalability.* As business and informational requirements change, relational data models are able to handle these changes quickly and easily. For this flexibility, the relational data model for databases is the most popular data model today.
2. *Simplicity.* A relational data model is a relatively simple model that is easy to communicate to both database users and database developers.
3. *Reduced information redundancy.* A relational data model requires each piece of data to be recorded only in one place, eliminating the need for information to be stored in multiple places in the organization. This also helps keep the information updated because the information only has to be updated once in one database, which can help avoid data inconsistency.

For the remainder of the chapter, we focus on the use of relational databases.

Definitions for Databases

Before we get into the details of how relational databases are created and used in an organization, it is useful to define a few terms related to databases.

- **Database management system (DBMS)**—The DBMS is defined as a computer program that creates, modifies, and queries the database. Specifically, the DBMS is designed to manage a database's storage and retrieval of information.

LO 4-1
Describe the
advantages of
relational databases.

- **Data dictionary**—The data dictionary describes the data fields in each database record such as field description, field length, field type (e.g., alphanumeric, numeric), and so on.
- **Database administrator**—The database administrator is responsible for the design, implementation, repair, and security of a firm's database.

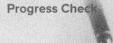
Progress Check

1. A database is an organized collection of data for various uses. Name three uses for a sales database at **Bed Bath & Beyond.**
2. Relational data models allow changes to the data model as information needs change. **General Motors** has recently expanded into China and been very successful. How does the use of a relational data model help General Motors' database designers and database users?

FUNDAMENTALS OF RELATIONAL DATABASES

Entities and Attributes

LO 4-2

Explain basic relational database principles.

First, it is important to describe entities and attributes of a relational database. As introduced in Chapter 3, a class (also called an entity) in the relational database model could be a person, place, thing, transaction, or event about which information is stored. Customers, sales, products, and employees are all examples of classes. Classes could be grouped into resources (R), events (E), and agents (A) in data modeling.[1] *Resources* are those things that have economic value to a firm, such as cash and products. *Events* are the various business activities conducted in a firm's daily operations, such as sales and purchases. *Agents* are the people who participate in business events, such as customers and salespeople.

Attributes are characteristics, properties, or adjectives that describe each class. Attributes for customer may include the Customer ID, Customer Last Name, Customer First Name, and Customer Address. Attributes for sales could be Invoice Number, Customer ID, Date, and Product Number. Attributes for products may include Product Number, Product Name, and Product Price.

There are three main constructs in a relational database: tables, attributes, and records. The primary construct is called a table or relation for data storage, with rows and columns much like a spreadsheet. Each table in a database represents either a class or a relationship among classes. Tables need to be properly linked to make a relational database. The columns in a table are called fields and represent the attributes or characteristics of the class or relationship. The rows in a table are called records or tuples. A record represents all the specific data values that are associated with one instance.

Keys and Relationships

Logical relationships within a relational database model are created by using primary keys and foreign keys. A simplistic illustration of a relational database for Gizmos and Gadgets (a reseller of smartphones) appears in Figure 4.1. As defined in Chapter 3, a **primary key (PK)** is an attribute or combination of attributes that uniquely identifies a specific row in a table. Notice the Customer ID in the Customer table is the primary key that uniquely

---

[1]The REA model was first conceptualized by William E. McCarthy in 1982. See W. E. McCarthy, "The REA Accounting Model: A Generalized Framework for Accounting Systems in a Shared Data Environment," *The Accounting Review,* July 1982, pp. 554–78.

Products of Gizmos and Gadgets.

The McGraw-Hill Companies/Ashley Zellmer, photographer

identifies the customer. In this case, the telephone number of the customer serves as the Customer ID. In Figure 4.1, the primary key that uniquely identifies a sale in the Sales table is the invoice number, and the primary key that uniquely identifies each product in the product table is the product number.

A **foreign key (FK)** in the relational database model serves as an attribute in one table that is a primary key in another table. A foreign key provides a logical

FIGURE 4.1

Illustration of a Relational Database Using Primary Keys and Foreign Keys for Gizmos and Gadgets, a Phone Reseller

Gizmos and Gadgets   June 12, 2017   Invoice #13131

To: Mark Wagstaff
168 Apple Rd., Rockville, MD 20852
602-966-1238

Product No.	Description	Price	Amount
1233	Apple iPhone 5g	399.00	399.00

                 Order Total   399.00

Customer Table			
Customer ID	**Customer Last Name**	**Customer First Name**	**Customer Address**
602-966-1238	Wagstaff	Mark	168 Apple Rd., Rockville, MD 20852
602-251-7513	Waite	Seth	2500 Campanile Dr., NY, NY 10001

Primary Key

Foreign Key

Sales Table			
Invoice No.	**Customer ID**	**Date**	**Product No.**
13131	602-966-1238	6/12/17	1233
13945	602-966-1238	8/28/17	1334
14995	602-251-7513	11/21/17	1233
15123	602-251-7513	12/11/17	5151
15127	602-251-7513	12/12/17	3135

Primary Key   Foreign Key

Primary Key

Product Table		
Product No.	**Product Name**	**Product Price**
1233	Apple iPhone 5g	399.00
1334	Motorola Droid	299.00
1233	Apple iPhone 5g	399.00
5151	iPhone cover	32.00
3135	Apple Charger	23.00

relationship, or a link, between two tables. For example, notice the link between the Customer table and the Sales table by use of the foreign key, Customer ID, in Figure 4.1. Also, notice the link between the Sales table and the Product table by use of the foreign key Product No. in the Sales table.

Basic Requirements of Tables

The approach of relational database imposes requirements on the structure of tables. If these basic requirements are not fulfilled or if data redundancy exists in a database, anomalies may occur. The requirements include the following:

- The **entity integrity rule**—the primary key of a table must have data values (cannot be null).
- The **referential integrity rule**—the data value for a foreign key must either be null or match one of the data values that already exist in the corresponding table.
- Each attribute in a table must have a unique name.
- Values of a specific attribute must be of the same type (example: alpha or numeric).
- Each attribute (column) of a record (row) must be single-valued. This requirement forces us to create a relationship table for each many-to-many relationship.
- All other nonkey attributes in a table must describe a characteristic of the class (table) identified by the primary key.

Progress Check

3. Describe how primary keys and foreign keys link tables in a relational database. *(Hint: Use Figure 4.1 to help describe how they work.)*

USING MICROSOFT ACCESS TO IMPLEMENT A RELATIONAL DATABASE

Introduction to Microsoft Access

Microsoft Access is a program in the Microsoft Office Suite. Access is a simple database management system that can be used to run databases for individuals and small firms. In practice, many larger firms choose more complicated database systems like MySQL server or Microsoft SQL Server. The Access system is composed of seven objects that are used to implement relational databases.

The basic building block of a database is the *table*. A table is used to store data, which consist of a series of rows (records) and columns (attributes) connected by relationships (links between tables). All data stored in the database will be stored in tables. Tables are linked by the use of foreign keys, forming an interconnected network of records that taken together are the relational database.

When users want to find answers to questions in the database, such as "how many customers do I have?" they use **queries**. Queries are a tool used to retrieve and display data derived from records stored within the database. This can range from listing all customers who live in Oregon, which is a subset (dynaset) of records in the customer table, to the balance in Accounts Payable, which must draw data from multiple tables. Calculations and data sorting are often performed with queries.

Forms are utilized by users to enter data into tables and view existing records. In viewing existing records, forms are powered by queries that allow data from multiple tables to be displayed on each form. Often, a firm that uses a fully electronic accounting information system will allow end users to directly update the database through the use of forms.

Reports are used to integrate data from one or more queries and tables to provide useful information to decision makers. Unlike a form, the report does not allow users to edit database information. In an accounting database, reports might consist of a sales invoice to be mailed to customers or the year-end balance sheet to show stakeholders the financial position of the firm. The applications of reports are limited only by data that have been stored in the database.

Access also allows for web-based forms, called **pages**, which allow data to be entered into the database in real time from outside of the database system. This type of application might be used to allow customers to place orders through the firm's website.

For more advanced users, Access offers **macros**. Macros are defined by users to automate processes such as opening a specific form.

Finally, Access's code can be altered by the use of **modules**. Some Microsoft applications come with modules built in that will be automatically added onto Access, like the **PayPal** module that facilitates integration with the organization's PayPal account. Other modules can be coded using Visual Basic script to alter the fundamental processes at the heart of Access.

Steve's Stylin' Sunglasses

Steve's Stylin' Sunglasses (SSS) is a retail store that designs and manufactures custom sunglasses. Every pair of sunglasses Steve, the owner, creates is unique and is therefore fairly expensive to buy. The excellent reputation for quality products and the stellar customer service provided by SSS have attracted new and returning customers.

To promote sales, Steve allows payments to be made periodically over time based on a zero-interest installment plan. However, a down payment is required. Though most customers pay for their sunglasses in full with either cash or credit card, some choose to take advantage of the payment plan option. Steve has noticed that the installment plan is utilized most frequently by customers buying multiple pairs of sunglasses at one time. Steve's policy on installment sales is that each payment from a customer must be clearly marked for one specific sale.

Because Steve is directly supervising two salespeople, who are paid on commission, he prefers to keep all sales separate to facilitate oversight of the revenue cycle. Steve does not collect any data on his customers until they make their first purchase at the store. However, he insists on storing data on every customer because each customer is entitled to free cleanings and adjustments.

Steve handles the bulk of the behind-the-scenes work at the store, including designing the sunglasses. As a result, he employs two salespeople—Frank and Sandra—who deal with the customers. When a customer walks through the door, the first available salesperson greets and assists that customer from the beginning to the end of the transaction, including helping select the best pair of sunglasses and ringing up the sale on the cash register. To that point, Frank and Sandra also act as the company's cashiers, and in that capacity, they take turns making weekly trips to **Bank of America** to deposit the cash receipts. The company has a few bank accounts with Bank of America.

A Data Model and Attributes for Steve's Stylin' Sunglasses' Sales Process

In Figure 4.2, we use a UML class diagram to draft a data model for the sales process of SSS. Notice that an REA data model presents classes in the UML diagram in three general categories: resources, events, and agents.

The central column in Figure 4.2 includes two events (i.e., business activities)—Sales and Cash Receipt. The Sales event conducted by SSS involves one resource (Inventory)

FIGURE 4.2
The Data Model for Sales Process of Steve's Stylin' Sunglasses

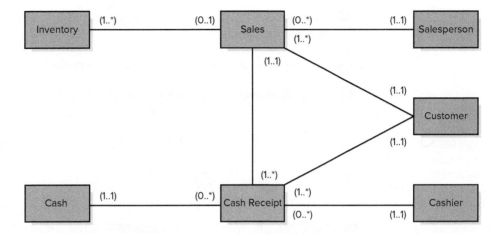

and two agents (Salesperson and Customer). The Cash Receipt event involves one resource (Cash) and two agents (Cashier and Customer). The two events are related. One would decrease the resource of SSS (selling inventories), which leads to the other that would increase the recourse of SSS (collecting cash). They are economic events involving exchanging resources with external agents (i.e., customers).

Please notice that the class Cash contains information of the bank accounts that SSS has. You can consider Cash as Bank Accounts in the diagram. To simplify, you may also consider each record in the Cash Receipt event as a check from a customer.

Multiplicities in Steve's Stylin' Sunglasses' Data Model

Figures 4.3, 4.4, and 4.5 explain the multiplicities regarding the sales event of Steve's Stylin' Sunglasses.

FIGURE 4.3
Explanations on Multiplicities Related to the Sales Event

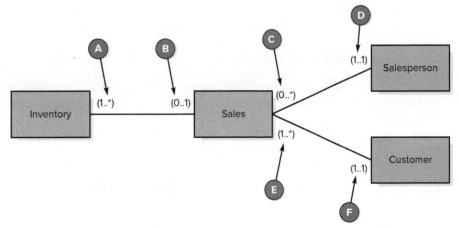

(A) SSS may sell more than one pair of sunglasses to a customer at one time.

(B) Every pair of sunglasses SSS creates is unique and could be sold once only. Zero means a pair of sunglasses could be designed but not yet sold.

(C) The shop employs two employees who can act as salespersons. At a minimum, a salesperson (new) may not handle any sale transaction yet, and at most, each salesperson could handle many sale transactions.

D One and only one salesperson greets and assists a customer from the beginning to the end of a sale transaction.

E SSS has repeat customers. Customer data are recorded after the first purchase.

F Each sale involves one and only one customer.

FIGURE 4.4
Explanations on Multiplicities Related to the Cash Receipt Event

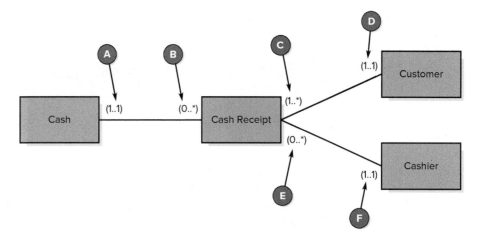

A Each cash receipt is deposited in one and only one bank account.

B Each bank account could have no deposit or many deposits from the cash receipt event.

C Each customer has the option for an installment plan (i.e., SSS will have many cash receipts from one customer). The "1" means a down payment is required.

D Each cash receipt is from one and only one customer.

E The shop employs two employees who can act as cashier. A cashier (new) may not handle any cash receipt yet, or a cashier could take charge of many cash receipts.

F Each cash receipt (e.g., a check from a customer) is handled by one and only one cashier.

FIGURE 4.5
Explanations on Multiplicities between the Sales and Cash Receipt Events

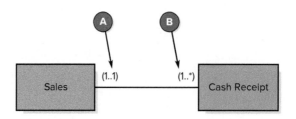

A Each cash receipt is for one and only one sale transaction.

B Each sale transaction may have at least one cash receipt (i.e., a down payment is required), and at most many cash receipts from customers (i.e., installment sales).

Given the data model in Figure 4.2, we assume the following attributes for each table.

Customer	[Customer_Number (PK), Customer_First_Name, Customer_Last_Name, Customer _Address, Customer_City, Customer_State, Customer_Zip, Customer_Email]
Salesperson	[Salesperson_Number (PK), Salesperson_First_Name, Salesperson_Last_Name, Salesperson_SSN]
Cashier	[Cashier_Number (PK), Cashier_First_Name, Cashier_Last_Name, Cashier_SSN]
Sales	[Sale_Number (PK), Sale_Date, Sale_Amount, Payment_Type, Customer_Number (FK), Salesperson_Number (FK)]
Cash_Receipt	[Receipt_Number (PK), Receipt_Date, Receipt_Amount, Customer_Number (FK), Cashier_Number (FK), Sale_Number (FK), Account_Number (FK)]
Cash	[Account_Number (PK), Bank_Name, Bank_Address, Bank_Contact_Person, Balance]
Inventory	[InventoryID_Number (PK), Description, Completion_Date, Cost, Price, Sale_Number (FK)]

Using Access to Implement a Simple Database for Steve's Stylin' Sunglasses

Getting Started in Access

Step 1.   Open Access.

Step 2.   Access will ask you to choose from available templates. Select "Blank database" (see Figure 4.6).

FIGURE 4.6
Starting Access

© Microsoft Access

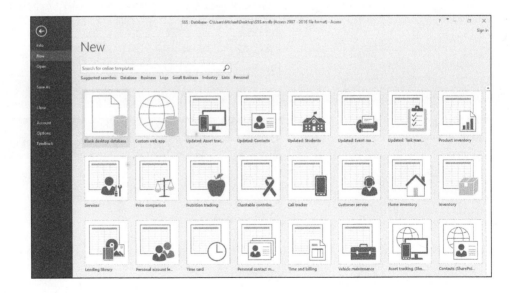

Step 3.   To change the name of the database, click File → Save Database As; then save the database as "SSS." You will likely get a message saying "All objects must be closed before you save the database" (see Figure 4.7). Click "Yes."

Step 4.   Ensure that the ribbon marked "Enable content" is enabled.

FIGURE 4.7
Save a Database in
Access

© Microsoft Access

Creating New Tables in Access

Refer to the tables and attributes designed based on the data model (Figure 4.2). This is the database we will be constructing. The first table is the Customer table.

Step 1. Click the tab Create → Table (see Figure 4.8). (Note: The Table Design button will create a table and open it in Design View. See Figure 4.9.)

FIGURE 4.8
Create a Table in
Access

© Microsoft Access

FIGURE 4.9
Create a Table in
Design View

© Microsoft Access

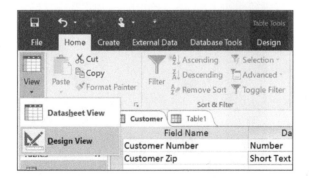

Step 2. Click the tab Home → View (dropdown menu) → Design View (see Figure 4.9).

Step 3. You will be prompted to Save As, so save the table as "Customer." This table will contain the records of Steve's Stylin' Sunglasses' customers. Note the Field Name, Data type, and Description columns. You will use these to configure the Customer table (see Figure 4.10).

FIGURE 4.10
The Design View of
the Customer Table

© Microsoft Access

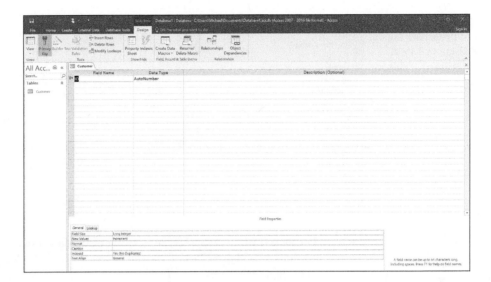

Step 4. The first attribute of the Customer table will be its primary key. Currently, the primary key is named ID. Highlight ID in the Field Name column and change it to "Customer Number." A field name names an attribute in a table. It may contain 64 characters and may not contain periods, exclamation points, or brackets because they are used in Visual Basic scripts. You should see a key icon next to the Customer Number (see Figure 4.11). If it is not there, right click and select "Primary Key" or look for the primary key button on the design tab of the ribbon.

FIGURE 4.11
Create the Primary
Key of the Customer
Table

© Microsoft Access

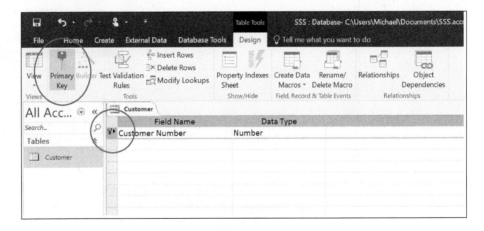

Step 5. Click on the dropdown button for the Data Type and select Number. This will force any data entered into this field to be in the form of a number. Take some time to familiarize yourself with the options on this menu. Description field (Figure 4.10), when used, allows useful information about the attribute to be provided to users.

Step 6. It is a good practice to set Field Properties for each attribute. For example, for Customer Number, we would set the Field Size to Long Integer and the Validation Rule to Like "######". By doing so, we will ensure that all Customer Numbers are six digits long (i.e., six pound signs). The Validation Text of "Customer # should be 6 numbers" provides an error message to tell users what they did wrong. Because this is a primary key, choose the Required field as "Yes" and the Indexed field as "Yes (No Duplicates)" (see Figure 4.12).

FIGURE 4.12
Field Properties for the Primary Key of the Customer Table

© Microsoft Access

Field Properties	
General	Lookup
Field Size	Long Integer
Format	
Decimal Places	Auto
Input Mask	
Caption	
Default Value	0
Validation Rule	Like "######"
Validation Text	Customer# should be 6 numbers
Required	Yes
Indexed	Yes (No Duplicates)
Text Align	General

Step 7.   For some fields, it is appropriate to use an Input Mask. For example, Customer Zip should have an Input Mask. To do this, select the attribute Customer Zip and click in the Input Mask area in the Field Properties box. You will see to the right a button with ". . ." on it. Click this button to bring up the Input Mask Wizard window as shown in Figure 4.13. Select Zip Code from the menu and click Next and Finish.

FIGURE 4.13
Input Mask for Customer Zip Field

© Microsoft Access

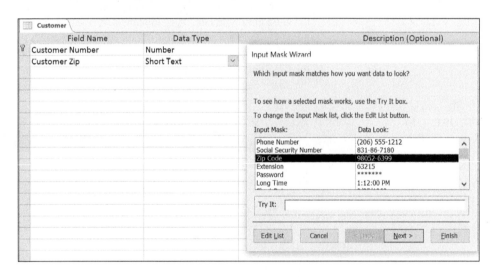

Step 8.   Create the rest of the tables and attributes given before, using appropriate data types and properties. Generally, validation rules are used for primary keys. The attributes of the Sales table are shown in Figure 4.14. For other fields such as Sale Date in the Sales table, you will also use Input Masks.

FIGURE 4.14
Attributes of the Sales Table

© Microsoft Access

Field Name	Data Type
Sale Number	Number
Sale Date	Date/Time
Sale Amount	Currency
Payment Type	Text
Customer Number	Number
Salesperson Number	Number

Creating Relationships in Access

In order to implement a relationship in Access, you must use a foreign key. Note that the names of the two fields (the primary key in one table and the foreign key in the other table) do not have to be the same. You will create links between these similar fields in Access' Relationship window.

Step 1.   To pull up the Relationship window, click Database Tools → Relationships (see Figure 4.15).

FIGURE 4.15
Open the Relationship Window in Access

© Microsoft Access

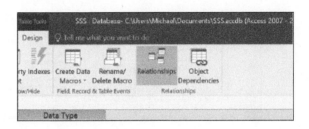

Step 2.   Click the Show Table button in the Design tab to pull up a list of all your tables. Select all your tables and press the Add button. Arrange the tables in the form similar to the data model.

Step 3.   Click each primary key that you want to link and drag it to its respective foreign key in another table. Be sure to check the "Enforce Referential Integrity" box for each relationship (see Figure 4.16).

FIGURE 4.16
Enforce Referential Integrity in Linking Tables

© Microsoft Access

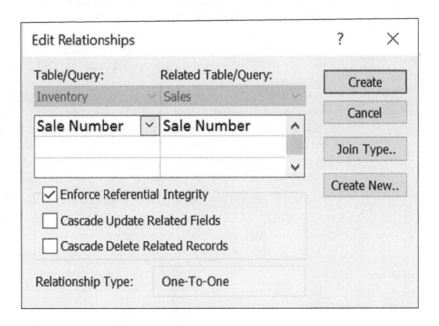

Step 4.   Upon completion of this process for all relationship among the tables, the Relationship window should look like Figure 4.17. A referential database has been created in Access for Steve's Stylin' Sunglasses.

FIGURE 4.17
A Database for Steve's Stylin' Sunglasses

© Microsoft Access

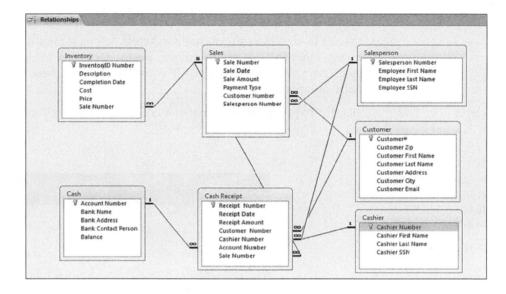

STRUCTURED QUERY LANGUAGE (SQL)

LO 4-3

Describe how to query using Structured Query Language (SQL).

SQL (usually pronounced "Sequel") stands for **Structured Query Language** and is a computer language designed to query data in a relational database. SQL is based on relational algebra and allows a user to query and update the database. In a database, while queries allow the user to access, read, and report on desired data, the responsibility of actually making physical changes to the relational database belongs to the database management system (DBMS). The four most basic operations—Create, Read, Update, and Delete (CRUD)—must be supported in a DBMS. SQL provides the "INSERT" operator (i.e., a command) to create new records, the "SELECT" operator to read or retrieve data, the "UPDATE" operator to update records, and the "DELETE" operator to delete existing records from the database.

The SELECT operator is used to begin a query. The SELECT operator tells the query which columns (or attributes) of a table should be included in the query result. A query includes a list of columns in the final result immediately following the SELECT operator. An asterisk (*) can also be used to specify that the query should return all columns of the queried tables. SELECT is the most useful operator in SQL, with optional keywords and clauses that include the following:

1. The FROM clause to the SELECT operator indicates the name of table(s) from which to retrieve data.

   SQL Example 1: Given the attributes in the Customer table in Figure 4.18, how is a query used to find the salesperson for each customer?

FIGURE 4.18
Customer

Customer#	Name	A/R Amt	SP#
C-1	Bill	345	E-12
C-2	Mick	225	E-10
C-3	Keith	718	E-10
C-4	Charlie	828	E-99
C-5	Ron	3,200	E-10

If we use the following SQL commands, we are asking SQL to select the Customer#, Name, and SP# attributes from the Customer Table:

> SELECT Customer#, Name, SP#
>
> FROM Customer;

We will get the following query result (Figure 4.19):

FIGURE 4.19

Customer#	Name	SP#
C-1	Bill	E-12
C-2	Mick	E-10
C-3	Keith	E-10
C-4	Charlie	E-99
C-5	Ron	E-10

2. The WHERE clause states the criteria that must be met to be shown in the query result. There are many search criteria that you can specify for the final result. Search criteria using relational operators, the BETWEEN operator, and the LIKE operator are very common in SQL commands (Figure 4.20).

FIGURE 4.20
Cash Receipt

Remittance Advice#	Amount	Bank Account#	Date	Customer Number	Cashier Number
RA-1	1,666	BA-6	25-JUL-2017	C-2	E-39
RA-2	10,000	BA-7	26-JUL-2017	C-2	E-39
RA-3	72,000	BA-7	15-AUG-2017	C-1	E-39
RA-4	32,600	BA-7	15-AUG-2017	C-5	E-39
RA-5	1,669	BA-6	25-AUG-2017	C-2	E-39

SQL Example 2:

If we use the following SQL command, we are asking SQL to retrieve all cash receipt information for customer C-2 from the table called "Cash Receipt."

> SELECT *
>
> FROM [Cash Receipt]
>
> WHERE [Customer Number] = 'C-2';

Please note that the asterisk (*) following the SELECT SQL statement is a wild card indicating all columns should be selected. The brackets are needed following the FROM and WHERE clauses because there are spaces in the table and attribute names. In addition, if any table name or attribute name contains one or more spaces, we have to use brackets such as [Cash Receipt] to make sure it is considered as one table or one attribute in SQL.

We will get the following query result (Figure 4.21):

FIGURE 4.21

Remittance Advice#	Amount	Bank Account#	Date	Customer Number	Cashier Number
RA-1	1,666	BA-6	25-JUL-2017	C-2	E-39
RA-2	10,000	BA-7	26-JUL-2017	C-2	E-39
RA-5	1,669	BA-6	25-AUG-2017	C-2	E-39

Notice the WHERE command eliminated those rows that did not have Customer Number equal to C-2.

SQL Example 3: Assume you would like to use a query to find the salesperson for each customer, and you would like to show the name of each salesperson as part of the result. Data are presented in Figures 4.22 and 4.23.

Customer#	Name	A/R Amt	SP#
C-1	Bill	345	E-12
C-2	Mick	225	E-10
C-3	Keith	718	E-10
C-4	Charlie	828	E-99
C-5	Ron	3,200	E-10

FIGURE 4.22
Customer

SP#	SP_Name
E-10	Howard
E-12	Pattie
E-34	Stephanie
E-99	David

FIGURE 4.23
Salesperson

If we use the following SQL commands, we are asking SQL to select the Customer#, Name, SP#, and SP_Name attributes from the Customer table and Salesperson table:

SELECT Customer#, Name, SP#, SP_Name

FROM Customer, Salesperson

WHERE Customer.SP#=Salesperon.SP#;

It is critical that we include WHERE here to link two tables. SP# is a foreign key in the Customer table. We use it to link the Salesperson table with the Customer table.

We will get the following query result (Figure 4.24):

FIGURE 4.24

Customer#	Name	SP#	SP_Name
C-1	Bill	E-12	Pattie
C-2	Mick	E-10	Howard
C-3	Keith	E-10	Howard
C-4	Charlie	E-99	David
C-5	Ron	E-10	Howard

The above example shows a "one to many" relationship. That is, each customer is served by a salesperson and each salesperson can serve many customers.

3. The GROUP BY operator is used with aggregate functions on the query results based on one or more columns.

SQL Example 4: Refer to the Cash Receipt table in SQL Example 2 (Figure 4.20). Assume you would like to know the total cash receipt amount from each customer. If you use the following SQL commands, you can get the result.

SELECT [Customer Number], SUM(Amount)

FROM [Cash Receipt]

GROUP BY [Customer Number];

The query results will be (Figure 4.25):

FIGURE 4.25

Customer Number	Amount
C-2	13,335
C-1	72,000
C-5	32,600

4. The ORDER BY clause identifies which columns are used to sort the resulting data. If there is no ORDER BY clause, the order of rows returned by a SQL query will not be defined.

> **SQL Example 5:** Refer to the Cash Receipt table in SQL Example 2 (Figure 4.20). If we use the following SQL commands instead, the amount of cash receipt would be ordered in ascending amount (ASC) or descending amount (DESC). The result (Figure 4.26) is different from that of Example 2.
>
> SELECT *
>
> FROM [Cash Receipt]
>
> WHERE [Customer Number] = 'C-2'
>
> ORDER BY Amount ASC;

FIGURE 4.26

Remittance Advice#	Amount	Bank Account#	Date	Customer Number	Cashier Number
RA-1	1,666	BA-6	25-JUL-2017	C-2	E-39
RA-5	1,669	BA-6	25-AUG-2017	C-2	E-39
RA-2	10,000	BA-7	26-JUL-2017	C-2	E-39

5. The INSERT INTO operator inserts data into a SQL table. For example, you can insert a row into the Cash Receipt table with the following SQL commands:

> INSERT INTO [Cash Receipt]
>
> VALUES ('RA-6', 5000, 'BA-7', '28-AUG-2017', 'C-2', 'E-39');

After insertion, the Cash Receipt table will have one more row and the result of the execution is as follows (Figure 4.27):

FIGURE 4.27
Cash Receipt

Remittance Advice#	Amount	Bank Account#	Date	Customer Number	Cashier Number
RA-1	1,666	BA-6	25-JUL-2017	C-2	E-39
RA-2	10,000	BA-7	26-JUL-2017	C-2	E-39
RA-3	72,000	BA-7	15-AUG-2017	C-1	E-39
RA-4	32,600	BA-7	15-AUG-2017	C-5	E-39
RA-5	1,669	BA-6	25-AUG-2017	C-2	E-39
RA-6	5,000	BA-7	28-AUG-2017	C-2	E-39

6. The UPDATE operator is for updating data in a SQL table. For example, you can use the following SQL UPDATE command to change the Amount value from 5000 to 6000 for the inserted entry of RA-6. You often need to use the command SET for the updated data value.

> UPDATE [Cash Receipt]
>
> SET Amount = 6000
>
> WHERE [Remittance Advice#] = 'RA-6';

7. The DELETE FROM operator deletes data from a SQL table. For example, to delete the entry previously inserted, you can use the following SQL commands:

> DELETE FROM [Cash Receipt]
>
> WHERE [Remittance Advice#] = 'RA-6';

After executing the DELETE command, the record of Remittance Advice# 'RA-6' will be deleted from the Cash Receipt table, and the table will look the same as the original one.

8. The SELECT DISTINCT clause selects a column without showing repetitive values.

   SQL Example 6: Refer to the Cash Receipt table in SQL Example 2(Figure 4.20). You can retrieve each customer number once from the Cash Receipt table with the following command:

   SELECT DISTINCT [Customer Number]

   FROM [Cash Receipt];

   You will get the following query result (Figure 4.28):

FIGURE 4.28

Customer Number
C-2
C-1
C-5

9. The BETWEEN operator can be used to specify the end points of a range. Possible criteria can be "WHERE Amount BETWEEN 1000 AND 2000" or "WHERE Date BETWEEN '01-JAN-2017' AND '31-DEC-2017'." Assuming that you are interested in finding out cash receipt entries made in July, then you can issue the following SQL command to retrieve those entries.

   SELECT *

   FROM [Cash Receipt]

   WHERE Date BETWEEN '01-JUL-2017' AND '31-JUL-2017'

   The query result will be (Figure 4.29):

FIGURE 4.29

Remittance Advice#	Amount	Bank Account#	Date	Customer Number	Cashier Number
RA-1	1,666	BA-6	25-JUL-2017	C-2	E-39
RA-2	10,000	BA-7	26-JUL-2017	C-2	E-39

10. Membership Operator (IN) allows you to test whether a data value matches the specified target values.

    SQL Example 7: Refer to the Cash Receipt table in SQL Example 2 (Figure 4.20). Assume you would like to know the total cash receipt amount from customers C-1 and C-2. If you use the following SQL commands, you can get the result shown in Figure 4.30, which is different from that of Example 4.

    SELECT [Customer Number], SUM(Amount)

    FROM [Cash Receipt]

    WHERE [Customer Number] IN ('C-1', 'C-2')

    GROUP BY [Customer Number];

    The query results will be:

FIGURE 4.30

Customer Number	Amount
C-1	72,000
C-2	13,335

In addition, there are six relational operators in SQL. Their definitions are listed here:

Relational Operators	Meaning
=	equal
! = or < >	not equal
<	less than
< =	less than or equal to
>	greater than
> =	greater than or equal to

Given the data in Figure 4.20, if you are interested in those entries with an amount ≥10000, you can use the following SQL commands.

> SELECT *
>
> FROM [Cash Receipt]
>
> WHERE Amount > = 10000;

You will get the following query result back (Figure 4.31):

FIGURE 4.31

Remittance Advice#	Amount	Bank Account#	Date	Customer Number	Cashier Number
RA-2	10,000	BA-7	26-JUL-2017	C-2	E-39
RA-3	72,000	BA-7	15-AUG-2017	C-1	E-39
RA-4	32,600	BA-7	25-AUG-2017	C-5	E-39

SQL language provides several convenient aggregate functions to be used in SQL commands. These aggregate functions include AVG, SUM, MAX, MIN, and COUNT. Their definitions are as follows:

- AVG(X): gives the average of column X.
- SUM(X): gives the summation of all rows that satisfy the selection criteria for column X.
- MAX(X): gives the maximum value of column X.
- MIN(X): gives the minimum value of column X.
- COUNT(X): gives the number of rows that satisfy the given condition.

To query the total amount and average amount from the Cash Receipt table, use

> SELECT SUM(Amount), AVG(Amount)
>
> FROM [Cash Receipt];

To query the largest amount entry from the Cash Receipt table, use

> SELECT MAX(Amount)
>
> FROM [Cash Receipt];

To query the total amount that occurred in July from the Cash Receipt table, use

> SELECT SUM(Amount)
>
> FROM [Cash Receipt]
>
> WHERE Date BETWEEN '01-JUL-2017' AND '31-JUL-2017';

SQL create commands, update commands, and many other SQL query commands as well as SQL functions are beyond the scope of this textbook. See, for example, www.w3schools.com/sql/ for a list of popular SQL query commands.

Progress Check

4. What does the SQL command SELECT * do?
5. What SQL command would you use to order an amount in descending order?
6. What SQL commands would you use if you wanted to query transactions made in July from the Cash Receipt table?

LO 4-4
Understand the purpose and basic framework for an enterprise system.

In fact, for a popular ERP product (SAP/ERP) installation, there are more than 10,000 tables that are all linked to each other!

ENTERPRISE SYSTEMS

Before enterprise systems were developed, each function within the organization (finance, accounting, human resources, procurement, manufacturing, etc.) had its own information system that met its own needs. However, imagine the challenge for a company like **General Motors** to predict, budget, and manage its costs for producing a new Corvette! The company would have to get production information from the manufacturing database, costs from the accounting database, and labor information and costs from the human resources database and attempt to integrate them. Because of these types of problems and the power of integrated information, enterprise systems were developed, including major, commercial enterprise systems such as SAP/ERP, Oracle ERP, and Microsoft Dynamics.

Enterprise systems (ESs), also known as enterprise resource planning (ERP) systems, are commercialized information systems that integrate and automate business processes across a firm's value chain located within and across organizations. Typically, an enterprise system uses a relational data model as a basis for the information system. The use of primary and foreign keys links the hundreds of tables that form the basis for the enterprise system.

As mentioned in Chapter 1, ESs accommodate the integration and support of the various business processes and information needs of a company by integrating multiple modules to help a manufacturer or other business manage the important parts of its business, including product planning, parts purchasing, inventory maintenance, supplier interaction, customer service, and order tracking. ESs can also include application modules for the accounting, finance, and human resources aspects of a business. ESs are applicable to all types of businesses. In fact, most universities now use enterprise systems to manage course registration and student accounts (including the payment of library fines and parking tickets!).

Figure 4.32 offers a list of potential modules available from SAP. You can quickly see the breadth of the offering that would come from a typical enterprise systems vendor.

Managers (and auditors) can trace the creation of information throughout business processes and also identify the participants in each process. Therefore, ES has a higher level of internal transparency compared to the typically isolated legacy systems. For example, once one user from the sales department enters a customer order, users from the inventory department can see this information immediately and begin to process the customer order. At the same time, users from the accounting department can use this information to prepare the customer invoice and recognize revenue once it has been earned. Database transactions in ES are often designed to track specific details of any given business transaction, including who entered the data into the system, who modified it, and who actually used it.

FIGURE 4.32
List of Modules
Available from SAP

List of SAP Modules Available for Implementation	
Financial Applications	
FI	Financial Accounting
CO	Controlling
EC	Enterprise Controlling
IM	Investment Management
PS	Project System
Human Resources	
PA	Personnel Administration
PT	Personnel Time Management
PY	Payroll
Logistics Applications	
SD	Sales and Distribution
MM	Materials Management
PP	Production Planning and Control
LE	Logistics Execution
QM	Quality Management
CS	Customer Service

The purported informational benefits of an enterprise system include enhanced completeness, transparency, and timeliness of information needed to manage effectively an organization's business activities.[2]

The enterprise system serves as the backbone of the company's internal business processes and serves as a connection with the external business processes for supply chain and customer relationship management systems.

Challenges of Enterprise System Implementation

Although the standard enterprise system software is packaged and technically sound, all types of challenges emerge from both a technical and organizational perspective when it comes time to custom-fit the software to a particular organization's needs. More specifically, organizations face many challenges in implementing enterprise systems, including the following:

1. Integrating various modules within the enterprise system.
2. Integrating with external systems such as the information system of a supplier and/or customer.
3. Integrating with the firm's own existing legacy systems.
4. Converting data from existing legacy systems to the enterprise system.
5. Getting any big project implemented at a firm. This might include scope creep (i.e., increasing the number of changes to the software initially planned), cost overruns, time delays, and so on. In addition, this means getting adequate training for employees and getting them to actually adopt the new software when they might feel their old system seemed to meet their needs just fine.

These challenges can be overwhelming and some are specifically addressed in Chapter 16. Here, we provide an illustration of a few of the high-profile examples of firms that had failed or challenged enterprise system implementations, as well as the resulting damage inflicted on the firm:

[2]H. Klaus, M. Rosemann, and G. G. Gable, "What Is ERP?," *Information Systems Frontiers* 2, no. 2 (2000), p. 141.

Hershey was not able to deliver Hershey Kisses for Halloween in 1999 right after the first attempt to implement its enterprise system.
© JILL JARSULIC/KRT/Newscom

1. **Hershey**

   Hershey spent $115 million on a failed enterprise system implementation attempt of SAP R/3, Siebel CRM, and Manugistics supply chain applications during the Halloween season, which caused huge candy disruptions in 1999. This failed attempt prevented Hershey from delivering $100 million worth of Hershey Kisses for Halloween that year, causing a third-quarter sales drop of 12.4 percent. Earnings that year were off by 18.6 percent (compared with the previous year), and that caused the stock price to fall by 8 percent.

2. **Nike**

   In 2000, a $400 million i2 upgrade to **Nike**'s supply chain and enterprise systems gave the shoe and athletic company $100 million in lost sales, a 20 percent stock dip, and a collection of class-action lawsuits.

3. **Hewlett-Packard (HP)**

   In 2004, **HP**'s enterprise system implementation went awry. Gilles Bouchard, then-CIO of HP's global operations, said, "We had a series of small problems, none of which individually would have been too much to handle. But together they created the perfect storm." The project eventually cost HP $160 million in order backlogs and lost revenue—more than five times the project's estimated cost.

4. **Enterprise System Failure at a University**

   During fall semester 2004, more than 27,000 students at the University of Massachusetts, Stanford University, and Indiana University were unable to find their classes and unable to collect their financial aid checks due to a flawed ERP system. However, after a couple frustrating days and weeks, everyone eventually got their checks and class schedules![3]

5. **Fox Meyer**

   Fox Meyer, once the nation's fourth-largest distributor of pharmaceuticals, blamed its enterprise system fiasco as the reason for its bankruptcy in 1996.

6. **Shane Co.**

   Shane Co., the family-owned jewelry retailer that sought bankruptcy in 2009, told a U.S. judge that the company's decline was triggered partly by delays and cost overruns for a $36 million SAP AG enterprise system.

Enterprise Systems Computing in the Cloud

LO 4-5
Assess how cloud computing facilitates enterprise systems.

Providing sufficient computing power in an organization to run an enterprise system can be challenging. In recent years, **cloud computing** has emerged as a potential alternative to host enterprise systems and other firm computing needs. Cloud computing is Internet-based computing, where shared resources, software, and information are provided to firms on demand. Just like an electrical grid can handle electricity needs on the fly, cloud

[3]www.cio.com/article/486284/10_Famous_ERP_Disasters_Dustups_and_Disappointments.

computing can handle computing needs on the fly. Cloud computing is simply a set of pooled computing resources that are delivered over the Internet.

Cloud computing can easily host enterprise system applications. Enterprise system applications can quickly scale to the requirements of the computing task by making hundreds of servers and related resources available when they are required. When using cloud computing, firms do not need to worry about buying more computers to meet increasing computing traffic demands or about huge computing traffic spikes. They will simply pay for the computing power they use, much like you pay for the amount of electricity you use in your home or work.

Cloud computing, of course, has disadvantages as well. Ensuring that any sensitive data are secure and backed up frequently by the host is often a concern of cloud computing clients. Making sure the host has minimal down time and adequate processing speed at all times are also concerns. But perhaps the biggest concern is that cloud computing requires the client to have a constant Internet connection. If, for some reason, the Internet connection goes down, the system will not function. This represents an obvious downside on a firm's business that uses cloud computing for its interfaces with their enterprise system.

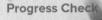

Progress Check

7. Why are enterprise systems so much better than legacy systems that firms are willing to invest the time, money, and effort to risk implementing such systems?
8. From Figure 4.32, which SAP modules would an accounting firm implement to track its billable hours for the audit staff?

Summary

- Relational databases offer efficient, effective databases for a firm. Their flexibility and scalability along with their simplicity offer powerful advantages for a firm and its information systems.
- Relational databases rely on primary and foreign keys to link tables.
- Structured Query Language (SQL) is used with relational databases to query the database.
- Enterprise systems are based on relational databases and link many different modules and functions of the firm to give integrated information to the firm's management and workers throughout the firm.
- Cloud computing is a recent innovation that could host a firm's enterprise systems such as SAP's cloud-based ERP software Business ByDesign.

Key Words

attributes (*85*)   Data elements that describe instances in a class, very much like fields in a database table; characteristics, properties, or adjectives that describe each class.

cloud computing (*104*)   Internet-based computing, where shared resources, software, and information are provided to firms on demand; using redundant servers in multiple locations to host virtual machines.

data dictionary (*85*)   Describes the data fields in each database record such as field description, field length, field type (e.g., alphanumeric, numeric), etc.

database (*84*)   A shared collection of logically related data for various uses.

database administrator (*85*)   The person responsible for the design, implementation, repair, and security of a firm's database.

database management system (DBMS) (84) A computer program that creates, modifies, and queries the database. Specifically, the DBMS is designed to manage a database's storage and retrieval of information.

enterprise system (ES) (102) A centralized database that collects data from throughout the firm. Commercialized information system that integrates and automates business processes across a firm's value chain located within and across organizations.

entity integrity rule (87) The primary key of a table must have data values (cannot be null).

foreign key (FK) (86) Attribute that allows database tables to be linked together; foreign keys are the primary keys of other tables placed in the current table to support the link between the two tables.

form (87) Forms are utilized by users to enter data into tables and view existing records.

hierarchical data model (84) Organizes data into a tree-like structure that allows repeating information using defined parent/child relationships.

macro (88) Macros are defined by Access users to automate processes such as opening a specific form.

module (88) Some Microsoft applications come with modules built in that will be automatically added onto Access.

network data model (84) A flexible model representing objects and their relationships; allows each record to have multiple parent and child records or M:N mapping, also known as many-to-many relationships.

pages (88) Access pages allow data to be entered into the database in real time from outside of the database system.

primary key (PK) (85) An attribute or a combination of attributes that uniquely identifies an instance of a class in a data model or a specific row in a table.

query (87) Query in Access is a tool used to retrieve and display data derived from records stored within the database.

referential integrity rule (87) The data value for a foreign key must either be null or match one of the data values that already exist in the corresponding table.

relational data model (84) Stores information in the form of related two-dimensional tables.

report (88) Reports in Access are used to integrate data from one or more queries and tables to provide useful information to decision makers.

Structured Query Language (SQL) (96) A computer language designed to retrieve data from a relational database.

Answers to Progress Check

1. There could be different answers for this question. Three possible answers are as follows:
   a. Which **Bed Bath & Beyond** products are selling the best.
   b. Which products the company needs to advertise or which need a price reduction.
   c. How many of which product to order for tomorrow, next week, and next month from its suppliers.

2. If relational data models are not used, database designers and database users have to predict information uses in the future, even when their business model (the way they make money) changes. This is one of the key reasons relational data models (and relational databases) are used.

3. The primary key of one table serves as a foreign key in another table. When they are matched together, they are able to link two distinct tables in preparation for querying, updating, or modifying.

4. The SQL statement "SELECT *" requests that all columns in a table be selected for use in the query.

5. The SQL clause "ORDER BY Amount DESC" would be used.

6. The following SQL commands should be used.

   SELECT *

   FROM [Cash Receipt]

   WHERE Date BETWEEN '01-JUL-2014' AND '31-JUL-2014';

7. The power of integration of the various modules and functions (e.g., accounting, marketing, procurement, manufacturing, etc.) across the organization makes an enterprise system particularly valuable to not only management, but also to workers throughout the enterprise.

8. The SAP module PT Personnel Time Management appears to be the most applicable module for tracking billable hours for the audit staff.

Appendix A

Creating a Form for Data Entry and Display

Forms are utilized to enter data into tables and view existing records. This appendix provides a tutorial to create a simple form for Steve's Stylin' Sunglasses (SSS) to enter customer information into the Customer table and display the customer records one by one.

Step 1. Open the SSS database in Microsoft Access.

Step 2. Display all the tables on the left-hand side of the database window, and highlight the Customer table. Click on the Form Wizard icon in the form section of the Create tab (Figure 4.A1).

FIGURE 4.A1
Create a Form in Access

© Microsoft Access

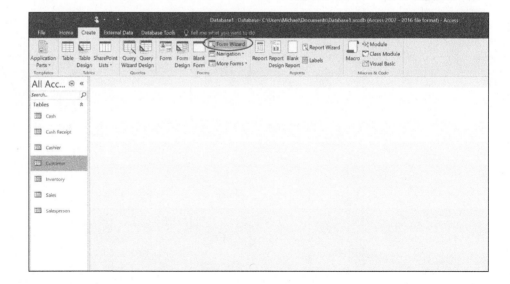

Step 3. In the pop-up Form Wizard window, select Customer table from the Table/Queries pull-down menu, and select all seven fields for inclusion in the form (Figure 4.A2).

FIGURE 4.A2
Select Fields Using
Form Wizard

© Microsoft Access

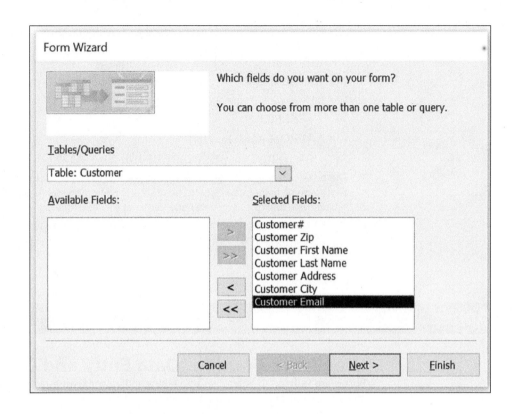

Step 4.   Click the Next button. You will see four types of form layouts. Choose "Columnar" as the form layout (Figure 4.A3).

FIGURE 4.A3
Select a Layout Using
Form Wizard

© Microsoft Access

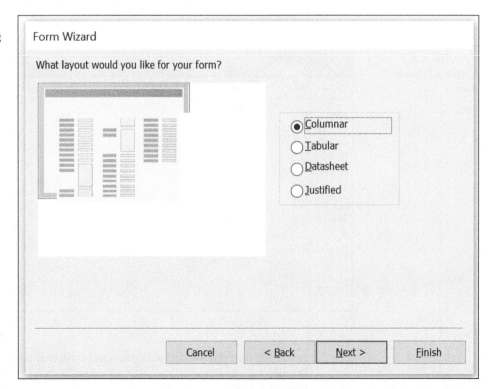

Step 5. Click the Next button. Name the title of the form "Customer Form" and select "Modify the form's design" as indicated in Figure 4.A4. Click Finish and a screen resembling Figure 4.A5 will appear.

FIGURE 4.A4
Give a Title to the Form

© Microsoft Access

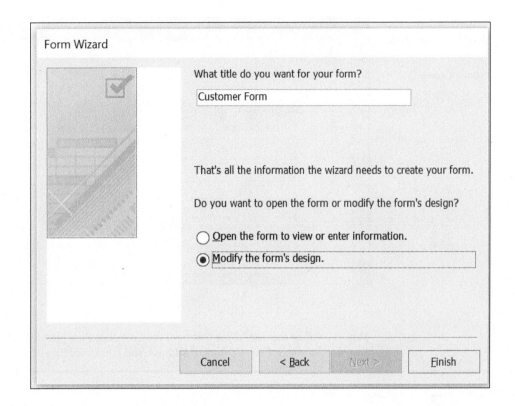

FIGURE 4.A5
Draft a Customer Form

© Microsoft Access

Step 6.   Figure 4.A5 is the design view of the Customer Form in which you can format the form. The Customer Zip text field looks too wide. Select the Customer Zip field and resize it (Figure 4.A6).

FIGURE 4.A6
Modify the Customer Form

© Microsoft Access

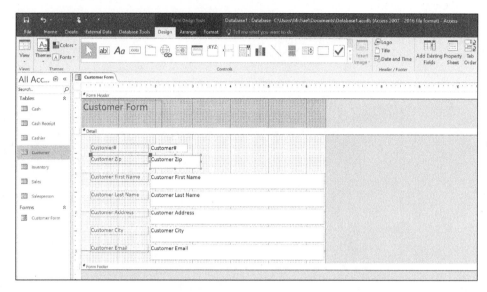

Step 7.   Adjust the size of the text field for Customer First Name, Customer Last Name, Customer City, Customer Address, and Customer Email. Make the form look like Figure 4.A7.

FIGURE 4.A7
Continue Modifying the Customer Form

© Microsoft Access

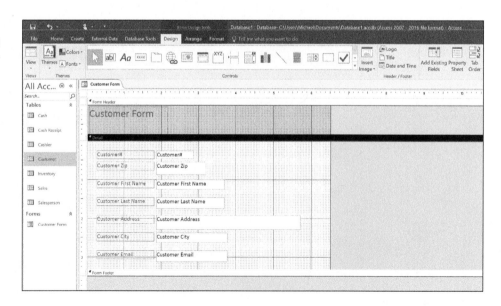

Step 8.   In order to enter data using the form, we need to switch to Form View. Click on the Form View icon in the View section of the File tab (Figure 4.A8).

FIGURE 4.A8
Switch from the
Design View to the
Form View

© Microsoft Access

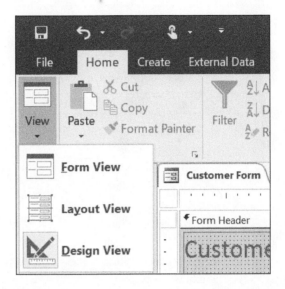

Step 9. In Form View, enter a new customer record as follows—Customer Number: 100001, Customer First Name: John, Customer Last Name: Smith, Customer Address: 2105 East Main Street, Customer Zip: 80202-4781, Customer City: Denver, Customer Email: Joh_S@gmail.com. If you would like to add the second record using this form, click on the triangle symbol icon on the record line at the bottom of the Customer Form. It will display another blank page for data entry.

Step 10. Close and save the Customer Form. Double-click on the Customer table on the left-hand side of the database window to open the table. You will see the new record has already been entered into the Customer table (Figure 4.A9).

FIGURE 4.A9
Form View of the
Customer Form

© Microsoft Access

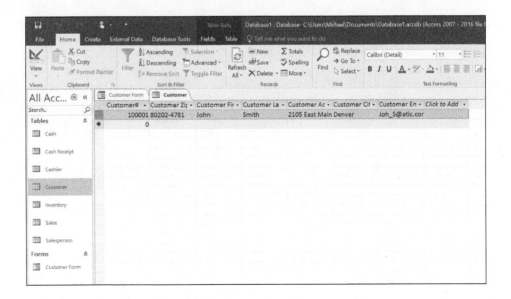

Step 11. Save and close the SSS file.

In this exercise, you learned how to create a form to enter customer information into the Customer table (steps 2 to 7) and how to review customer information one by one using the form (step 9).

■ connect

Multiple Choice Questions

1. In the hierarchical data model, the mapping from parent to child is: **LO 4-2**
   a. 1:1 (one-to-one).
   b. 1:N (one-to-many).
   c. N:N (many-to-many).
   d. N:1 (many-to-one).

2. Advantages of relational data models generally include: **LO 4-1**
   a. reduced information redundancy.
   b. low cost.
   c. ease of implementation.
   d. efficiency.

3. A class in a relational database model is defined as: **LO 4-2**
   a. the sum of a whole.
   b. characteristics or properties of a table.
   c. person, place, thing, transaction, or event about which information is stored.
   d. being or existence, especially when considered as distinct, independent, or self-contained.

4. Which statement about enterprise systems is correct? **LO 4-4**
   a. Most enterprise systems are designed mainly for accounting and finance functions.
   b. **SAP, Oracle**, and **Microsoft** all offer products for enterprise systems.
   c. Most enterprise systems are designed for the service industry.
   d. Small companies do not use enterprise systems at all.

5. Refer to Figure 4.2; if Steve's Stylin' Sunglasses accepts installments without requiring a down payment, the multiplicities between Sales and Cash Receipts should be changed to: **LO 4-2**
   a. Sales (0..1) - (1..*) Cash Receipts.
   b. Sales (1..1) - (0..*) Cash Receipts.
   c. Sales (1..1) - (1..1) Cash Receipts.
   d. Sales (0..*) - (1..1) Cash Receipts.
   e. None of the above is correct.

6. The FROM clause to the SELECT statement used in SQL indicates: **LO 4-3**
   a. the name of the table(s) from which to retrieve data.
   b. the name of the column(s) from which to retrieve data.
   c. the name of the database(s) from which to retrieve data.
   d. the name of the query from which to retrieve data.

7. The WHERE clause to the SELECT statement used in SQL states the criteria that must be met: **LO 4-3**
   a. to run a query.
   b. to be included as an attribute in the table.
   c. to be included in the database.
   d. to be shown in the query result.

8. The "ORDER BY Amount ASC" clause to the SELECT statement used in SQL suggests that: LO 4-3

   a. the amount of the query result will be listed in ascending order.

   b. the amount of the query result will be listed in descending order.

   c. the data attribute ASC be shown in order.

   d. none of the above.

9. SAP modules available for implementation include: LO 4-4

   a. Payroll, Personnel Time Management, and Enterprise Management.

   b. Payroll, Financial Accounting, and Enterprise Management.

   c. Financial Accounting, Payroll, and Sales and Distribution.

   d. Sales and Distribution, Financial Accounting, and Procurement.

10. Cloud computing: LO 4-5

    a. takes energy from the sun and clouds.

    b. is Internet-based computing, where shared resources, software, and information are provided to firms on demand.

    c. requires a firm to make an extensive investment in hardware and software to meet firm needs.

    d. can meet computing needs today but is not expected to meet tomorrow's computing needs.

11. What kind of relationship does a network data model represent? LO 4-1

    a. One-to-one relationship

    b. One-to-many relationship

    c. Many-to-one relationship

    d. Many-to-many relationship

12. Which of the following is a valid primary key for a cash receipt table? LO 4-2

    a. Purchase order number

    b. Check number

    c. Cash receipt number

    d. Receipt amount

13. Which of the following is used in SQL to begin a query? LO 4-3

    a. BEGIN

    b. SELECT

    c. INPUT

    d. INSERT

14. The GROUP BY operator in SQL is used to: LO 4-3

    a. aggregate functions on the query results based on one or more columns.

    b. identify which columns are used to sort the resulting data.

    c. state the criteria that must be met to be shown in the query result.

    d. indicate the name of the table from which to retrieve data.

15. When using Microsoft Access, the main function of "Table" is to: LO 4-2

    a. store data.

    b. report data.

    c. retrieve data.

    d. analyze data.

Discussion Questions

1. Explain the differences among hierarchical, network, and relational data models. What makes the relational data model the most popular data model in use today? **LO 4-1**

2. What are the basic requirements of a relational database? **LO 4-2**

3. Structured Query Language (SQL) is used to retrieve data from a database. Why would an accountant need to learn SQL? **LO 4-3**

4. Figure 4.32 lists the modules available from SAP. List and explain which modules would be most appropriate for either **Maytag** or a manufacturing company you are familiar with. **LO 4-4**

5. Given the description of **Hershey**'s failed enterprise system implementation from the chapter, which of the four challenges of the enterprise system described in the chapter seem to best explain what happened? Use **Google** or **Yahoo!** to get more details on this case to help answer this question. **LO 4-4**

Problems

Cash

Account#	Type	Bank	Balance
BA-6	Checking	Boston5	253
BA-7	Checking	Shawmut	48,000
BA-8	Draft	Shawmut	75,000
BA-9	Checking	Boston5	950

connect 1. Use the Cash table above to show the output for the following SQL query:

> SELECT Account#, Balance
>
> FROM Cash
>
> WHERE Balance < 50000;

connect 2. Use the Cash table above to show the output for the following SQL query:

> SELECT Account#, Balance
>
> FROM Cash
>
> WHERE Bank = 'Boston5'
>
> ORDER BY Amount DESC;

connect 3. Use the Cash table above to write a SQL query to show a list of checking accounts. Hint: Filter the results on the Type field.

connect 4. Use the Cash table above to write a SQL query to show the total of all of the balances. Hint: Use the SUM function.

5. Consider the UML diagram used to model Steve's Stylin' Sunglasses' (SSS) sales data. Draw a new UML diagram assuming that SSS sells mass-produced brand-name sunglasses instead of custom sunglasses.

connect 6. Think about data collected and used by **Netflix**. **LO 4-1, LO 4-2**

    a. Identify three tables that would contain customer or subscription data.

    b. For each table identified in a, list five attributes (you may include primary and foreign keys as well as non-key attributes).

    c. Describe each attribute using elements from a data dictionary (e.g., description, field length, field type, etc.).

    d. Why would Netflix be interested in storing and tracking these attributes (e.g., to enhance customer service or future customer sales, to sell more affiliated products to customers, etc.)?

7. Cloud computing has plenty of appeal for many firms, especially those that have immense computing needs. Why do you think some might be reluctant to have their data and computing power originating from the cloud? **LO 4-5**

8. Use the **Access_Practice.accdb** database to complete the following tasks in Access. LO 4-2

   a. The database contains three tables containing information about this company's sales process: Inventory, Sales, and SalesItems. Use the Relationships window to link the tables together.

   b. The SalesItems table records the quantity and price of each item sold on each sale (sales may include more than one item). Calculate the extended amount of sale (call it Amt) for each item (Quantity * UnitPrice). Include InvoiceID, InventoryID, Quantity, and UnitPrice in the query. Name the query Item_Extension_Calculation.

   c. Calculate the total dollar amount of *each sale*. Include InvoiceID, InvoiceDate, CustomerID, and EmployeeID from the Sales table and the Amt from the Item_Extension_Calculation query. Name the query Sale_Amount_Calculation.

   d. Calculate total sales for *each inventory item*.

   e. Calculate *total sales*.

   f. Calculate the month in which each sale occurred. Include InvoiceID and InvoiceDate from the Sales table. Name the query Sales_Months. *(Hint:* Look for the Month function in the expression builder.)

   g. Calculate the sum of sales for each month.

9. This problem continues Problem 8. Use the **Access_Practice.accdb** database that you have been working on to complete the following tasks. LO 4-2

   a. Go to the Relationships screen and connect the five tables, enforcing referential integrity.

   b. Calculate the total sales for each customer. Include CustomerID and CompanyName from the Customer table and the calculated sale amount from the Sale_Amount_Calculation query. Name the query Total_Customer_Sales.

   c. Generate an e-mail user name for each employee using the first letter of the employee's first name and the first five letters of the employee's last name, e.g., Rod Smith = > rsmith. Include EmployeeID, EmployeeFirstName, and EmployeeLastName in the query. Name the query Employee_Email_Generator.

   d. Calculate the total sales for each month.

   e. Determine which customer had the highest average sales amount. *(Hint:* Sort in descending order.)

   f. Assume the employees earn a 5 percent commission on sales. Calculate the total commission due to each employee. Use two queries to do these calculations.

Background for Problems 10 to 14

Ellen Novotny started an online bookstore in 2017. You are Ellen's best friend and promised to help her. Ellen asked you to create a small database to track the information on books and authors. You created the following tables: Author, Book, and Author_Book. The table Author_Book is a relationship table to link the Author table and Book table because of the many-to-many relationship between the two tables. That is, each author may write many books and each book may have multiple authors. In general, each customer can purchase many books in a single transaction. Also, copies of the same book can be sold to different customers. Once an order is processed, the books are shipped right away. Based on these tables you have (see below), help Ellen to extract the information she needs from the database.

Author

Author ID	Last Name	First Name	Email	Phone number
AU-1	Adams	Eric	Eric168@yahoo.com	(714) 833-2419
AU-2	Brown	Jennifer	jenifferb@gmail.com	(619) 596-0012
AU-3	Davis	Keith	keithd@gmail.com	(212) 342-5680
AU-4	Newport	Kevin	kevinn@hotmail.com	(301) 947-7741
AU-5	Pham	John	johnpham@gmail.com	(617) 645-3647
AU-6	Sviokla	Julia	jsviokla@yahoo.com	(805) 498-1688

Book

Book ID	Title	Area	Year	Edition	Publisher
B-1	Accounting Principles	Financial Accounting	2016	8	Wiley
B-2	Cost Management	Management Accounting	2017	3	McGraw-Hill
B-3	Accounting Information Systems	Information Systems	2017	2	McGraw-Hill
B-4	Individual Taxation 2017	Taxation	2018	6	Pearson
B-5	Intermediate Accounting	Financial Accounting	2016	1	Wiley
B-6	Advanced Accounting	Financial Accounting	2017	1	McGraw-Hill

Author_Book

Author ID	Book ID
AU-1	B-2
AU-1	B-5
AU-2	B-6
AU-3	B-2
AU-3	B-3
AU-4	B-2
AU-5	B-4
AU-6	B-1
AU-6	B-6

Customer

Customer ID	Last Name	First Name	Email
C-1	Black	Emily	Ewb2003@yahoo.com
C-2	Brown	Jack	jackjack@gmail.com
C-3	Easton	Anderson	anderson.easton@gmail.com
C-4	Jennix	May	jennixm@hotmail.com
C-5	Venable	Judy	Judy.Venable@gmail.com
C-6	White	Ashley	Ashley2015@yahoo.com
C-7	Williams	Eric	Williams_e@yahoo.com

Sales_Line_Item

Sales Date	Customer ID	Book ID	Quantity	Unit price
9/1/2017	C-7	B-3	1	$205
9/1/2017	C-7	B-1	1	$221
9/1/2017	C-1	B-6	30	$195
9/2/2017	C-5	B-2	60	$199
9/2/2017	C-5	B-5	25	$210
9/2/2017	C-3	B-2	1	$245
9/2/2017	C-3	B-6	1	$215
9/2/2017	C-3	B-4	1	$160
9/3/2017	C-2	B-1	1	$221

10. Ellen asks you to give her a list of the books that each author wrote. Write a complete SQL statement to provide the information to Ellen, including author names, book titles, publishers, and the years of publication.

11. Ellen wants to know how many books each author wrote. Write a SQL statement to provide such information to Ellen.

12. You are going to send e-mails to inform the customers that the books ordered have been shipped. Write a SQL statement to obtain the complete information on the book title(s), unit price(s), and the number of each book purchased to be sent to the customers.

13. Ellen wants to know how many copies of each book were sold. Write a SQL statement to obtain the necessary information you think Ellen wants. LO 4-3

14. Ellen wants to know the dollar amount of total sales made on September 1, 2017. Write a SQL statement to obtain the necessary information you think Ellen wants. LO 4-3

connect 15. The Cash Receipt table below contains seven attributes. Which of those could possibly be foreign keys? LO 4-2

Cash Receipt

Remittance Advice #	Date	Amount	Customer #	Check #	Invoice #	Cashier #
RA-220	11/02/2016	2549.90	C-12	201	S-101	E-13345
RA-278	11/10/2016	699.90	C-5	1457	S-108	E-13347
RA-276	11/30/2016	1209.70	C-9	392	S-107	E-13345
RA-289	11/30/2016	949.95	C-28	2558	S-105	E-13346

connect 16. A sales invoice typically includes the date of sale, salesperson, customer data, items included in the sale, and amount. Which foreign keys should be added to the following table to link all of these data elements? LO 4-2

Sales

Invoice #	Date	Amount
S-101	10/05/2016	2549.90
S-105	11/01/2016	949.95
S-107	11/02/2016	1209.70
S-108	11/06/2016	699.90

Additional problems are available in connect only.

Chapter **Five**

Sales and Collections Business Process

A look at this chapter

This chapter examines the sales and cash collection process. We use a comprehensive example to develop activity and structure models of the process. We show how the activity model in conjunction with business rules can be used to develop, implement, and monitor control activities. We show how the structure model can be used to develop a relational database to support information processing requirements. The chapter includes a comprehensive exercise in which students prepare UML class models and then develop the corresponding Microsoft Access database to prepare specific financial information.

A look back

Chapters 2 and 3 described types of business process models and introduced basic modeling tools to guide the student's development of modeling skills. Chapter 4 introduced relational databases and Microsoft Access. We use those skills to examine activity and structure models for the sales and collection process.

A look ahead

In the next chapter, we examine the purchasing and cash disbursement process. We again use the basic modeling tools from Chapters 2, 3, and 4 to examine activity and structure models and corresponding database structures for the process.

© James Leynse/Getty Images

In April 2008, **Starbucks** started offering additional benefits to registered Starbucks Card holders when they use their cards at Starbucks stores in the United States and Canada:

1. Complimentary customization on select syrups and milk alternatives (e.g., soy milk).
2. Complimentary Tall beverage of choice with the purchase of one pound of whole bean coffee.
3. Free refills on brewed coffee during the same visit.
4. Two hours daily of free, in-store Wi-Fi.
5. The opportunity to join Starbucks in supporting charitable causes.

Speaking about this sales initiative, Starbucks CEO Howard Schultz said, "Already, one in seven customers uses the Starbucks

Card, and now we are taking the first steps toward recognizing these customers by providing them value beyond any other coffeehouse. It is the personal relationship our customers have with our brand, our stores, and our baristas that is the foundation of our success. Through this initiative, we are making it even easier to make the Starbucks Experience your own."

At the same time, Starbucks introduced its Pike Place Roast, aimed at providing its customers a "unique, consistent, and fresh brewed coffee experience." It also began making coffee in smaller batches to ensure that its coffee is always fresh.

Starbucks' senior management clearly recognizes the importance of its sales process, and the continuing improvement of its customers' experiences, to its success and long-term growth. What kinds of information do you think Starbucks needs to manage and improve its sales process?

Chapter Outline

Sales and Collection Process

Sunset Graphics Example

Company Overview

Sunset Graphics' Sales and Collection Process Description

Sunset Graphics' Activity Models

Basic Sales Activity Model

Refining the Model to Show Collaboration

Refining the Model to Consider Exceptions

Business Rules and Sunset Graphics' Sales and Collection Process Controls

Sunset Graphics' Structure Models

UML Class Model for Quotes

UML Class Model for Adding Orders

UML Class Model for Adding Cash Receipts

UML Class Model for Adding Categorical Information

UML Class Model for Supporting Relational Database Planning

Sunset Graphics' Relational Database

Relational Database Planning for Attributes

Create Database and Define Tables

Set Relationships

Comprehensive Exercise: Baer Belly Bikinis' Sales to Retailers

Appendix A: Generic REA Model with Multiplicities for the Sales and Collection Process

Learning Objectives

After reading this chapter, you should be able to:

5-1   Describe the business activities that comprise the sales and collection process.

5-2   Develop an activity model of the sales and collection process using BPMN.

5-3   Understand and apply different activity modeling options.

5-4   Develop business rules to implement controls for the sales and collection process.

5-5   Develop a structure model for the sales and collection process using UML class diagrams.

5-6   Use multiplicities to implement foreign keys in relational tables.

5-7   Implement a relational database from the UML class diagram of the sales and collection process.

LO 5-1

Describe the business activities that comprise the sales and collection process.

SALES AND COLLECTION PROCESS

The sales and collection process includes business activities related to selling products and services, maintaining customer records, billing customers, and recording payments from customers. It also includes activities necessary to manage accounts receivable, such as aging accounts and authorizing credit. Certainly, the sales and collection processes generate accounting transactions to record revenue, accounts receivable, and cash receipts. They also affect cost of goods sold and inventory for companies that sell merchandise.

Figure 5.1 describes typical accounting transactions resulting from the sales and collection process. **Sales** are typically made in exchange for **cash** or credit. The transaction may also require collection of sales tax. A cash sale increases cash. A credit sale results in an account receivable. **Accounts receivable** are monies owed to the firm from the sale of **products** or services. A sale of goods also results in a corresponding recognition of cost of goods sold expense and reduction of inventory. When the customer subsequently pays for the goods or services sold on credit, cash is increased and accounts receivable are reduced.

We apply the tools introduced in Chapters 2, 3, and 4 to a comprehensive example of the sales and collection process. For this example, we take on the role of business analysts helping a small business, Sunset Graphics Inc., document its business processes. In this chapter, we first describe the sales and collection activities using BPMN, and then we define the typical information structure using UML class diagrams. Finally, we use the UML class diagrams to build a database to collect and report sales and collection information. Throughout, we describe business rules that establish potential process controls.

FIGURE 5.1

Accounting Transactions for the Sales and Collection Process

Oct 1	Accounts Receivable	1,350.54	
	Sales Tax Payable		100.04
	Sales		1,250.50
	Sold products on credit to Smith, Inc. Invoice No. 459		
Oct 1	Cash	1,452.87	
	Sales Tax Payable		107.62
	Sales		1,345.25
	Sold products for cash		
Oct 1	Cost of goods sold	750.30	
	Inventory		750.30
	Recording cost of sales		
Oct 31	Cash	1,350.54	
	Accounts Receivable		1,350.54
	Received payment from Smith, Inc. for Invoice No. 459		

SUNSET GRAPHICS EXAMPLE

Company Overview

Virgil and Linda B (their family name is Bartolomucci, but everyone calls them Mr. and Mrs. B) started their company more than 20 years ago and have grown it into a successful graphic design and printing business. They design and sell signs and banners, lettering and vinyl graphics for vehicles and boats, corporate promotional items, and silk-screened T-shirts and embroidered gear, among other products. Recently, Virgil and Linda decided that they wanted to try and step back from the day-to-day operations. Before they did that, they decided that it was time to review their business processes to develop better documentation, improve processes, and establish consistency in customer service. They also wanted to be sure that effective internal controls were in place because they wouldn't be on site as often.

Sunset Graphics' Sales and Collection Process Description

Because most of its products are designed to customer specifications, Sunset usually prepares a **quote** for the **customer** that carefully describes the products and services it will provide. If the customer likes the quote, he or she will place the **sales order** for all or part of the quoted products and services. At that point, Sunset may order any products not in inventory from its suppliers. When it receives the products, Sunset then applies the graph-

Designing for customer specifications.
© Ingram Publishing/SuperStock

ics. When the entire order is complete, Sunset delivers the products to the customer. In some cases, Sunset applies the graphics or installs the products at the customer's site. When the job is complete, it bills the customer and either collects payment immediately or allows the customer to pay within 30 days, depending on the customer's credit.

SUNSET GRAPHICS' ACTIVITY MODELS

LO 5-2
Develop an activity model of the sales and collection process using BPMN.

Basic Sales Activity Model

After talking with Virgil and Linda B about their sales and collection process, our first task was to draw a simple activity model using BPMN. As shown in Figure 5.2, the start of the process occurs when the customer requests a quote. Then, a series of tasks takes place in sequence until the customer pays for the products and services and the process ends. Sunset records sales when the products and services are delivered to the customer. Although some customers do not place orders after getting a quote, Virgil allowed that most do.

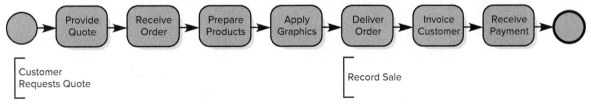

FIGURE 5.2
Basic Sales Activity Model

LO 5-3
Understand and apply different activity modeling options.

Refining the Model to Show Collaboration

Business process analysis is an iterative process. After thinking about the basic model, Linda remarked that much of their business involved interaction with customers, and the basic model doesn't really show that interaction. We agreed, but said that BPMN also allows *pools* that show different participants in a process. *Message flows* (shown by dashed arrows) between pools describe the interaction between participants.

To illustrate, we prepared Figure 5.3 that shows the customer's activities in one pool and Sunset Graphics' activities in the other pool. We explained that each pool needs a start and end event, and the *sequence flow* (shown by the solid arrows) within a pool continues from the start event to the end event without a break. This type of activity model is called a **collaboration** model in BPMN, and the interaction between participants is called **choreography.**

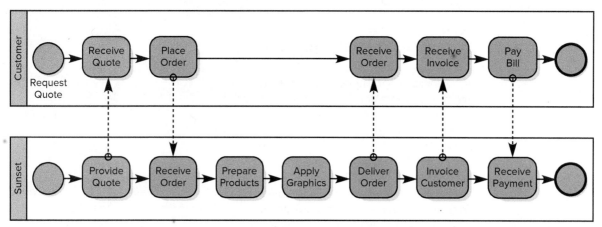

FIGURE 5.3
Collaboration Sales Activity Model

Linda said that this model more clearly shows the interactions, but she really did not care about customers' activities. She was just concerned about the choreography of interactions between the pools and the orchestration of Sunset's activities (the sequence of activities within one pool is called an **orchestration**). We understood and changed the model. Figure 5.4 now hides the customer's activities, but it shows the important message flows between participants. We told Linda that we could also hide Sunset's activities and just show the choreography between participants, but she liked this model.

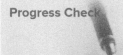

Progress Check

1. What information does the collaboration model in Figure 5.4 tell you that is different from the basic model shown in Figure 5.2?
2. From your own experience, describe how you would change Figure 5.4 to reflect another sales and collection process.

Refining the Model to Consider Exceptions

Virgil then asked how we would model potential exceptions to the typical process flow. For example, he said that sometimes Sunset's suppliers don't have the products that Sunset needs to complete the job, and it has to notify the customer and cancel the job. We weren't ready to model details of the purchasing process yet, but we could model it generally as a *collapsed* **subprocess** and also allow for the exception. A collapsed subprocess contains a series of steps that are hidden from view. Because this was getting more complicated, we temporarily dropped the pools and revised the basic sales model.

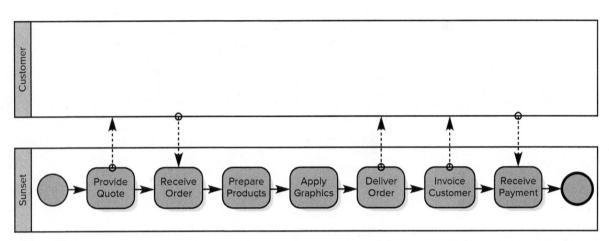

FIGURE 5.4
Collaboration Sales Activity Model

Figure 5.5 now models the purchasing exception when products are not available. We show the exception that occurs when the product is not available as an *intermediate* **error event** attached to the subprocess. When the exception occurs, the customer is notified and the process ends. Under normal conditions, the process continues as before.

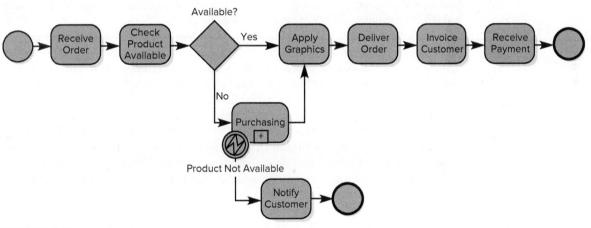

FIGURE 5.5
Sales Activity Model with Exception

Virgil loved it. He said that is exactly what happens at times. Then, he asked about the invoice customer and review payment tasks. He said they don't always get paid immediately and sometimes have to send another invoice. Because he was starting to understand BPMN, he asked if we could also use a boundary event to show that the payment was not received on time. We applauded him for how well he understood the tools. Yes, we can use an *intermediate timer boundary event* to show the exception. Virgil says that he waits 2 weeks after the payment due date to send a new invoice. Figure 5.6 adds the intermediate timer boundary event to the process. The timer event would be triggered when the payment is not received within 2 weeks.

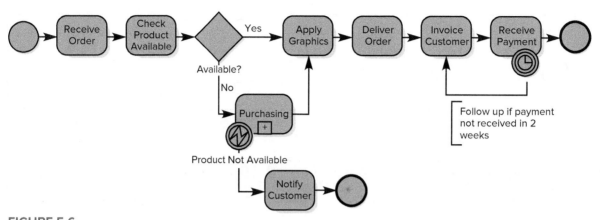

FIGURE 5.6
Sales Activity Model with Intermediate Boundary Events

LO 5-4
Develop business rules to implement controls for the sales and collection process.

BUSINESS RULES AND SUNSET GRAPHICS' SALES AND COLLECTION PROCESS CONTROLS

Next, we wanted to talk about controls over the sales and collection process because Virgil and Linda planned to step back from the day-to-day operations. We said that we would like to implement controls by developing business rules for the process. We explained to Virgil and Linda that a business rule is a compact statement that constrains some aspect of business activity. Business rules help ensure that information systems operate in a consistent and effective manner to achieve organizational objectives.

Virgil remarked that business rules seemed similar to internal controls. He quickly pulled out his laptop and went to the COSO website, www.coso.org.[1] He paraphrased its definition, "Internal control is broadly defined as a process designed to provide reasonable assurance regarding the effectiveness and efficiency of operations, reliability of financial reporting, and compliance with applicable laws and regulations." We answered that business rules are not processes; they are constraints on the process. However, you could think of business rules as control activities. COSO describes control activities as including approvals, authorizations, verifications, reconciliations, reviews of operating performance, security of assets, segregation of duties, and other activities designed to address risks to achievement of the entity's objectives. After thinking about it, Virgil agreed. He understood that business rules implement specific control activities for a particular business process. He just wasn't sure how to do it.

We explained that business rules are developed by identifying three elements: event, condition, and action. The first step is to identify important business events. Then, we need to know your conditions that would affect your intention or objective for each event. Finally, we determine the appropriate actions to take based on the conditions. For example, we've already listed important business events in the activity models, so let's examine Sunset's sales and collection process in Figure 5.4 and develop some possible business rules.

Both Virgil and Linda were now involved, so we started with the first step in the process: provide quote. We asked what their intention was for this step. They replied that they wanted to provide quotes accurately and promptly because the quote was extremely important in winning the customer's business. We then asked about the constraints that should be applied to the activity because a Sunset partner would prepare the quotes in the future. Virgil responded that the partner should provide the quote to the customer within 1 day of the customer's request. Linda added that they wanted to control approvals so that

[1]See Chapter 11 for more complete explanation of COSO (Committee of Sponsoring Organizations of the Treadway Commission) and internal control elements.

a manager approved large value quotes. That way, they could be sure that Sunset would not be overextended by taking on a large job that it could not accomplish on time.

Next, we asked about the accounting information system controls over the process. We explained that **access controls** limit who can use and change records in the system. This helps implement appropriate segregation of duties. Virgil said that the partners who provide quotes should not also manage the inventory and set prices, so they should not have access that would allow them to modify product and price information. Finally, we said we need **application controls** to ensure data integrity and an audit trail. For example, we need to control the assignment of quote numbers to make sure all of them are accounted for. Plus, we need to establish appropriate ranges or limits for each value that Sunset's partners can add or change in the system.

With Virgil and Linda's direction, we were able to develop an initial set of business rules for the sales and collection process. They articulated their intentions for every step in the process, and then we set business rules to segregate duties and limit partner authority appropriately. Table 5.1 shows the initial set of business rules for Sunset's sales and collection process.

Process Steps	Intention	Partner Authority/Action	Access Controls	Application Controls
Provide Quote	Provide quotes promptly and accurately.	Partner must provide quote within 1 business day of request; manager must approve quotes > $5,000.	Partners preparing quotes cannot modify established product and service prices.	System must provide quote number control, default values, range and limit checks, and create audit trail.
Receive Order	Record order promptly and accurately; ensure customer credit is authorized.	Partner must record order within 1 hour of receipt; manager must approve orders > $5,000; credit manager must approve credit order > $1,000.	Partners accepting orders cannot modify established product and service prices; partners accepting orders cannot approve request for customer credit > $1,000.	System must provide order number control, default values, range and limit checks, and create audit trail; system links quote to order.
Prepare Products and Apply Graphics	Prepare products promptly; ensure products match order; ensure quality products.	Partner must check all products for defects and show defective products/graphics to manager; partner must prepare products and apply graphics to meet required delivery schedule.	Partners preparing products cannot modify order.	System must allow the partner to modify only the status information; system must assign current date by default.
Deliver Order	Deliver order on date requested; ensure customer accepts delivery.	Partner delivering order must verify that delivery matches order.	Partners delivering products cannot modify order.	System must supply delivery information and not allow modification.
Invoice Customer	Invoice customer promptly; monitor until paid.	Partner must invoice customer no later than 3 business days after delivery.	Partner preparing invoice cannot modify order; before preparing the invoice, make sure the product has been delivered.	System must supply invoice number; invoice information must be filled in automatically from order.
Receive Payment	Record and deposit receipt promptly.	Partner receiving payment must record receipt immediately and deposit intact on same day.	Partner receiving payment cannot modify order or invoice.	System must supply receipt number, default to current date, default payment value to order amount.

TABLE 5.1

Using Business Rules to Implement Internal Controls

LO 5-5

Develop a structure model for the sales and collection process using UML class diagrams.

SUNSET GRAPHICS' STRUCTURE MODELS

We proceeded to examine Sunset Graphics' information requirements by preparing UML class diagrams that describe their sales and collection process. As described in Chapter 3, the primary purpose of a UML model of the sales and collection process is to create a blueprint for the development of a relational database to support the collection, aggregation, and communication of process information. To develop UML class diagrams, we follow the **REA** framework (resources, events, and agents) as a proven approach to describing business processes in a way that meets both accounting and broad management information requirements.

UML Class Model for Quotes

Virgil and Linda B outlined Sunset's process for preparing quotes for customers. They call their employees partners. In this case, a Sunset partner works with the customer to document how Sunset will meet the customer's requirements. The Sunset partner will prepare the quote, and the customer will confirm the quote. The quote specifies the prices and quantities of Sunset's products and services to be delivered. So, our preliminary model shows Sunset's **resources** (Products), the Quote **event**, and the two **agents** (Sunset Partner and Customer) that participate in the event.

In Figure 5.7, we've numbered the three relevant associations: (1) the Sunset Partner to Quote event association, (2) the Customer to Quote event association, and (3) the Quote events to Products resource association. The multiplicities for association number 1 indicates that each Sunset Partner may participate in a minimum of zero Quotes and a maximum of many Quotes, but each Quote involves only one Sunset Partner.[2] Similarly, for association number 2, each Customer may participate in zero to many Quotes and each Quote is prepared for only one Customer. For association number 3 each Quote specifies prices and quantities for at least one product (minimum of one and maximum of many). Each product may be listed on many quotes (but some products may not yet be listed on quotes). Associations 1 and 2 represent **one-to-many relationships** between classes. Association number 3 represents a **many-to-many relationship**. As we discuss later, the nature of these relationships determines how the associations are implemented in the relational database.

FIGURE 5.7
UML Class Diagram for Quotes

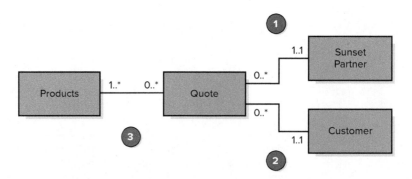

UML Class Model for Adding Orders

Next, Virgil and Linda B described how Sunset's quotes typically result in one or more orders from the customer. Of course, the same customer is involved in both the quote and the order, but a different Sunset partner could take the order. Sunset does not always prepare quotes prior to taking an order because some of its products are ready for delivery

---

[2] When describing multiplicities, we refer to the instances of the class—for example, Quotes refers to the individual quotes that are instances of the Quote class (or rows in the Quote table).

and do not need to be customized. When the customer places the order, Sunset has a formal commitment from the customer that will result in a sale when Sunset completes the delivery. Sunset does not deliver products and services until the order is complete, so there is a one-to-one relationship between orders and subsequent sales.

Figure 5.8 adds the Order event. We highlight association 4 because it links the Customer's order to the previous quote. Other associations with Order are similar to associations with Quote. The multiplicities for association 4 indicate that each Quote is related to a minimum of zero Orders, which may happen if the Customer does not place an order but also indicates that orders follow quotes in time (i.e., there can be delay between the quote and the customer order). Each Quote may be related to more than one Order if the Customer places partial orders, such as when the customer needs certain products and services immediately but others can wait. Orders are related to a minimum of zero Quotes and a maximum of one Quote.

FIGURE 5.8
UML Class Diagram for Orders and Quotes

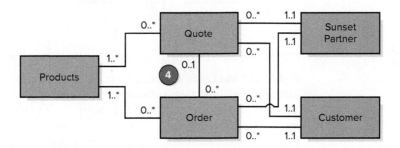

UML Class Model for Adding Cash Receipts

Linda B then remarked that some customers pay Sunset as soon as it delivers the products and services. However, Virgil said that Sunset's business and government customers are usually offered credit terms. In some situations, the customers may send one check for several orders. In any case, a Sunset partner records the **cash receipt** from the customer. All cash receipts are deposited in their primary bank account daily.

Figure 5.9 adds the Cash Receipt event and the Cash resource (e.g., bank accounts) to the UML class diagram. As with Orders and Quotes, a Sunset Partner and Customer both participate in the Cash Receipt event, and the multiplicities for these associations are similar to the earlier associations between agents and events. We've highlighted the association between Orders and Cash Receipts *events* (number 5) and the association between the Cash Receipts event and the Cash resource (number 6). For association number 5, the multiplicities indicate that each Cash Receipt is linked with a minimum of one Order and a maximum of many Orders (one customer payment for multiple orders), and each Order is linked to a minimum of zero (not paid yet) and a maximum of one (paid in full) Cash Receipt. Thus, the delivered Orders for which there are no Cash Receipts define Sunset's accounts receivable. For association number 6, the multiplicities indicate that each Cash Receipt is deposited into one account (Cash resource), and each account could have many Cash Receipts.

Progress Check

3. Describe when a Sales/Order might be preceded by the Quote activity.
4. Could the order event be divided into two events: Orders and Sales? If so, when does this make sense?

FIGURE 5.9
UML Class Diagram
for Orders and Cash
Receipts

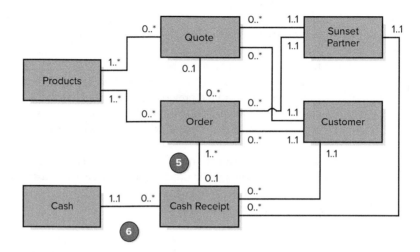

UML Class Model for Adding Categorical Information

Both Virgil and Linda now agree that the model generally represents their sales and collection process, but they wondered how to include product categories and order status information that they use for management. For example, they categorize their products into t-shirts and gear for silk screening and embroidery, lettering material for vehicles and boats, sign and banner material, customer artwork, and printing materials (card stock and stationery items). Additionally, they have a number of different categories for their promotional products. They also track the status of their orders (e.g., waiting for supply, pending graphic application, ready for delivery, and delivered).

We replied that companies often apply guidelines, constraints, and descriptive information to their resources, events, and agents to help manage the business process. Additionally, companies need to summarize the economic activity to support management's information requirements. Generically, these other classes can be called **type images**.[3] For Sunset, we can model product category and order status information by adding two classes to the basic model, as shown in Figure 5.10.

In Figure 5.10, the Product Category and Order Status classes allow Sunset to establish appropriate categories for the related classes (i.e., Products for Product Categories and Orders for Order Status). Association number 7 highlights the two associations between the underlying class and its type image. The multiplicities for both associations reflect that each category/status can apply to many instances of the underlying class. For example, each Product Category comprises many Products. Once implemented in a relational database, these type images allow process information to be summarized by category.

Type images could also support control activities by designating responsibilities. For example, a Sunset Partner could be assigned inventory management responsibility for one or more Product Categories, as shown by association number 5. The multiplicities for association number 8 indicate that one Sunset Partner is assigned to each Product Category, but some Sunset Partners could be assigned to manage multiple Product Categories.

LO 5-6
Use multiplicities to
implement foreign
keys in relational
tables.

UML Class Model for Supporting Relational Database Planning

Virgil B had no more questions about the UML class diagrams of Sunset's sales and collection process, but he did wonder how the model would be implemented in the relational

[3]See, e.g., G. Geerts and W. McCarthy, "Policy Level Specifications in REA Enterprise Information Systems," *Journal of Information Systems* 20, no.2 (2006), pp. 37–63.

FIGURE 5.10
UML Class Diagram for Orders and Cash Receipts with Type Images

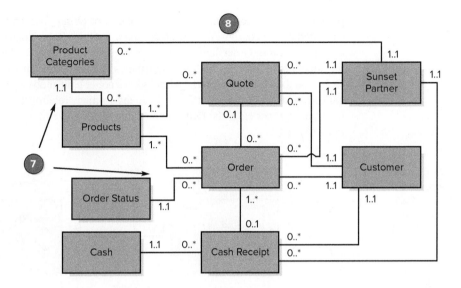

database. He knew that relational databases implement links between tables through foreign keys.[4] "How do you know where to put the foreign keys," he asked.

We said that once you understand the multiplicities, it is pretty easy to determine where to put the foreign keys. Let's use some of the associations that we've already discussed as examples. Figure 5.11 shows the one-to-many relationship between Customers and Orders. We've included some sample attributes for the classes. The «pk» notation indicates the primary keys; the «fk» notation indicates the foreign keys. Thus, *Cust_num* (customer number) is the primary key for the Customer table, and *Order_num* (order number) is the primary key for the Order table. The multiplicities indicate that each Customer can be linked with multiple Orders, but each Order only involves one Customer. Foreign keys are primary keys of linked tables, so either the *Cust_num* is a foreign key in the Orders table or the *Order_num* is the foreign key in the Customer table. Remember that properly designed relational tables cannot have multivalued fields. Thus, the *Order_num* cannot be a foreign key in the Customer table because each Customer can participate in multiple Orders. Instead, the *Cust_num* must be placed in the Orders table as the foreign key, as shown in Figure 5.11.

FIGURE 5.11
Using Multiplicities to Determine Foreign Key Implementation for One-to-Many Relationships

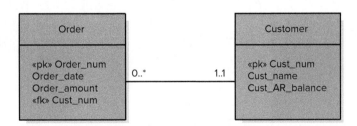

Next, we have to determine what to do with the many-to-many relationships, as shown between Order and Products in Figure 5.12. In this case, we need to turn the many-to-many relationship into two one-to-many relationships that can be easily implemented in a relational database. To do that, we define the Order Items class and model a *composition* association between Orders and Order Items as shown in Chapters 3 and 4. Note that the

---

[4]See Chapter 4 for a complete discussion of foreign keys and referential integrity.

primary key of Order Items is the combination of *Order_num* and *Prod_num* (called concatenated key or composite key): *Order_num* in Order Items links to *Order_num* in Orders and *Prod_num* in Order Items links to *Prod_num* in Products. The Order Items table will include *quantity ordered* and *price* attributes because those attributes depend on both the Order and the Product ordered.[5] Although we could have modeled Order Items on the original UML class diagram, identifying the many-to-many relationship serves the same purpose because, in either case, the Order Items table would have to be defined when the model is implemented.[6]

FIGURE 5.12
Implementing Many-to-Many Relationships

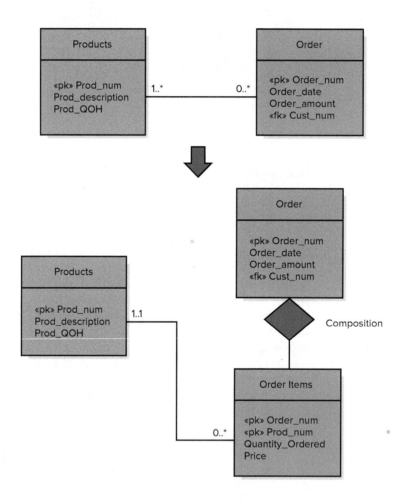

5. Refer to Figure 5.10. Where does the foreign key go for the Customer to Cash Receipt association?
6. Where would the foreign keys go in the Order to Cash Receipt association?

---

[5] Think about your cash register receipt at the grocery store—one sale includes many items.

[6] Additionally, the Order Items class cannot exist without the Order class, and because it can be derived from other classes, some argue that it should not be modeled.

LO 5-7
Implement a relational database from the UML class diagram of the sales and collection process.

SUNSET GRAPHICS' RELATIONAL DATABASE

Virgil and Linda B were now interested in seeing how the structure model would be implemented in a relational database for Sunset. For this example, we use Microsoft Access, but the process would be similar for any database-driven system. We encourage students to use the following description to implement a relational database to support information requirements for the sales and collection process.

Relational Database Planning for Attributes

During the model development process, we reviewed Sunset's existing documents to determine specific data requirements for each class/table. We then followed the guidance in the previous section to determine allocation of foreign keys. This resulted in a list of tables, attributes, data types, field sizes and primary and foreign keys, as shown in Table 5.2.

PK/FK	Attribute Name	Type	Size
	Table: tblBankAccounts		
PK	Account_number	Text	10
	Bank_routing_number	Text	10
	Bank_balance	Currency	8
	Bank_name	Text	15
	Bank_branch	Text	15
	Bank_phone_number	Text	15
	Table: tblCashReceipts		
PK	Receipt_number	Text	10
	Receipt_date	Date/Time	8
	Receipt_amount	Currency	8
FK	Customer_number	Text	10
	Customer_check_number	Text	10
FK	Received_by	Text	10
FK	Bank_account_number	Text	10
	Receipt_deposit_date	Date/Time	8
	Table: tblCustomers		
PK	Customer_number	Text	15
	Customer_name	Text	30
	Customer_address	Text	30
	Customer_address_2	Text	30
	Customer_city	Text	20
	Customer_state	Text	2
	Customer_zip	Text	5
	Customer_contact	Text	30
	Customer_phone	Text	15
	Customer_established_date	Date/Time	8
	Customer_last_activity	Date/Time	8

PK/FK	Attribute Name	Type	Size
	Customer_balance	Currency	8
	Table: tblOrderItems		
PK	Order_number	Text	10
PK	Product_number	Text	10
	Order_quantity	Integer	2
	Order_price	Currency	8
	Table: tblOrders		
PK	Order_number	Text	10
	Order_date	Date/Time	8
FK	Customer_number	Text	10
FK	Quote_number	Text	10
FK	Order_taken_by	Text	10
	Order_required_by	Date/Time	8
	Order_delivered	Date/Time	8
	Order_total_amount	Currency	8
	Order_instructions	Memo	—
FK	Receipt_number	Text	10
FK	Order_status	Text	10
	Table: tblOrderStatus		
PK	Order_status_code	Text	10
	Order_status_description	Text	255
	Table: tblPartners		
PK	Partner_number	Text	10
	Partner_first_name	Text	15
	Partner_last_name	Text	15
	Partner_hire_date	Date/Time	8
	Partner_SocSecNo	Text	11
	Partner_Address	Text	50

TABLE 5.2
Sunset Database Table and Attribute Definitions

(continued)

PK/FK	Attribute Name	Type	Size
	Partner_Address2	Text	50
	Partner_City	Text	20
	Partner_State	Text	2
	Partner_Zip	Text	10
	Partner_phone	Text	14
	Partner_cellphone	Text	14
	Table: tblProductCategory		
PK	Product_category_number	Text	10
	Product_category_description	Text	255
	Product_category_manager	Text	10
	Product_category_notes	Memo	—
	Table: tblProducts		
PK	Product_number	Text	10
	Product_description	Text	255
	Product_price	Currency	8

PK/FK	Attribute Name	Type	Size
	Product_unit_of_sale	Text	10
	Product_category	Text	10
	Product_quantity_on_hand	Integer	2
	Product_notes	Memo	—
	Table: tblQuoteItems		
PK	Quote_number	Text	10
FK	Product_number	Text	10
	Quote_quantity	Integer	2
	Quote_price	Currency	8
	Quote_notes	Text	255
	Table: tblQuotes		
PK	Quote_number	Text	10
	Quote_date	Date/Time	8
FK	Customer_number	Text	10
FK	Quote_by	Text	10
	Quote_amount	Currency	8

TABLE 5.2
(continued)

Create Database and Define Tables

The next step is to create a new, blank Microsoft Access database and create the tables described in Table 5.2 with the following steps:

1. Create the Table Design as shown in Figure 5.13 by selecting the CREATE tab; then select the Table Design icon on the ribbon bar.
2. Define each attribute listed for the table in Table 5.2 by typing the field name, selecting the data type, and setting the field size, as shown in Figure 5.14.
3. Set the primary key by selecting the appropriate field and clicking the Primary Key icon on the ribbon bar, as shown in Figure 5.15.
4. Save the table.
5. Repeat until all the tables are defined.

FIGURE 5.13
Create the Table Design

© Microsoft Access

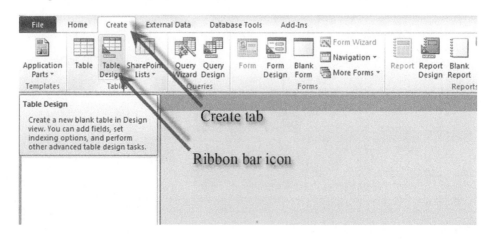

FIGURE 5.14
Define the Fields in
the Table

© Microsoft Access

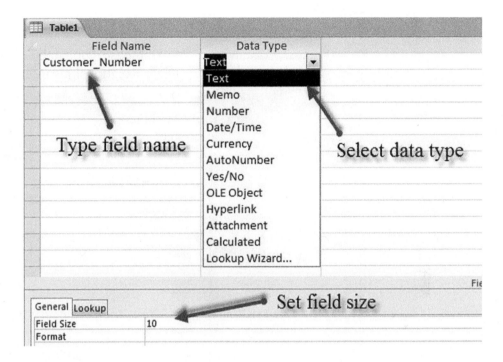

FIGURE 5.15
Set the Primary Key
for the Table

© Microsoft Access

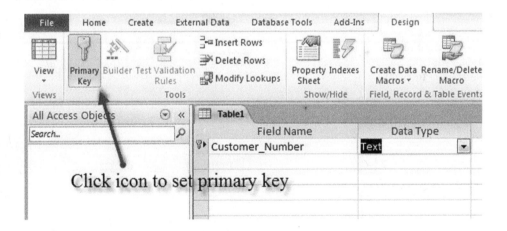

Set Relationships

After the tables are defined, the next step is to establish the links between tables. Click on the DATABASE TOOLS tab and select the Relationships icon on the ribbon bar as shown in Figure 5.16. Then, as shown in Figure 5.17, add all the tables to the relationships screen and connect foreign keys to primary keys so that the relationships mimic the UML class diagram shown in Figure 5.9.

FIGURE 5.16
Set Relationships

© Microsoft Access

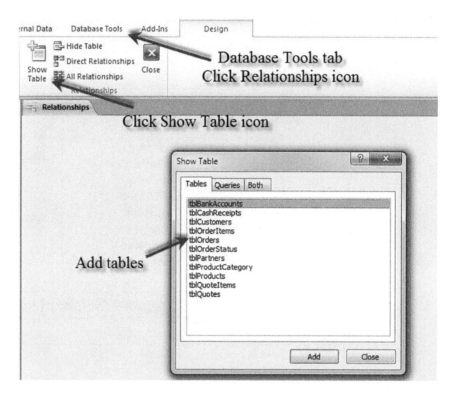

FIGURE 5.17
Partially Linked Tables with Referential Integrity Enforced

© Microsoft Access

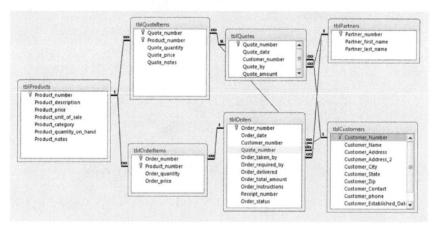

COMPREHENSIVE EXERCISE: BAER BELLY BIKINIS' SALES TO RETAILERS

Baer Belly Bikinis Inc. (BBB) is a small business located in Santa Monica, California. It sells swimwear and related products to specialty stores throughout the United States. It also sells its products to individuals over a company website. Paige Baer founded BBB almost 10 years ago after she graduated from the Fashion Institute of Design and Merchandising. She recognized the need for swimsuits sold as separates. Her business has grown rapidly, and now BBB has a large following of customers who want to be able to mix and match to find their ideal swimsuit. Currently, BBB products are carried in more than 1,000 specialty swimwear boutiques and online retailers.

During an initial interview with Paige Baer, she outlined BBB's business processes. She acknowledged that she doesn't know much about accounting and information technology.

As the business grew, her accounting suffered and information systems were added piece-meal. So, she is looking forward to an assessment of her requirements and recommendations that would position BBB for substantial further growth.

First, Paige described BBB sales to independent boutique retailers. BBB uses a group of independent sales representatives to sell its products to boutique retailers around the country. These sales representatives are not BBB employees. They are paid commissions based on the dollar volume of sales. After working with the sales representatives, individual retailers call BBB to place their order for the upcoming season. BBB will then ship the products when they become available. The retailers are expected to pay for shipments within 30 days. BBB offers a prompt payment discount for payment within 10 days.

The following material summarizes BBB's activities to prepare for and conduct the sales process:

- Summer
  - BBB finalizes designs for next year's products and prepares catalog materials with information on its future products.
- Fall to Spring
  - BBB sales representatives (independent agents working on commissions) visit retailers to develop sales. (BBB's payment of commissions to sales representatives is outside the scope of this case, although you should include the Sales Reps in your model and database.)
  - BBB's retailer customers place orders for one of two deliveries in season: (1) early spring (April) and (2) early summer (May/June). BBB records information on its retailers before they place any orders.
- Upon receipt of finished goods from their manufacturer in April and May, BBB ships products to retailers.
- Retailers' payments are due 30 days after shipment and include shipping costs. Some retailers pay late. Some take advantage of the prompt payment discounts.

BBB Finished Goods Inventory

BBB tracks its inventory by catalog number (catalog#). Each product is identified by color code, use (e.g., tops or bottoms), and type (e.g., the specific design of the piece). The color codes reflect the color and fabric design options, and they can change each year. At the beginning of the season, the quantity on hand of each item is zero. The quantity on hand increases when BBB gets deliveries from its manufacturer (outside the scope of this case) and decreases as it ships the products to the retailers to fill orders.

BBB Shipments

BBB makes one shipment for each retailer order and records revenue when the products are shipped. Warehouse employees prepare the shipments. All shipments are made under BBB's contract with a shipping company. BBB charges customers for the cost of the shipment, so the amount due from the retailers depends on the wholesale price of each item, the quantity shipped, and the shipping cost for the shipment. Payments to the shipping company are outside the scope of this case.

BBB Cash Receipts

Retailer customers send payment by check according to the payment terms (BBB standard payment terms are 2% 10 days net 30, meaning they receive a 2% discount on any amount they pay within 10 days with the net balance due within 30 days). The payment from the retailer customer always applies to only one order, but sometimes the retailers send multiple checks for that order. A BBB employee (accounts receivable) logs cash receipts from retailers. At the end of the day, the cash receipts are deposited intact into one bank account (BBB's main account). Each cash receipt is tracked by unique sequential cash receipt number.

Exercise Requirements

1. Based on the preceding information and the following attributes list, prepare a UML class model and corresponding table listing describing BBB's sales to retailers. List the tables in the following order: resources, events, agents, type images, and linking tables. Identify the primary keys and foreign keys in each table.
2. [optional] Based on the preceding information, prepare a BPMN activity model that describes BBB's Sales to Retailers process. The model should begin with retailers placing orders and end when BBB collects payments for the sales to the retailers.
3. Your instructor will provide an Excel spreadsheet with the BBB information. Create a new Access database, and import each worksheet in the spreadsheet into the database. Set appropriate primary keys.
4. After importing all the data, create relationships among tables to implement your data model.
5. Prepare queries to answer the following questions:
   a. What was BBB's total revenue?
   b. What is BBB's account receivable balance for each retailer customer as of the end of June?
   c. Which BBB product generated the largest sales volume? (List all products in descending order of sales dollars).

Attribute Listing for BBB

Bank Name	Finished Inventory Quantity on Hand
Cash Account Balance April 1	Flat Rate Ship Charge
Cash Account Description	Inventory Type Use
Cash Account#	Order Date
Cash Receipt#	Order Employee#
Customer Address	Order#
Customer City State Zip	Quantity Ordered
Customer Name	Receipt Amount
Customer Phone	Receipt Date
Customer#	Requested Date
Delivery Date	Retail Price
Employee Address	Sales Rep Area
Employee City	Sales Rep Email Address
Employee Department	Sales Rep Name
Employee First Name	Sales Rep Phone
Employee Hire Date	Sales Rep#
Employee Last Name	Ship Date
Employee Pay Amount	Shipping Employee#
Employee Phone	Shipping Cost
Employee Salary/Wage	Size of Inventory Item
Employee Zip	Standard Cost of Inventory Item
Employee#	Supervisory Employee#
Fabric Color Code	Type Code
Fabric Color Name	Wholesale Price
Fabric Cost per Yard	Yards Fabric Required for This Inventory Type
Finished Inventory Catalog#	
Finished Inventory Description	

Summary

- From an accounting standpoint, we must account for sales, accounts receivable, and cash collection in the sales and collection process.
- Sunset Graphics Inc. provides an ongoing example of how to model the sales and collection process.
- Activity models can show the basic steps in the process and the collaborations between the company and its customers, as well as exceptions to the process.
- Business rules implement internal control activities.
- There is a standard structure model pattern for the sales and collection process that shows the economic reality of the process.
- The standard pattern is tailored to a specific organization by adding type images to collect management information.
- The structure model provides a blueprint for a relational database that will collect, store, and report sales and collection information.
- The comprehensive exercise reinforces the concepts presented in the chapter.

Key Words

access controls (*125*)   Limit who can use and change records in the system; for example, passwords control who can use an application.

accounts receivable (*120*)   Monies owed by customers for prior sales of goods or services. In a data modeling context, accounts receivable are calculated as each customer's sales less corresponding cash receipts.

agents (*126*)   The people or organizations who participate in business events, such as customers and salespeople.

application controls (*125*)   Ensure data integrity and an audit trail; for example, new invoices are assigned sequential numbers; specific to a subsystem or an application to ensure the validity, completeness, and accuracy of the transaction.

cash (*120*)   The organization's monies in bank or related accounts. The instances of the class are individual accounts. This is considered a resource.

cash receipts (*127*)   Record receipts of cash from external agents (e.g., customers) and the corresponding deposit of those receipts into cash accounts. This is considered an event.

choreography (*122*)   The interaction (message flows) between two participants (modeled as pools) in a process modeled using BPMN.

collaboration (*122*)   A BPMN model showing two participant pools and the interactions between them within a process.

customer (*121*)   The external agent in the sales and collection process.

error event (*123*)   An intermediate event in a BPMN model showing processing for exceptions to the normal process flow.

events (*126*)   Classes that model the organization's transactions, usually affecting the organization's resources, such as sales and cash receipts; Important occurrences that affect the flow of activities in a business process. BPMN includes symbols to define start, intermediate, and end events.

many-to-many relationship (*126*)   Exists when instances of one class (e.g., sales) are related to many instances of another class (e.g., inventory) and vice versa. These relationships are implemented in Access and relational databases by adding a linking table to convert the many-to-many relationship into two one-to-many relationships.

one-to-many relationship (*126*) Exists when instances of one class are related to multiple instances of another class. For example, a customer can participate in many sales, but each sale involves only one customer.

orchestration (*122*) In BPMN, the sequence of activities within one pool.

product (*120*) Class representing the organization's goods held for sale, that is, the organization's inventory. This is considered a resource.

quote (*121*) Description of the products and/or services to be provided to a customer if ordered.

REA (*126*) Resource-event-agent framework for modeling business processes, originally developed by William McCarthy.

resources (*126*) Those things that have economic value to a firm, such as cash and products.

sales (*120*) Events documenting the transfer of goods or services to customer and the corresponding recognition of revenue for the organization.

sales order (*121*) Event documenting commitments by customers to purchase products. The sales order event precedes the economic event (sale).

subprocess (*122*) Represent a series of process steps that are hidden from view in BPMN. The use of subprocesses in modeling helps reduce complexity.

type image (*128*) Class that represents management information (such as categorizations, policies, and guidelines) to help manage a business process. Type image often allows process information to be summarized by category.

Appendix A

Generic REA Model with Multiplicities for the Sales and Collection Process

GENERIC PATTERN WITH MULTIPLICITIES

Figure 5.A1 shows a generic sales and collection process UML diagram. There are two resources, *inventory* and *cash;* there are two events, *sales* and *cash receipts;* and there are two agents, *employees* (internal agent) and *customers* (external agent). In this example, let's assume that the inventory is something tracked by universal product code (UPC). UPC are those bar codes you see on literally millions of products, such as soap, breakfast cereal, and packages of cookies. The cash resource represents the various bank accounts that would make up this enterprise's cash balance on its balance sheet. The sales event records information about individual sales transactions (e.g., transaction number, date, total dollar amount). The cash receipt event records information about payments received from customers and deposited into one of the bank accounts (e.g., receipt number, receipt date, receipt dollar amount, customer check number). The employees agent records information about the enterprise's employees, including those employees who handle sales transactions. The customers agent records information about actual and potential customers (let's assume that customer information is recorded in some cases when customers ask for product information and before they participate in their first sale, and let's also assume that the company only receives cash from customers).

FIGURE 5.A1
Generic Sales and
Collection UML
Diagram

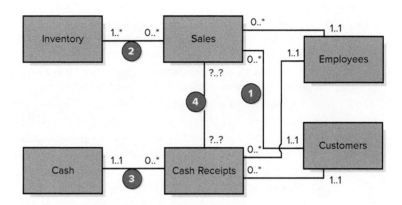

Consider association 1 between *customers* and *sales.* The multiplicities indicate that each customer participates in a minimum of zero and a maximum of many sales. Does this seem reasonable? The minimum of zero means that we can record information about customers before they participate in any sale. On the other side of the association, the multiplicities indicate that each sale involves one and only one customer. Again, does this seem reasonable? Notice that the multiplicities for the other associations between agents and events are the same. In fact, these are the typical multiplicities for those associations. There are circumstances where they might be different, but those circumstances occur infrequently.

Next, consider association 2 between the *sales* event and *inventory* resource. The multiplicities indicate that each sale involves a minimum of one and a maximum of many inventory items. For example, you visit your local **Starbucks** and buy one coffee, a tea for your friend, plus two scones. The multiplicities also indicate that each inventory item can be sold zero times or many times. Starbucks has to put an item on its menu before it can be sold, so it could have inventory items that have not yet been sold. But the same inventory item can be sold many times—as long as the quantity on hand is greater than zero. The multiplicities on this association are typical when the inventory is carried at a type of product level, such as when the inventory is identified by UPC. If the company sells high-value items, the multiplicities would differ. (How?)

Now, consider association 3 between the *cash receipt* event and the *cash* resource. These multiplicities indicate that each cash receipt (e.g., one check from a customer) is deposited into one and only one account, and each account is associated with a minimum of zero cash receipts and a maximum of many cash receipts. These multiplicities reflect typical business practices. Cash receipts are deposited into one account (when you deposit money via an ATM, you are putting it in one account, right?).

Finally, consider the duality association 4 between the *sales* and *cash receipt* events. The question marks indicate that these multiplicities depend on the nature of the business. Some businesses require payment at the time of the sale. Some allow payment terms. Some provide revolving accounts for their customers. Some collect payments in advance of the sale (e.g., magazine subscriptions). So, there are no typical multiplicities for this association.

Although we discourage memorization of data modeling elements, students often find that multiplicities are easier to understand once they see the typical sets for particular associations. We therefore recommend that students recognize and use the standard patterns for multiplicities as shown in Figure 5.A1, remembering that those standard multiplicities could change depending on the particular circumstances of the business.

Answers to Progress Check

1. The collaboration model shown in Figure 5.4 highlights the interactions between Sunset Graphics and its customers. Figure 5.2 shows the sequence of activities for the sales process without identifying information coming into or out of each activity.

2. The answer depends on the choice of firm. Take **Amazon.com,** for example. Amazon collects payments at the time of the order and does not invoice customers.

3. Companies that provide quotes typically build or tailor their products to the specific customer requirements compared to companies that simply sell available products.

4. The order event could be separated into orders and sales when one order could result in multiple sales or one sale could involve multiple orders.

5. The foreign key for the Customer to Cash Receipt association in Figure 5.9 would be posted in the Cash Receipt table.

6. The foreign key for the Order to Cash Receipt association in Figure 5.9 would be posted in the Order table.

▓ connect®

Multiple Choice Questions

1. Which of the following is not an activity within the sales and collection process? **LO 5-1**
    a. Selling products and services
    b. Billing customers
    c. Managing inventory
    d. Recording payments from customers
    e. All of the above are sales and collection activities.

2. The sales and collection process is the point of contact between the firm and which set of external business partners? **LO 5-1**
    a. Investors
    b. Customers
    c. Employees
    d. Vendors
    e. All of the above

3. Which of the following sales and collection process activities can result in the creation of an account receivable? **LO 5-1**
    a. Receiving a sales order from a customer
    b. Shipping ordered products to the customer
    c. Billing the customer
    d. Recording payment from the customer
    e. None of the above

4. Which of the following describes message flows between pools? LO 5-2
   a. Orchestrations
   b. Sequence flows
   c. Choreography
   d. Intermediate events
   e. None of the above

5. Which of the following statements is true? LO 5-2, LO 5-3
   a. Each pool must have a start event.
   b. Sequence flows are shown by arrows with a solid line.
   c. Message flows are shown by arrows with a solid line.
   d. Each pool must have more than one swimlane.
   e. Both a and b are true.

6. Which of the following is not a purpose of a subprocess in BPMN? LO 5-3
   a. Reducing complexity
   b. Presenting higher-level process descriptions
   c. Creating alternative activities
   d. Developing a reusable model
   e. All of the above are purposes of subprocesses in BPMN.

7. What is the purpose of an intermediate error event? LO 5-3
   a. Indicates a change in flow due to a process exception
   b. Indicates the end of a process
   c. Indicates the start of a collapsed subprocess
   d. Describes the activities that will occur when there is not an error
   e. None of the above

8. Which of the following is an example of a business rule implementing access controls? LO 5-4
   a. The warehouse containing inventory must be locked when the inventory manager is not present.
   b. User's recording collections cannot modify sales records.
   c. The computer system shall generate an audit trail.
   d. Internal auditors shall be used.
   e. Both a and b are business rules implementing access controls.

9. Which of the following is not part of the REA framework? LO 5-5
   a. Agents
   b. Type images
   c. Resources
   d. Events
   e. All of the above are part of the REA framework.

10. How do you implement a one-to-many relationship in a relational database? LO 5-6
    a. Post a foreign key.
    b. Create a new table.
    c. Combine two fields to create a primary key.
    d. Create an association.
    e. None of the above

Use this diagram to answer multiple choice questions 11 through 32.

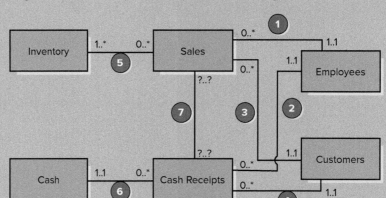

11. Refer to the association marked with the number 1 in the preceding diagram. Which of the following is the best description of the association? **LO 5-5, LO 5-6**

   a. Each employee participates in at least one sale.

   b. Each employee participates in a minimum of zero sales.

   c. Each employee participates in a maximum of one sale.

   d. Each employee participates in at least two sales.

   e. None of these are a description of the association.

12. Refer to the association marked with the number 1 in the preceding diagram. Which of the following is the best description of the association? **LO 5-5, LO 5-6**

   a. Each sale may involve multiple employees.

   b. Each sale may involve no employees.

   c. Each sale is associated with a minimum of one employee.

   d. Each sale is associated with a maximum of many employees.

   e. None of these are a description of the association.

13. Refer to the association marked with the number 2 in the preceding diagram. Which of the following is the best description of the association? **LO 5-5, LO 5-6**

   a. Only cashiers handle cash receipts.

   b. Each employee is associated with many cash receipts.

   c. One employee may be associated with many cash receipts.

   d. Each employee is associated with a minimum of one cash receipt.

   e. None of these are a description of the association.

14. Refer to the association marked with the number 2 in the preceding diagram. Which of the following is the best description of the association? **LO 5-5, LO 5-6**

   a. Each cash receipt may involve multiple employees.

   b. Each cash receipt may involve no employees.

   c. Each cash receipt is associated with only one employee.

   d. Each cash receipt is associated with a maximum of many employees.

   e. None of these are a description of the association.

15. Refer to the association marked with the number 3 in the preceding diagram. Which of the following is the best description of the association? **LO 5-5, LO 5-6**

   a. Each customer participates in a maximum of one sale.

   b. Each customer participates in at least one sale.

   c. Each customer participates in a minimum of zero sales.

    d. Each customer eventually participates in at least two sales.

    e. None of these are a description of the association.

16. Refer to the association marked with the number 3 in the preceding diagram. Which of the following is the best description of the association? **LO 5-5, LO 5-6**

    a. Each sale is associated with a minimum of one customer.

    b. Each sale may involve multiple customers.

    c. Each sale is associated with a maximum of many customers.

    d. Each sale may involve no customers.

    e. None of these are a description of the association.

17. Refer to the association marked with the number 3 in the preceding diagram. What is the best interpretation if the minimum multiplicity next to Customers is 0 instead of 1? **LO 5-5, LO 5-6**

    a. Some customers don't pay.

    b. Some customers place orders but don't pick up their items.

    c. Some sales are made in cash and customer information is not recorded.

    d. Some customers never buy anything.

    e. None of these interpret this situation appropriately.

18. Refer to the association marked with the number 4 in the preceding diagram. Which of the following is the best description of the association? **LO 5-5, LO 5-6**

    a. Each customer pays in cash at the time of the sale.

    b. Each customer is associated with a maximum of many cash receipts.

    c. Each customer is associated with more than one cash receipt.

    d. Each customer is associated with a minimum of one cash receipt.

    e. None of these are a description of the association.

19. Refer to the association marked with the number 4 in the preceding diagram. Which of the following is the best description of the association? **LO 5-5, LO 5-6**

    a. Each cash receipt may involve no customers.

    b. Each cash receipt is associated with only one customer.

    c. Each cash receipt may involve multiple customers.

    d. Each cash receipt is associated with a maximum of many customers.

    e. None of these are a description of the association.

20. Refer to the association marked with the number 5 in the preceding diagram. Which of the following is the best description of the association? **LO 5-5, LO 5-6**

    a. Each sale may involve a maximum of many inventory items.

    b. Each sale may involve a minimum of zero inventory items.

    c. Each sale involves one inventory item.

    d. Each sale may involve two inventory items.

    e. None of these are a description of the association.

21. Refer to the association marked with the number 5 in the preceding diagram. Which of the following is the best example of a business rule that constrains the association? **LO 5-4, LO 5-5**

    a. Sales are allowed if they include at least one inventory item.

    b. Sales are prohibited if they include more than one inventory item.

    c. Sales must include at least one inventory item.

    d. Sales are allowed with the manager's approval in advance.

    e. None of these are the best example of a business rule.

22. Refer to the association marked with the number 5 in the preceding diagram. Which of the following is the best description of the association? LO 5-5, LO 5-6

    a. Each inventory item must be sold at least once.

    b. Each inventory item may be sold many times.

    c. Each inventory item is associated with a minimum of one sale.

    d. Each inventory item is associated with a maximum of one sale.

    e. None of these are a description of the association.

23. Refer to the association marked with the number 6 in the preceding diagram. Which of the following is the best description of the association? LO 5-5, LO 5-6

    a. Each cash receipt is deposited into multiple cash accounts.

    b. Each cash receipt is associated with a minimum of zero cash accounts.

    c. Each cash receipt is associated with a maximum of many cash accounts.

    d. Each cash receipt is deposited into one cash account.

    e. None of these are a description of the association.

24. Refer to the association marked with the number 6 in the preceding diagram. Which of the following is the best description of the association? LO 5-5, LO 5-6

    a. Each cash account may be associated with many cash receipts.

    b. Each cash account is associated with one cash receipt.

    c. Each cash account is associated with a minimum of one cash receipt.

    d. Each cash account is associated with a maximum of one cash receipt.

    e. None of these are a description of the association.

25. Refer to the association marked with the number 7 in the preceding diagram. Assume that customers pay for all sales in full at the end of the month. Which of the following is the multiplicity that should be found next to the cash receipts class? LO 5-5, LO 5-6

    a. 0..*

    b. *..*

    c. 0..1

    d. 1..1

    e. 1..*

26. Refer to the association marked with the number 7 in the preceding diagram. Assume that customers pay for all sales during the month in full at the end of the month. Which of the following is the multiplicity that should be found next to the sales class? LO 5-5, LO 5-6

    a. 0..*

    b. *..*

    c. 0..1

    d. 1..1

    e. 1..*

27. Refer to the association marked with the number 7 in the preceding diagram. Assume that customers pay for all sales during the month in full at the end of the month. Which of the following is the best example of a business rule that constrains the association? LO 5-4, LO 5-5

    a. Customers are allowed to pay for sales on credit.

    b. Customers must pay for sales at the time of the sale.

    c. Customers are prohibited from paying for sales on credit.

    d. Customers may delay payment for a sale upon approval by the manager.

    e. None of these are an example of an appropriate business rule for the association.

28. Refer to the association marked with the number 5 in the preceding diagram. What is the best description of the type of inventory that this company sells? **LO 5-5, LO 5-6**

    a. High-value items such as automobiles

    b. Customized products

    c. Items identified by UPC (bar codes)

    d. Tickets to concerts

    e. None of these correctly describes the type of inventory.

29. Assume you are implementing a database from the preceding diagram. How many tables would the database include? **LO 5-5, LO 5-6, LO 5-7**

    a. 6

    b. 7

    c. 5

    d. 4

    e. You can't tell from the information provided.

30. Assume you are implementing a database from the preceding diagram. Which of these is the best way to implement the relationship identified by the number 3? **LO 5-5, LO 5-6, LO 5-7**

    a. Post the primary key of customers in sales as a foreign key.

    b. Post the primary key of sales in customers as a foreign key.

    c. Create a linking table between sales and customers.

    d. All of these are acceptable.

    e. None of these are acceptable.

31. Assume you are implementing a database from the preceding diagram. Which of these is the best way to implement the relationship identified by the number 6? **LO 5-5, LO 5-6, LO 5-7**

    a. Post the primary key of cash in cash receipts as a foreign key.

    b. Post the primary key of cash receipts in cash as a foreign key.

    c. Create a linking table between cash and cash receipts.

    d. All of these are acceptable.

    e. None of these are acceptable.

32. Assume you are implementing a database from the preceding diagram. Which of these is the best way to implement the relationship identified by the number 5? **LO 5-5, LO 5-6, LO 5-7**

    a. Post the primary key of sales in inventory as a foreign key.

    b. Post the primary key of inventory in sales as a foreign key.

    c. Create a linking table between sales and inventory.

    d. All of these are acceptable.

    e. None of these are acceptable.

Discussion Questions

1. The sales and collection process generates revenue, accounts receivable, and cash flow information for a firm's financial statements. What other information do you think managers would like to collect? **LO 5-1**

2. What kinds of businesses collect cash before recording the corresponding sales? How would that different sequence affect internal control requirements? **LO 5-1**

3. Draw a basic sales activity model using BPMN for a fast-food restaurant. Draw a second basic sales activity model using BPMN for a traditional restaurant. Discuss similarities and differences. How would you add taking reservations to the second model? **LO 5-2**

4. Draw a collaboration diagram that shows two pools and the message flows between a fast-food restaurant and its customers. How would you change that diagram for a traditional restaurant? **LO 5-2, LO 5-3**

5. Draw UML class diagrams for fast-food and traditional restaurants. Discuss similarities and differences. How would you add taking reservations to the second model? LO 5-2, LO 5-3

6. Using Amazon.com as an example, prepare a collaboration sales activity model. What is the difference between an online process and a traditional brick-and-mortar store process? LO 5-3

7. From your experience, think about the sales process for an online or brick-and-mortar store. Describe some business rules that help provide internal controls over that process. LO 5-4

8. What classes and associations would be included in a model that describes the information needed for a query that calculates the accounts receivable balance for each customer? Describe differences in the information for the *open-invoice method*, where customers pay according to specific invoices, versus the *balance-forward method*, where customers pay balances on monthly statements. LO 5-5

Problems

connect

1. The Beach Dude (BD) employs a legion of current and former surfers as salespeople who push its surfing-oriented products to various customers (usually retail outlets). This case describes BD's sales and collection process.

    Each BD salesperson works with a specific group of customers throughout the year. In fact, they often surf with their customers to try out the latest surf gear. The BD salespeople act laid-back, but they work hard for their sales. Each sale often involves hours of surfing with their customers while the customers sample all the latest surf wear. Because BD makes the best surfing products, the customers look forward to the visits from the BD salespeople. And they often buy a lot of gear. Each sale is identified by a unique invoice number and usually involves many different products. Customers pay for each sale in full within 30 days, but they can combine payments for multiple sales.

    BD manages its clothing inventory by item (e.g., XL BD surfer logo T-shirts), identified by product number, but it also classifies the items by clothing line (the lines are differentiated by price points as well as the intended use of the clothing, e.g., surfing products, casual wear, etc.). LO 5-5, LO 5-6, LO 5-7

    a. Draw a UML class diagram that describes the Beach Dude's sales and collection process.

    b. Using Microsoft Access, implement a relational database from your UML class diagram. Identify at least three fields per table.

    c. Describe how you would create queries in the relational database to determine the Beach Dude's accounts receivable.

connect

2. The Bob White Karate Studio has been a local fixture for almost 40 years. The studio offers training in American Kenpo Karate to students from 3 years old to 80 years old. Students select one of several programs: (a) monthly payments, (b) semi-annual payments, or (c) the black belt program. Each of these programs allows them to take group classes as well as one or more private lessons with a qualified black belt instructor, depending on the program selected. For example, the monthly program includes one private lesson, the semi-annual program includes three private lessons, and the black belt program includes one lesson per week until the student attains black belt rank. Additionally, students may purchase additional private lessons, as well as uniforms, sparring gear, and various studio insignia and clothing items. The additional half-hour private lessons are priced as packages, which include 5, 10, 20, 40, or 60 lessons, and the price also varies depending on whether the lessons are provided by senior or junior instructors. When students purchase a package, they are assigned to a particular instructor for the duration of the package. Students typically pay for anything they buy at the time of their purchase, but established students are sometimes allowed to purchase on credit. In that case, they generally must pay within 2 weeks. While all studio employees are also instructors, only a few employees handle sales transactions and accept payments. LO 5-2, LO 5-3, LO 5-5, LO 5-6, LO 5-7

    a. Draw a BPMN activity diagram that describes the Bob White Karate Studio's sales and collection process.

    b. Prepare a UML class diagram with classes, associations, and multiplicities.

c. Using the preceding information and the following attributes list, prepare a listing of the relational tables necessary to support this sales and collection process. List the tables in the following order: resources, events, agents, type images, and linking tables.

Attributes:

Cash account#	Program#
Cash account balance	Program description
Credit card number for this sale	Program price
Date sale paid	Quantity of instructors of this type
Employee/instructor#	Quantity of this inventory item purchased on this sale
Employee name	
Employee rank	Sale#
Instructor type	Sale amount
Inventory item#	Sale date
Inventory item description	Sale paid (Y/N)
Inventory item price	Student#
Inventory item quantity on hand (QOH)	Student current rank
Private lesson package#	Student name
Private lesson package description	Student original enrollment date
Private lesson package price	

3. Beach Rentals (BR) maintains an inventory of rental houses near universities and leases those houses to student renters. This case describes their rental business process. BR agents—former marketing majors renowned for their fast-talking and flamboyant lifestyles—work with potential renters and sign the rental contracts for BR.

BR tracks its houses by city, neighborhood, and distance from campus. BR assigns one specific BR agent to each neighborhood to manage rentals for all houses in that neighborhood, but each BR agent may be assigned to multiple neighborhoods. BR cashiers collect the rent and are bonded for security purposes. Because cashiers never become agents (or vice versa), BR tracks BR cashiers separately from BR agents, although both are identified by employee numbers.

BR sets rental rates to its student customers by considering such matters as number of bedrooms and age of the house. Additionally, BR applies a monthly rental surcharge to each house that depends solely upon its neighborhood designation; for example, upscale neighborhoods have higher surcharges and less desirable neighborhoods have lower surcharges. The same surcharge applies for the life of the lease. Every house has a rental surcharge, and all houses in a particular neighborhood have the same surcharge.

Prospective renters, usually students, contact BR to inquire about renting a house. When a potential renter contacts BR, a BR agent is assigned to assist him or her. That BR agent remains the person's point of contact for as long as he or she continues to deal with Beach Rentals. BR records information on each potential renter as soon as he or she contacts BR to inquire about a house.

BR agents negotiate the rental contracts with the students. Each rental contract must last at least 6 months, and 12-month contracts get a 5 percent discount. BR also charges a damage fee that is due along with the first month's rent when the rental contract is signed. The BR agent earns a 10 percent commission on each rental contract, and BR tracks the year-to-date (YTD) commission earned for each of the BR agents. Of course, the BR agents compete with one another to see who earns the highest commissions, and BR fosters the competition by giving an annual award to its "best" agent.

When multiple students want to rent one house, BR requires that they designate the primary renter—the one who will be responsible for paying the rent. BR also gathers information about all the other occupants of the house and designates them as secondary renters. All the student renters, however, sign the rental contract, and BR assigns a unique renter number to each occupant. The students may not change primary renter for the term of a contract. BR cashiers collect the rental payments monthly from the primary renters. BR records information concerning employees, house owners, bank accounts, and neighborhoods in the database before the renters are involved in any events. LO 5-5, LO 5-6, LO 5-7

a. Prepare a UML class diagram with classes, associations, and multiplicities.

b. Using the preceding information and the following attributes list, prepare a listing of the relational tables necessary to support this sales and collection process. List the tables in the following order: resources, events, agents, type images, and linking tables.

c. Using the list of relational tables and Microsoft Access, define the relational tables and establish the relationships among tables necessary to implement Beach Rentals' sales and collection process in Access.

Attributes:

Agent employee#	Monthly rent
Agent name	Neighborhood name
Agent real estate license status	Number of bedrooms
Bank account#	Number of houses in this city
Bank account balance	Rent discount for 12-month contract
Bank name and address	Rental contract#
Cash receipt $ amount	Rental contract begin date
Cash receipt#	Rental contract duration in months
Cashier employee#	Rental surcharge amount
Cashier name	Renter bank and routing numbers
City name	Renter name
Damage fee	Renter number#
House street address	YTD rental commissions
House zip code	

Additional problems are available in connect only.

Chapter **Six**

Purchases and Payments Business Process

A look at this chapter

This chapter examines the purchases and payments process. We continue the comprehensive example to develop activity and structure models of the process. We show how the activity model in conjunction with business rules can be used to develop, implement, and monitor control activities. We show how the structure model can be used to develop a relational database to support information processing requirements.

A look back

Chapter 5 examined the sales and collection processes. It began the comprehensive example that we use to examine typical process activities and data structures.

A look ahead

In the next chapter, we examine the conversion process, whereby companies transform raw material into finished goods. We again use the basic modeling tools from Chapters 2 and 3 and database design methods presented in Chapter 4 to examine activity and structure models for the process.

© MachineHeadz/Getty Images.

In a 2002 interview,[1] David Norton, **Starbucks**' vice president of logistics, talked about its global supply chain: "Rapid global growth requires comprehensive, integrated strategies focused on the needs of our retail stores, license and joint venture partners. We have a formal process for developing both strategic and operating plans which ensures we link manufacturing, procurement, and logistics to the needs of the business."

Norton went on to describe the role of technology: "Technology has become increasingly a staple of the supply chain rather than a driver. There have been few significant advances on the physical distribution side of the supply chain in years. In the information arena, the pattern seems to be over-commit and under-deliver. Systems are generally harder, more costly, and take longer to implement than has been the promise. The evolution of systems over the past 15 years might be even characterized as a journey from homegrown proprietary systems through best-of-breed/homegrown combinations, and finally to monolithic ERP environments. And

[1] Reported January 1, 2002, www.SupplyChainBrain.com.

my experience is that the integrated, monolithic ERP environments simply lack the flexibility to meet unique business requirements. We believe the best place to be today is combining the best of different applications. And our IT professionals here at Starbucks are comfortable with this because of advances in business integration systems/tools that enable this approach."

Finally, describing what it takes to design and operate integrated supply chain management tools, Norton noted, "A lot of folks come into the business and don't understand that you need a solid item master, a solid price master, a solid customer master, a solid order management system, a solid inventory system—all tied in nicely with AP [accounts payable] and AR [accounts receivable]—and if you don't have any of that stuff right, you can just about forget everything else."

Clearly, technology is important to Starbucks for the management of its supply chain. What kinds of information do you think Starbucks needs to manage and improve its supply chain?

Chapter Outline

Purchases and Payments Process

Sunset Graphics Example

Company Overview

Sunset Graphics' Purchases and Payments Process Distribution

Sunset Graphics' Activity Models

Basic Purchases Activity Model

Refining the Model to Show Collaboration

Business Rules and Sunset Graphics' Purchases and Payments Process Controls

Sunset Graphics' Structure Models

Basic UML Class Diagram for Purchases and Payments

Refining the UML Class Diagram for Purchases and Payments

Sunset Graphics' Relational Database

Relational Database Planning for Attributes

Creating the Database and Defining the Tables

Comprehensive Exercise: Baer Belly Bikinis' Purchases of Fabric

Appendix A: Generic REA Model with Multiplicities for the Purchases and Payments Process

Learning Objectives

After reading this chapter, you should be able to:

6-1 Describe the business activities that comprise the purchase and payment process.

6-2 Develop an activity model of the purchase and payment process using BPMN.

6-3 Understand and apply different activity modeling options.

6-4 Develop business rules to implement controls for the purchase and payment process.

6-5 Develop structure models for the purchase and payment process using UML class diagrams.

6-6 Implement a relational database from the UML class diagram of the purchase and payment process.

LO 6-1
Describe the business activities that comprise the purchase and payment process.

PURCHASES AND PAYMENTS PROCESS

The purchases and payments process includes business activities related to buying inventory from **suppliers** maintaining supplier records, and making payments to suppliers for trade accounts payable while taking appropriate **purchase discounts**. The purchases and payments process generates accounting transactions to record **purchases, accounts payable,** and **cash disbursements.** The process also affects inventory values as purchases are added to inventory. Figure 6.1 describes typical transactions resulting from the purchases and payments process.

We will apply the tools introduced in Chapters 2, 3, 4, and 5 to a comprehensive example of the purchases and payments process. We first describe the process activities using BPMN, and then we define the typical information structure using UML class diagrams. Finally, we use the UML class diagrams to build a database to collect and report relevant process information. We also describe business rules that establish potential process controls.

FIGURE 6.1
Accounting Transactions for Purchases and Payments Process

Oct 1	Purchases (or Inventory)*		1,495.50	
	Accounts Payable			1,495.50
	Purchased inventory on credit from Richardson & Sons, Inc.			
	Invoice 1125 dated Oct 1, terms 2/10, net 30			
Oct 11	Accounts Payable		1,495.50	
	Purchase Discounts			29.91
	Cash			1,465.59
	Paid Richardson & Sons, Inc. for Invoice 1125 dated Oct 1			
	less 2% discount			
	* Debit to Purchases or Inventory account depends on whether the			
	company uses a periodic or perpetual inventory system.			

SUNSET GRAPHICS EXAMPLE

Company Overview

As described in Chapter 5, Virgil and Linda B own and operate Sunset Graphics. They design and sell signs and banners, lettering and vinyl graphics for vehicles and boats, corporate promotional items, and silk-screened T-shirts and embroidered gear, among other products. Recently, they decided that it was time to review their business processes to develop better documentation, improve processes, and establish consistency in customer service. They also wanted to be sure that effective internal controls were in place. This comprehensive example assumes that we are business analysts who are helping Virgil and Linda accomplish these goals.

Sunset Graphics' Purchases and Payments Process Description

Linda B does most of the buying and also pays most of the bills for Sunset, so she explained the process. When Sunset needs to purchase items, it usually follows a straightforward process:

1. Research prices and product availability.
2. Select the best price and availability combination, and send a **purchase order** to the supplier.

3. Receive the items from the supplier (and record the purchase and accounts payable).
4. Pay the supplier according to the credit terms.

SUNSET GRAPHICS' ACTIVITY MODELS

LO 6-2
Develop an activity
model of the purchase
and payment process
using BPMN.

Basic Purchases Activity Model

After talking with Linda B about their purchases and payments process, our first task was
to draw a simple business process model using BPMN. As shown in Figure 6.2, the start
of the process occurs when Sunset needs to purchase items to fulfill a customer order or to
replenish inventory. Then, a series of tasks takes place in sequence until Sunset pays for
the items and the process ends. Sunset records purchases and updates inventory when it
receives the items.

FIGURE 6.2
Basic Purchases
Activity Model

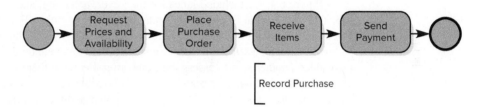

LO 6-3
Understand and apply
different activity
modeling options.

Refining the Model to Show Collaboration

After reviewing models for the sales and collection process in Chapter 5, Linda was starting to understand these models. She remarked that she liked the **collaboration** model better because it shows the interactions with the external parties that Sunset relies on. So, she
asked if we could prepare a collaboration model of the purchases and payments process.
Of course, we said we could. In this case, the *pools* would show suppliers and Sunset,
with *message flows* (shown by dashed arrows) between pools describing the interaction
between participants. In fact, if you are primarily interested in the interactions, you don't
need to model the **orchestration** within either pool. To illustrate, we prepared Figure 6.3,
which shows the two pools for the suppliers and Sunset Graphics and the **choreography**
between them.

FIGURE 6.3
Collaboration
Purchases Activity
Model

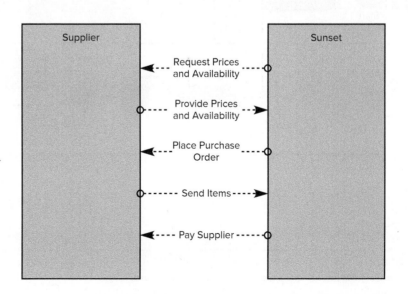

Linda thought that this model offered a good overview of their typical purchase and payment process. It showed the choreography of interactions between the pools. However, she reminded us that she would not be doing most of Sunset's buying and bill paying in the future. Because she was delegating those jobs, she thought that she should separate the buying duties from the payment duties for better internal control. She wondered if we could prepare a model that shows the process while highlighting different jobs within Sunset. We said that we could, and we reminded her about lanes in BPMN that allow us to model those different jobs.

Linda thought that showing the different jobs would provide better process documentation. However, she also noted that sometimes they do not get acceptable items from the supplier and have to send them back. She asked if we could also allow for that in the model. We prepared Figure 6.4 to show her a model with lanes that also allows for the return of deficient items.

In Figure 6.4, we included lanes for the buyer, receiving, and accounts payable (A/P) jobs that will exist at Sunset after Linda delegates her duties. We combined the Request Prices and Availability and Place Purchase Order activities in the original model shown in Figure 6.2 with a **subprocess** because we want to expand on those activities later. We also added another step to assess the items after receiving them from the supplier. Then, we included a **gateway** to branch into two possible courses of action. If the items are not acceptable, Sunset returns them to the supplier and the process ends. If the items are

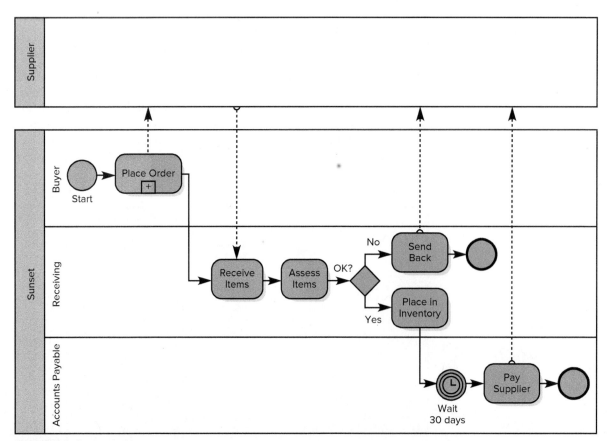

FIGURE 6.4
Expanded Collaboration Purchases Activity Model with Lanes

acceptable, they are placed in inventory; 30 days later (depending on credit terms), Sunset sends a payment to the supplier. Because there are two possible paths that do not reconnect, we include two end events.

Because we added some new notation, we explained what the new symbols mean. The gateway is modeled with the diamond. In this case, the gateway branches into two exclusive paths. We noted that with BPMN 2.0, gateways don't represent activities, so we needed to include the assessment activity, Assess Items, before the gateway. We also included an **intermediate timer event** (the **intermediate event** symbol with clock hands) to represent the time delay, Wait 30 days, before payment. **Timer events** represent a delay in the flow of a process. They can indicate a delay to (1) a specific date, such as December 31; (2) a relative time, such as 30 days; or (3) a relative repetitive date, such as next Friday at 5:00 p.m.

Progress Check

1. In Figure 6.4, at what point would Sunset record the purchase?
2. From your own experience, describe how you would change Figure 6.4 to reflect another purchases and payments process. What if the customer purchased over the Internet and paid by credit card?

LO 6-4

Develop business rules to implement controls for the purchase and payment process.

BUSINESS RULES AND SUNSET GRAPHICS' PURCHASES AND PAYMENTS PROCESS CONTROLS

Next, we wanted to talk about planning controls over the purchases and payments process to give Virgil and Linda more confidence in the integrity of the process when they stepped back from the day-to-day operations. As with the sales and collection process, we want to define controls by developing business rules for the process. First, we need to identify important business events and define Sunset's intention or objective for each event. Then, we determine the appropriate actions to take based on the conditions. For example, we've already listed important business events in the business process models, so let's examine Sunset's purchases and payments process in Figure 6.4 and develop some possible business rules.

Again, Virgil and Linda summarized their objectives for the steps in the process. Of course, their overall goal was to purchase needed items from reliable suppliers at the best possible prices to meet required delivery schedules. They also wanted to be sure that these suppliers were paid on time, taking prompt payment discounts where appropriate, so they could maintain positive, long-term relationships. Because they were not going to directly supervise the process anymore, they wanted to be sure that effective controls were applied.

We outlined some standard controls over the purchases and payments process, suggesting segregation of ordering, receiving, and payment duties.

Adding new purchases to inventory.
© *Digital Vision/Getty Images*

Process Steps	Intention	Partner Authority/ Action	Access Controls	Application Controls
Place Order	Order products from reliable suppliers at the best available prices to meet required delivery time.	Manager approval required for orders >$5,000; partner ordering products must not manage inventory.	Partner preparing purchase orders cannot modify product inventory records, receive items, or pay suppliers.	System must provide purchase order number control, default values, and range and limit checks and must create an audit trail.
Receive Items	Record receipt of items promptly and accurately.	Partner receiving items must not be same partner who ordered the items.	Partner receiving items cannot modify purchase orders or inventory records; they cannot view purchase order quantity ordered information.	System must only allow partner to enter the number of items received, subject to range and limit checks on quantities received; date of receipt defaults to current date.
Assess Items	Reject defective items; record acceptance promptly and accurately.	Partner assessing items must not be same partner who ordered the items.	Partner assessing items cannot modify purchase orders or inventory records.	System must only allow partner to record the assessment; date of assessment defaults to current date.
Place in Inventory	Place accepted items in proper inventory locations promptly.	Partner placing the items in inventory must not be same partner who ordered the items.	Partner placing items in inventory cannot modify purchase orders.	System must specify where items are to be placed.
Send Items Back	Return defective items to suppliers promptly.	Manager approval required for defective items return.	Partner returning items cannot modify supplier information.	System must supply supplier return address.
Pay Supplier	Pay suppliers accurately, taking cost-effective discount terms.	Partner making payment must not be partner who ordered items or received/ accepted items.	Partner making payments cannot modify purchase orders and receipt/ acceptance records.	System must supply supplier payment information and amount of payment; payment date defaults to current date.

TABLE 6.1
Using Business Rules to Implement Internal Controls

We reiterated that *access controls* limit which of their partners can view and change records in the system and help implement appropriate segregation of duties. We also need *application controls* to ensure data integrity and an audit trail. For example, we need to control the assignment of purchase order and receiving report numbers to make sure all of them are accounted for. Plus, we need to establish appropriate ranges or limits for each value that Sunset's partners can add or change in the system.

With Virgil and Linda's direction, we developed an initial set of business rules for the purchases and payments process. They articulated their intentions for every step in the process, and then we set business rules to segregate duties and limit partner authority appropriately. Table 6.1 shows the initial set of business rules for Sunset's purchases and payments process. We noted that we would need to set application controls for almost every attribute updated during data entry.

LO 6-5
Develop structure models for the purchase and payment process using UML class diagrams.

SUNSET GRAPHICS' STRUCTURE MODELS

Linda B seemed pleased with the business process models so far. However, Virgil B was more interested in planning Sunset's new database. He'd already set up the sales and collection tables in Access, and he was waiting for the purchases and payments model so he could set up these tables, too. So, we proceeded to examine Sunset Graphics' purchases and payments information requirements. As described in Chapter 3, the primary purpose of our UML class diagram of the purchases and payments process is to create a blueprint for the development of a relational database to support the collection, aggregation, and communication of process information. As in Chapter 5, we follow the **REA** framework (**resources, events,** and **agents**) as a proven approach to describing business processes in a way that meets both accounting and broad management information requirements.

Basic UML Class Diagram for Purchases and Payments

We quickly reviewed Sunset's requirements for the purchases and payments process with Virgil B. In this case, a Sunset Partner (agent) selects the Supplier (agent) and issues a Purchase Order (event) as indicated by the number 1 on Figure 6.5. The Purchase Order specifies the prices and quantities of Products (resource) ordered. The Supplier (agent) sends, and a Sunset Partner (agent) receives (Receipts event), the products (resource) as indicated by the number 2 on Figure 6.5. The **receipt** triggers the recognition of the purchase and the corresponding account payable in the accounting records. Then, when the payment is due, a Sunset Partner (agent) pays (cash disbursement event) the Supplier (agent) from a Cash account (resource) as indicated by the number 3 on Figure 6.5.[2] The payment reduces accounts payable.

We showed Virgil the basic model, and he noticed that this model looked very similar to the sales and collection process model. Although the events were different, the resources and the Sunset Partner agent were the same. We said that this was a typical purchases and payments process. We always start with this basic diagram when we model the purchases and payments process, and then we modify it to reflect the unique information structure of a particular company. The Purchase Orders event represents Sunset's commitment to purchase **products** and pay the supplier, although commitments do not affect the financial statements. The Receipts event does affect the financial statements because it records the purchase for those items received and accepted and records the increases to accounts payable. The Cash Disbursement event also affects financial statements because it records decreases to **cash** and decreases to accounts payable.

FIGURE 6.5
Basic UML Class Diagram for Purchases and Payments

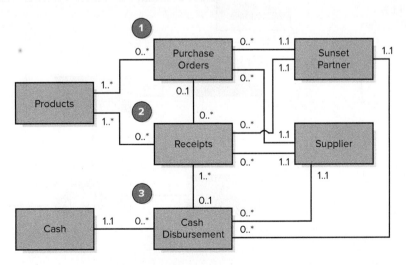

[2]Note that UML class diagrams reflect data structure and do not necessarily reflect the sequence of events.

Virgil said that he thought he understood multiplicities pretty well from our sales and collection process models, but he wanted to review a couple of them to make sure. For example, the multiplicities for the association between Purchase Orders and Products specify a **many-to-many relationship.** Each purchase order requests a minimum of one and a maximum of many products, and each product might not yet have been ordered and could be ordered many times.[3] We said that was correct but asked Virgil to explain the multiplicities for the Purchase Orders to Receipts association. He thought about it for a minute because he was not sure why a Purchase Order could be associated with multiple Receipts or why a Receipt could be related to a minimum of 0 Purchase Orders. We answered that we thought some Receipts were purchased over-the-counter from suppliers without first issuing a Purchase Order. Additionally, we thought that some Purchase Orders could result in partial shipments from the Supplier. Virgil responded that he could see how the model reflected those assumptions, but our assumptions were not correct. He said that Sunset always records a Purchase Order, even for over-the-counter purchases, and does not accept partial shipments.

Refining the UML Class Diagram for Purchases and Payments

Because Virgil said that Sunset always records Purchase Orders for a purchase and never accepts partial shipments, we revised the diagram. Because there is always a **one-to-one relationship** between Purchase Orders and Receipts, we can collapse the two classes into one and simplify the diagram (even though receipts happen after the orders). The new Purchases (event) class in Figure 6.6 would record purchase orders and include an attribute to indicate that the products were received. This is similar to the way we modeled Orders in the sales and collection process.

Each Purchase is associated with a minimum of 0 and a maximum of 1 Cash Disbursement because Sunset usually pays for purchases 30 days after receipt and pays in full. Each Cash Disbursement is associated with a minimum of 0 and a maximum of many Purchases because Sunset writes checks for other purposes and combines payments for multiple purchases from the same supplier when possible.

FIGURE 6.6
**Revised UML
Class Diagram
for Purchases and
Payments**

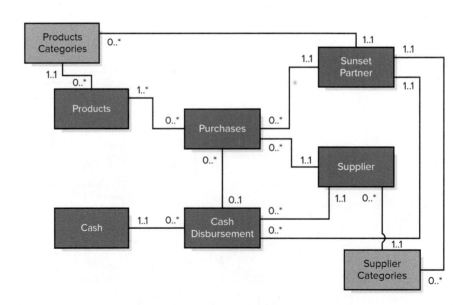

[3]We assume that products are identified before they are ordered.

Because we were refining the diagram, we added the **type image** for Product Categories that we also identified in the sales and collection process. Virgil then said that they also categorize their suppliers, so he suggested that we add a type image for Supplier Categories. He was really starting to understand UML class diagrams. We also added the association between Sunset Partners and Product Categories to reflect the assignment association that we identified in the sales and collection process.

Virgil agreed that Figure 6.6 accurately reflected their purchases and payments process. He was anxious to get started on defining the database. He recognized the composition association between Purchases and Purchase Items reflected by the many-to-many relationship between Purchases and Products. He said he understood how to post the foreign keys (see Chapters 3 and 4).

Progress Check

3. Describe when you would define two events—purchase orders and purchases—instead of combining them.
4. Review Figure 6.6 and explain when you might consider an association between Product Categories and Supplier Categories.

LO 6-6

Implement a relational database from the UML class diagram of the purchases and payments process.

SUNSET GRAPHICS' RELATIONAL DATABASE

Virgil and Linda B were both interested in implementing the purchases and payments UML class diagram in a relational database for Sunset. Again, we use Microsoft Access, but the process would be similar for any database-driven system. We encourage students to use the following description to implement a relational database to support information requirements for the purchases and payments process.

Relational Database Planning for Attributes

During the model development process, we reviewed Sunset's existing documents to determine specific data requirements for each class/table. We then followed the guidance in Chapter 3 to determine allocation of foreign keys. This resulted in a list of tables, attributes, data types, field sizes, and primary and foreign keys as shown in Table 6.2.

PK/FK	Attribute Name	Type	Size
	Table: tblBankAccounts		
PK	Account_number	Text	10
	Bank_routing_number	Text	10
	Bank_balance	Currency	8
	Bank_name	Text	15
	Bank_branch	Text	15
	Bank_phone_number	Text	15
	Table: tblCashDisbursements		
PK	Check_Number	Text	10
	Check_Amount	Currency	8
	Check_Date	Date/Time	8
FK	Supplier_Number	Text	10

PK/FK	Attribute Name	Type	Size
FK	Account_Number	Text	10
FK	Partner_Number	Text	10
	Table: tblPartners		
PK	Partner_number	Text	10
	Partner_first_name	Text	15
	Partner_last_name	Text	15
	Partner_hire_date	Date/Time	8
	Partner_SocSecNo	Text	11
	Partner_Address	Text	50
	Partner_Address2	Text	50
	Partner_City	Text	20
	Partner_State	Text	2

TABLE 6.2
Sunset Database Table and Attribute Definitions

(continued)

PK/FK	Attribute Name	Type	Size
	Partner_Zip	Text	10
	Partner_phone	Text	14
	Partner_cellphone	Text	14
	Table: tblProductCategory		
PK	Product_category_number	Text	10
	Product_category_description	Text	255
	Product_category_manager	Text	10
	Product_category_notes	Memo	—
	Table: tblProducts		
PK	Product_number	Text	10
	Product_description	Text	255
	Product_price	Currency	8
	Product_unit_of_sale	Text	10
FK	Product_category	Text	10
	Product_quantity_on_hand	Integer	2
	Product_notes	Memo	—
	Table: tblPurchaseItems		
PK	Purchase_Order_number	Text	10
PK	Product_number	Text	10
	Purchase_Order_quantity	Integer	2
	Purchase_Order_price	Currency	8
	Received_quantity	Integer	2
	Accepted_quantity	Integer	2
	Table: tblPurchases		
PK	Purchase_Order_Number	Text	10
	Purchase_Order_Date	Date/Time	8

PK/FK	Attribute Name	Type	Size
FK	Prepared_by	Text	10
FK	Supplier_Number	Text	10
	Received_Date	Date/Time	8
	Purchase_Order_Amount	Currency	8
	Required_by	Date/Time	8
FK	Check_Number	Text	10
	Memo	Memo	—
	Table: tblSupplierCategory		
PK	Supplier_category_number	Text	10
	Supplier_category_description	Text	255
	Supplier_category_purchases_YTD*	Currency	8
	Supplier_category_notes	Memo	—
	Table: tblSuppliers		
PK	Supplier_Number	Text	15
	Supplier_Name	Text	25
	Supplier_Contact_Name	Text	20
	Suppllier_Address	Text	30
	Supplier_Address_2	Text	30
	Supplier_City	Text	20
	Supplier_State	Text	2
	Supplier_Zip	Text	5
	Supplier_phone	Text	15
	Supplier_web_site	Hyperlink	—
FK	Supplier_Category	Text	10

* Year to date

TABLE 6.2
(continued)

Creating the Database and Defining the Tables

The next step is to create a new, blank Microsoft Access database and create the tables described in Table 6.2. Then, establish *relationships* between the tables as shown in Figure 6.7 and as described in Chapter 5. At that point, Sunset's purchases and payments process database is set up.

FIGURE 6.7
Linked Tables with
Referential Integrity
Enforced

© Microsoft Access

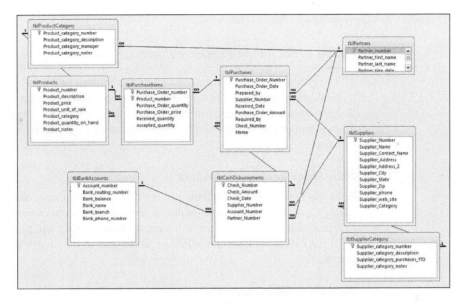

COMPREHENSIVE EXERCISE: BAER BELLY BIKINIS' PURCHASES OF FABRIC

As outlined in Chapter 5, Baer Belly Bikinis Inc. (BBB) is a small business located in Santa Monica, California. It sells swimwear and related products to specialty stores throughout the United States. It also sells its products to individuals over a company website. Paige Baer founded BBB almost 10 years ago after she graduated from the Fashion Institute of Design and Merchandising. She recognized the need for swimsuits sold as separates. Her business has grown rapidly, and now BBB has a large following of customers who want to be able to mix and match to find their ideal swimsuit. Currently, BBB products are carried in more than 1,000 specialty swimwear boutiques and online retailers.

During an initial interview with Paige Baer, she outlined BBB's business processes. She acknowledged that she doesn't know much about accounting and information technology. As the business grew, her accounting suffered and information systems were added piecemeal. So, she is looking forward to an assessment of her requirements and recommendations that would position BBB for substantial further growth.

This case examines BBB purchases of fabric. BBB's production staff selects the fabric and materials for the swimsuits. This case also examines BBB purchases of and miscellaneous supplies and services.

BBB Purchases of Fabric

BBB works closely with local fabric vendors to determine the color themes for each season's products. When BBB has received enough orders from the retailer customers to estimate the quantity of swimsuits and products to manufacture, BBB then orders the required quantities of fabric and related materials from the fabric vendors. BBB pays each fabric vendor at the end of the month for all purchases during the month. For each fabric order, there is one receipt. For each receipt of fabric, there is one order. Consequently, the order and purchases (receipts) can be modeled as one event.

Assessing fabric purchase requirements.
© Todd Wright/Blend Images/Getty Images

Details of the Fabric Purchase Process

1. The Production supervisor places an order for fabric according to internal estimates of production quantities (the estimates are not part of the project).
2. Fabric vendors ship fabric in bulk to BBB usually within 2 weeks of the order.
3. A Shipping and Warehouse employee receives the bulk fabric and verifies quantities received.

BBB Miscellaneous Purchases

BBB also purchases miscellaneous services and supplies, such as electricity, water, sewage, garbage, phone, and janitorial services. It also pays monthly rent on the building, purchases office supplies, hires photo shoot models and photographers, and so on. BBB pays its miscellaneous suppliers at the end of the month for all purchases during the month.

BBB Cash Disbursements

BBB assigns sequential numbers to each check issued. All checks for purchases (both fabric and miscellaneous) are written on its main bank account.

Exercise Requirements

1. Based on the preceding information and the following attributes list, prepare a UML class model and corresponding table listing describing BBB's purchases and payments process. List the tables in the following order: resources, events, agents, type images, and linking tables. Identify the primary keys and foreign keys in each table. [optional] Prepare a second UML model that combines the fabric and miscellaneous purchases events and the fabric and miscellaneous vendor agents. Show how you might model a way to differentiate among the types of vendors.
2. [optional] Based on the preceding information, prepare a BPMN activity model that describes BBB's purchases and payments process. The model should begin with BBB placing orders with its vendors and end when BBB makes payments for the purchases to the vendors.
3. Your instructor will provide an Excel spreadsheet with the BBB information. Create a new Access database, and import each worksheet in the spreadsheet into the database. Set appropriate primary keys.
4. After importing all the data, create relationships among tables to implement your data model.
5. Prepare queries to answer the following questions:

   a. What were BBB's total purchases of fabric in the second quarter (April to June)?
   b. What is BBB's accounts payable balance for each fabric as of April 15?
   c. Based on the information available, what is the quantity on hand in yards for each fabric color code as of April 15?

Attribute Listing for BBB

Bank Name	Employee#
Cash Account#	Employee Address
Cash Account Balance Beginning (April 1)	Employee City
Cash Account Description	Employee Department
Check#	Employee First Name
Check Amount	Employee Hire Date
Check Pay Date	Employee Last Name

Employee Pay Amount	Fabric Vendor State
Employee Phone	Fabric Vendor Type
Employee Salary/Wage	Fabric Vendor Zip
Employee Zip	Miscellaneous Purchase#
Fabric Color Code	Miscellaneous Purchase Amount
Fabric Color Name	Miscellaneous Purchase Date
Fabric Cost per Yard	Miscellaneous Purchasing Employee#
Fabric Inventory Quantity on Hand	Miscellaneous Vendor#
Fabric Purchase Date Received	Miscellaneous Vendor Address 1
Fabric Purchase Order#	Miscellaneous Vendor Address 2
Fabric Purchase Order Date	Miscellaneous Vendor Company
Fabric Purchase Quantity in Yards	Miscellaneous Vendor Item Number
Fabric Purchase Received By	Miscellaneous Vendor State
Fabric Purchase Total Amount	Miscellaneous Vendor Zip
Fabric Vendor#	Order Employee#
Fabric Vendor Address 1	Pay Employee#
Fabric Vendor Address 2	Vendor Type
Fabric Vendor Company	
Fabric Vendor Item Number	

Summary

- From an accounting standpoint, we must account for purchase orders, the receipt of goods and services (purchases), accounts payable, and cash disbursements (payments) in the purchases and payments process.
- Sunset Graphics Inc. provides a continuing example of how the purchases and payments process is modeled.
- BPMN activity diagrams can provide the basic sequence of tasks or can be extended to describe specific organizational responsibilities for tasks.
- Business rules implement controls over the purchases and payments process.
- UML class diagrams for the purchases and payments process are built on the standard REA pattern and look very similar to sales and collection process structure diagrams.
- Type images categorize information about agents and resources and show assignments.
- The structure models are the blueprint from which relational databases are designed and implemented.
- A comprehensive example reinforces the concepts presented in the chapter.

Key Words

accounts payable (*152*)   Amounts owed to suppliers for goods and services received. In a data modeling context, accounts payable are calculated based on receipts (purchases) from each supplier less the corresponding payments (cash disbursements) to those suppliers.

agents (*157*)   The people or organizations who participate in business events, such as customers and salespeople.

cash (*157*)   The organization's monies in bank or related accounts. The instances of the class are individual accounts. This is considered a resource.

cash disbursements (*152*)   Record payments of cash to external agents (e.g., suppliers) and the corresponding reduction in cash accounts. This is considered an event.

choreography (*153*)   The interaction (message flows) between two participants (modeled as pools) in a process modeled using BPMN.

collaboration (*153*)   A BPMN model showing two participant pools and the interactions between them within a process.

events (*157*)   Classes that model the organization's transactions, usually affecting the organization's resources, such as sales and cash receipts; Important occurrences that affect the flow of activities in a business process. BPMN includes symbols to define start, intermediate, and end events.

gateway (*154*)   Shows process branching and merging as the result of decisions. Basic gateways are depicted as diamonds. Usually, gateways appear as pairs on the diagram. The first gateway shows the branching, and the second gateway shows merging of the process branches.

intermediate event (*155*)   Occurs between start and end events and affects the flow of the process.

intermediate timer event (*155*)   Intermediate events that indicate a delay in the normal process flow until a fixed amount of time has elapsed.

many-to-many relationship (*158*)   Exists when instances of one class (e.g., sales) are related to many instances of another class (e.g., inventory) and vice versa. These relationships are implemented in Access and relational databases by adding a linking table to convert the many-to-many relationship into two one-to-many relationships.

one-to-one relationship (*158*)   Exists when instances of one class (e.g., sales) are related to only one instance of another class (e.g., cash receipts) and each instance of the other class is related to only one instance of the original class.

orchestration (*153*)   In BPMN, the sequence of activities within one pool.

product (*157*)   Class representing the organization's goods held for sale, that is, the organization's inventory. This is considered a resource.

purchase discount (*152*)   An offer from the supplier to reduce the cost of a purchase if payment is made according to specified terms, usually within a specified time.

purchase order (*152*)   A commitment event that precedes the economic purchase event. It records formal offers to suppliers to pay them if the supplier complies with the terms of the purchase order.

purchases (*152*)   Records the receipt of goods or services from a supplier and the corresponding obligation to pay the supplier. These are considered events.

REA (*157*)   Resource-event-agent framework for modeling business processes, originally developed by William McCarthy.

receipt (*157*)   Same as the purchases event.

resources (*157*)   Those things that have economic value to a firm, such as cash and products.

subprocess (*154*)   Represents a series of process steps that are hidden from view in BPMN. The use of subprocesses in modeling helps reduce complexity.

suppliers (*152*)   In the UML diagram of the purchases and payments process, the external agents from whom goods and services are purchased and to whom payments are made.

timer events (*155*)   Indication of a delay in the flow of a process to a specific date, an elapsed time (for example, 30 days), or a relative repetitive date, such as every Friday.

type image (*159*)   Class that represents management information (such as categorizations, policies, and guidelines) to help manage a business process. Type image often allows process information to be summarized by category.

Appendix A

Generic REA Model with Multiplicities for the Purchases and Payments Process

GENERIC PATTERN WITH MULTIPLICITIES

Figure 6.A1 shows a generic purchases and payments process UML diagram. There are two resources, *inventory* and *cash;* there are two events, *purchases* and *cash disbursements;* and there are two agents, *employees* (internal agent) and *suppliers* (external agent).

FIGURE 6.A1
Generic Purchases and Payments UML Diagram

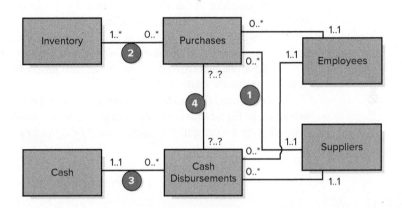

In this example, let's assume that the inventory is something tracked by universal product code (UPC). UPC are those bar codes you see on literally millions of products, such as soap, breakfast cereal, and packages of cookies. The cash resource represents the various bank accounts that would make up this enterprise's cash balance on its balance sheet. The purchases event records information about individual purchase transactions (e.g., transaction number, date, total dollar amount). The cash disbursement event records information about payments made to suppliers from one of the bank accounts (e.g., check number, check date, check dollar amount). The employees' agent records information about the enterprise's employees, including those employees who handle purchases transactions. The suppliers agent records information about actual and potential suppliers (let's assume that supplier information is recorded in some cases before the firm orders anything from them, and let's also assume that the company only writes checks to suppliers).

Figure 6.A1 shows the generic REA model. You should immediately notice the similarity with the sales and collection process diagram shown in Appendix A of Chapter 5. Consider association 1 between *suppliers* and *purchases.* The multiplicities indicate that each supplier participates in a minimum of zero and a maximum of many sales. Does this seem reasonable? The minimum of zero means that we can record information about suppliers before they participate in any sale. On the other side of the association, the multiplicities indicate that each purchase involves one and only one supplier. Again, does this seem reasonable? Notice that the multiplicities for the other associations between agents and events are the same. In fact, these are the typical multiplicities for those associations. There are circumstances where they might be different, but those circumstances occur infrequently.

Next, consider association 2 between the *purchases* event and *inventory* resource. The multiplicities indicate that each purchase involves a minimum of one and a maximum of many inventory items. The multiplicities also indicate that each inventory item can be purchased zero times or many times. The multiplicities on this association are typical when the inventory is carried at a type of product level, such as when the inventory is identified by UPC code.

Now, consider association 3 between the *cash disbursement* event and the *cash* resource. These multiplicities indicate that each cash disbursement (e.g., one check) is paid from one and only one account, and each account is associated with a minimum of zero cash disbursements and a maximum of many cash disbursements. These multiplicities reflect typical business practices. Think about paying bills using your bank's online banking feature. You log on, select the account, and then pay the bill. The amount of the payment is subtracted from that one account.

Finally, consider the duality association 4 between the *purchases* and *cash disbursement* events. The question marks indicate that these multiplicities depend on the nature of the business as well as the terms of the particular purchase. Payments could be made before, after, or at the same time as the purchase. One payment could be made for several purchases, or one purchase could involve several payments. So, there are no typical multiplicities for this association.

We recommend that students recognize and use the standard patterns for multiplicities as shown in Figure 6.A1, remembering that those standard multiplicities could change depending on the particular circumstances of the business.

Answers to Progress Check

1. Sunset would record the purchase when the items are received and accepted, so the purchase is recognized with the Place in Inventory activity.

2. If they purchased over the Internet, they would pay when they placed the order. The Pay Supplier activity would then occur during the Place Order process.

3. You would define two events when there is not a one-to-one relationship between purchase orders and purchases.

4. You would link Product Categories and Supplier Categories if summary information depended on both the product and supplier categories, for example, year-to-date sales for this product category and this supplier category.

▥ connect

Multiple Choice Questions

1. Which of the following is not an activity in the purchases and payments process? LO 6-1
   a. Request prices
   b. Receive items
   c. Pay for items
   d. Bill customers
   e. All of the above are activities in the purchases and payments process.

2. Which activity results in an increase to accounts payable? LO 6-1
   a. Request prices
   b. Place purchase order
   c. Receive items
   d. Return rejected items
   e. Send payment

3. *Choreography* describes which of the following? LO 6-2, LO 6-3
   a. Sequence of activities in a process
   b. Message flows between pools
   c. Process gateways
   d. Both a and c
   e. Both b and c

4. Which of the following is not an example of an application control? LO 6-4
   a. Range checks ensure that purchases are limited to valid amounts.
   b. Employee making disbursements cannot modify purchase orders.
   c. System supplies supplier address for the payment.
   d. System creates audit trail documenting all changes.
   e. All of the above are examples of application controls.

5. Which of the following describes the purpose of an intermediate timer event? LO 6-3
   a. Indicates receipt of a message
   b. Indicates branching
   c. Indicates delay
   d. Both a and c
   e. Both b and c

6. Which of the following is a resource in a purchases and payments structure model? LO 6-5
   a. Employee labor
   b. Receipt of goods
   c. Paying by check
   d. Inventory
   e. Supplier

7. Which of the following is an agent in a purchases and payments structure model? LO 6-5
   a. Employee labor
   b. Receipt of goods
   c. Cash disbursement
   d. Inventory
   e. Supplier

8. Which of the following is an event in a purchases and payments structure model? LO 6-5
   a. Cash
   b. Inventory
   c. Employee
   d. Cash disbursement
   e. None of the above

9. Which of the following events would indicate recording of a purchase in the AIS? **LO 6-5**

    a. Issue Purchase Order

    b. Receive Goods

    c. Make Payment

    d. Transfer Inventory

    e. None of the above

10. In a typical relational database supporting the purchase and payment process, which of the following tables is likely to have the most foreign keys? **LO 6-5**

    a. Employee table

    b. Supplier table

    c. Inventory table

    d. Cash disbursement table

    e. Cash table

Use the following diagram to answer Questions 11 through 27.

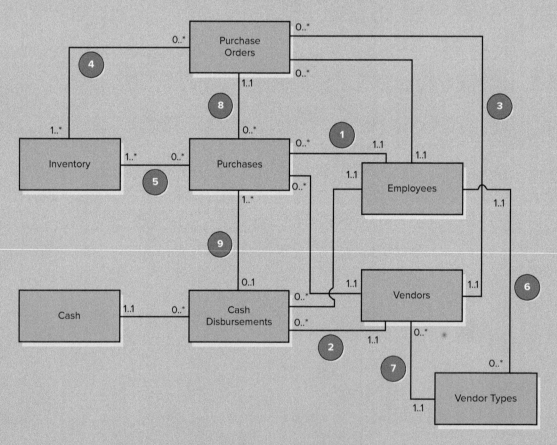

11. Refer to the association marked with the number 1 in the preceding diagram. Which of the following is the best description of the association? **LO 6-5**

    a. Each employee participates in a minimum of zero purchases.

    b. Each employee participates in at least one purchase.

    c. Each employee participates in a maximum of one purchase.

    d. Only employees in the shipping and receiving department receive purchases.

    e. None of these are a description of the association.

12. Refer to the association marked with the number 1 in the preceding diagram. Which of the following is the best description of the association? **LO 6-5**

    a. Each purchase is received by multiple employees.

    b. Each purchase is received by one employee.

    c. Each purchase can be received by a maximum of many employees.

    d. Each purchase can be received by a minimum of zero employees.

    e. None of these are a description of the association.

13. Refer to the association marked with the number 2 in the preceding diagram. Which of the following is the best description of the association? **LO 6-5**

    a. Each vendor always receives multiple cash disbursements.

    b. Each vendor receives a minimum of zero cash disbursements.

    c. Each vendor receives a maximum of one cash disbursement.

    d. Each vendor is paid by check.

    e. None of these are a description of the association.

14. Refer to the association marked with the number 2 in the preceding diagram. Which of the following is the best description of the association? **LO 6-5**

    a. Each cash disbursement is made to many vendors.

    b. A cash disbursement can be made to zero vendors

    c. Each cash disbursement is made to a maximum of one vendor.

    d. Each cash disbursement is made to a minimum of zero vendors.

    e. None of these are a description of the association.

15. Refer to the association marked with the number 3 in the preceding diagram. Which of the following is the best description of the association? **LO 6-5**

    a. Vendors may receive many purchase orders.

    b. Vendors must receive at least one purchase order.

    c. Vendors receive a minimum of one purchase order.

    d. Vendors receive a maximum of one purchase order.

    e. None of these are a description of the association.

16. Refer to the association marked with the number 3 in the preceding diagram. Which of the following is the best description of the association? **LO 6-5**

    a. Each purchase order is issued to many vendors.

    b. Each purchase order is issued to zero vendors.

    c. Each purchase order is issued to a maximum of many vendors.

    d. Each purchase order is issued to a minimum of one vendor.

    e. None of these are a description of the association.

17. Refer to the association marked with the number 4 in the preceding diagram. Which of the following is the best description of the association? **LO 6-5**

    a. Each purchase order specifies a type of inventory.

    b. Each purchase order is associated with a maximum of many inventory items.

    c. Each purchase order is associated with a minimum of zero inventory items.

    d. Some purchase orders do not list inventory items.

    e. None of these are a description of the association.

18. Refer to the association marked with the number 4 in the preceding diagram. Which of the following is the best description of the association? LO 6-5

    a. Each inventory item is ordered one time.

    b. Each inventory item is ordered zero times.

    c. Each inventory item is ordered on a minimum of zero purchase orders.

    d. Each inventory item is ordered on a minimum of one purchase order.

    e. None of these are a description of the association.

19. Refer to the association marked with the number 4 in the preceding diagram. Which of the following is the best way to implement the association in a relational database? LO 6-5, LO 6-6

    a. Post the primary key of purchase orders as a foreign key in inventory.

    b. Post the primary key of inventory in purchase orders as a foreign key.

    c. Create a linking table with a concatenated primary key.

    d. Record the date of the purchase order in the inventory table.

    e. None of these are a description of the correct implementation.

20. Refer to the association marked with the number 5 in the preceding diagram. Which of the following is the best description of the association? LO 6-5

    a. Each inventory item is associated with a minimum of one purchase.

    b. Each inventory item is purchased one time.

    c. Each inventory item is purchased zero times.

    d. Each inventory item is associated with a minimum of zero purchases.

    e. None of these are a description of the association.

21. Refer to the association marked with the number 5 in the preceding diagram. Which of the following is the best description of the association? LO 6-5, LO 6-6

    a. Purchases increase the quantity-on-hand of inventory items.

    b. Each purchase includes a minimum of zero inventory items.

    c. Each purchase includes a minimum of two inventory items.

    d. A purchase may be associated with a maximum of one inventory item.

    e. None of these are a description of the association.

22. Refer to the association marked with the number 5 in the preceding diagram. Which of the following is the best way to implement the association in a relational database? LO 6-5

    a. Create a linking table with a concatenated primary key.

    b. Post the primary key of purchases as a foreign key in inventory.

    c. Post the primary key of inventory in purchases as a foreign key.

    d. Post the purchases primary key in inventory and the inventory primary key in purchases.

    e. None of these are a description of the correct implementation.

23. Refer to the association marked with the number 6 in the preceding diagram. Which of the following is the best description of the association? LO 6-5

    a. Some employees are also vendor types.

    b. Employees only deal with authorized vendor types.

    c. Some employees are assigned to work with specific vendor types.

    d. Some vendor types are not issued purchase orders.

    e. None of these are a description of the association.

24. Refer to the association marked with the number 6 in the preceding diagram. Which of the following is the best way to implement the association in a relational database? LO 6-5
    a. Post the primary key of vendor types in employees as a foreign key.
    b. Post the primary key of employees as a foreign key in vendor types.
    c. Create a linking table with a concatenated primary key.
    d. The association does not require foreign keys.
    e. None of these are a description of the correct implementation.

25. Refer to the association marked with the number 7 in the preceding diagram. Which of the following is the best description of the association? LO 6-5
    a. Some vendors are not in a vendor type.
    b. Employees do not deal with vendors that are not in a vendor type.
    c. Vendors are classified by type.
    d. Each vendor type must contain at least one vendor.
    e. None of these are a description of the association.

26. Assume that you are drawing an activity (BPMN) diagram of the process. Which of the following is not true about your diagram? LO 6-5
    a. The issue purchase order task occurs before the receive purchases task.
    b. The purchases task could be modeled as a looping task to show multiple purchases following one purchase order.
    c. The process starts when a customer places a sales order.
    d. The process ends when the vendor is paid.
    e. All of these are true about the diagram.

27. Assume that you are drawing a collaboration activity (BPMN) diagram of the process. Which of the following would not be message flows on your diagram? LO 6-5
    a. Purchase order
    b. Delivery (of the purchase)
    c. Check/cash disbursement
    d. Inventory update
    e. All of these are message flows for the diagram.

Discussion Questions

1. Business rules implement internal controls. Review Table 6.1 and describe which business rules implement segregation of duties. Classify each of those business rules as obligatory, prohibited, or allowed as described in Chapter 3. LO 6-4

2. **Walmart** uses a vendor-managed inventory system, where the inventory is owned and managed by the vendor until it is delivered from Walmart's distribution center to the stores. What implications does this system have for Walmart's purchases and payments process? LO 6-1

3. Draw an activity model using BPMN for the process that you followed when you purchased your textbooks for the current semester. LO 6-2, LO 6-3

4. Refer to Figure 6.5. Describe the types of businesses that would employ a similar diagram for their purchases and payments processes. What other alternative approaches are there? Describe some businesses that would use these alternatives for the purchases and payments process structure. LO 6-2

5. Recall that type images apply guidelines, constraints, and descriptive information, as well as categorizing the economic resources, events, and agents for a business process. Figure 6.6 shows two examples of type images for Sunset Graphics. Are there other possible type images that could be added to the diagram to help Sunset's managers manage the purchases and payments process? LO 6-5

6. Some larger companies and government entities issue contracts for major purchases and then issue specific purchase orders to their contractors according to the terms of the contract. The contract can specify prices and payment terms as well as other administrative procedures. How would the use of contracts affect the standard process flow as shown in Figure 6.2? How would it affect the UML class diagram for the purchases and payments process? LO 6-5

7. Sunset Graphics often buys inventory after receiving a sales order from the customer. Suppose you are asked to prepare one UML class diagram that combines both the sales and collection process and the purchases and payments process. What would be shared among those processes? What would be unique to each process? Why? LO 6-5

8. What classes and associations would be included in a model that describes the information needed for a query that calculates the accounts payable balance for each supplier? Describe the logic of that query. (In other words, what steps would you follow to compute that balance?) LO 6-5, LO 6-6

Problems

connect 1. The following narrative describes the purchase and payment process for The Tablet Store. Use the narrative to answer the questions below. The Tablet Store recently opened to sell iPads and other tablet computing devices. It purchases its tablets directly from the manufacturers (e.g., Apple, Samsung, and Dell). To order tablets, a Tablet Store employee submits a purchase order to the manufacturer electronically. Each purchase order could stipulate several different models of tablets from one manufacturer. The manufacturers typically deliver the tablets to the store within two weeks after they receive the purchase order. The Tablet Store pays for each shipment within 30 days after receipt. If there are multiple orders to the same manufacturer, the Tablet Store occasionally combines payments, issuing one check for multiple receipts. All of the Tablet Store checks are drawn on one bank account. LO 6-5, LO 6-6

a. Draw a UML class diagram that describes the Tablet Store's purchases and payments process.

b. Using Microsoft Access, implement a relational database from your UML class diagram. Identify at least three fields per table.

c. Describe how you would use the relational database to determine the Tablet Store's accounts payable.

connect 2. The following narrative describes the purchase and payment process for Quick Jet Inc. Use the narrative to answer the questions below. Quick Jet Inc. provides air taxi service to the wealthy, including celebrities, sports stars, and business executives. Quick Jet employees negotiate long-term leases with airplane leasing companies. Each lease involves one plane. Quick Jet categorizes its planes according to passenger capacity and normal flying range. Quick Jet makes monthly lease payments for its planes. If it leases multiple planes from the same lease company, it combines payments. LO 6-2, LO 6-3, LO 6-5

Maintenance

The company has no maintenance staff of its own, so it also contracts with a number of airplane maintenance companies to perform the routine maintenance required to keep its fleet airworthy. It issues orders against the contracts for specific maintenance required for the planes. To comply with FAA regulations, it tracks the details of the specific maintenance performed on each plane. To facilitate the tracking, each maintenance order specifies the maintenance services for one plane. Quick Jet pays for all the maintenance performed by each maintenance contractor within 15 days, according to the terms of the contracts, and may combine payments.

Miscellaneous Purchases

Quick Jet also provides each of its pilots with credit cards so they can purchase fuel and miscellaneous supplies at the various airports they use. The pilots turn in detailed lists of their purchases that identify the supplier, the date, the amount purchased, and the prices, as well as the plane for which the items were purchased. Each list is assigned a miscellaneous purchase number. Quick Jet pays the credit card bills in full each month upon receipt from the credit card company.

Other Information

Quick Jet keeps information about the plane leasing companies, the plane maintenance contractors, miscellaneous suppliers, and the credit card companies in one vendor file. However, it tracks plane leases, maintenance contracts, maintenance orders, and miscellaneous purchases separately (separate events). Quick Jet categorizes its employees according to their job assignments (e.g., pilots, purchasing employees, A/P clerks). It also categorizes vendors according to the services/goods they provide. It puts information about its agents, resources, and type images in the database before linking to other classes.

a. Draw a BPMN activity diagram that describes Quick Jet's purchases and payments process.

b. Prepare a UML class diagram with classes, associations, and multiplicities.

c. Using the preceding information and the following attributes list, prepare a listing of the relational tables necessary to support this sales and collection process. List the tables in the following order: resources, events, agents, type images, and linking tables.

Attributes:

Cash account#	Plane#
Cash account balance	Plane maintenance contract#
Check#	Plane maintenance contract date
Check amount	Plane maintenance contract duration
Check date	Plane maintenance item performed on this order for this plane
Date this misc. purchase billed by credit card company	Plane maintenance order#
Employee#	Plane maintenance order date
Employee hire date	Plane miles since last maintenance
Employee name	Plane type
Employee type	Plane type passenger capacity
Employee type description	Plane type range in miles
Lease#	Vendor#
Lease date	Vendor Name
Lease monthly payment amount	Vendor type
Misc. supply purchase#	Vendor type description
Misc. supply purchase date	Year-to-date (YTD) purchases from this vendor type
Number of vendors of this type	

3. The following narrative describes a purchase and payment process and a sales and collection process for BR Management Company. Use the narrative to answer the questions below. BR Management Company (BRMC) operates apartment complexes and earns revenues by renting out the apartments in those complexes. BRMC assigns an agent/manager to each complex (one manager can manage several complexes) to handle day-to-day operations, such as maintaining the property and signing rental contracts. This case describes the maintenance and rental processes. **LO 6-5**

Complexes and Apartments

BRMC has acquired 15 and built several more apartment complexes over the past 2 years. It identifies complexes by address and apartments by the combination of address and apartment number. BRMC categorizes each apartment according to a number of factors, including the quality of its furnishings, number of rooms, and size. There are 27 apartment categories at present, each identified by unique category number. Because each complex presents a unique set of luxury appointments and amenities, BRMC determines the standard monthly rental fee by considering both the apartment category and complex; for example, 2 bedroom 1 bath apartments (category 21) rent for $850 per month in the Broadway complex, but the same category apartments rent for $1,450 per month in the Naples complex.

Maintenance

BRMC keeps its apartments and complexes in top condition. The BRMC agents monitor the condition of the facilities. Whenever the condition falls below BRMC standards, the agents hire contractors to bring the apartment back up to specifications. BRMC classifies each maintenance job by job type, and it matches the job type to the contractor type that can best perform the job. The BRMC agent then selects one specific contractor for the job from that contractor type. Each contractor may belong to several contractor types. Each maintenance job involves either one apartment or the common areas of the complex. BRMC tracks the maintenance performed on apartments and complex common areas.

Rentals

BRMC agents negotiate rental contracts with tenants. Each rental contract governs one year-long lease of an apartment. Although there is a standard monthly rental fee for each apartment in each building, agents may negotiate higher or lower rents if they see the need to do so. It is important to have a full record of the actual rent for all apartments. When there is more than one tenant per apartment, every tenant must sign the rental contract. BRMC assigns a unique tenant ID number to each tenant and issues them ID cards to control access.

Cash Receipts and Disbursements and Other Information

To simplify the case, the cash resource, the cashier agent, and the cash receipt and disbursement events (although they would certainly exist) are eliminated. You should *not* model those in your solution. All agents, resources, and types are put into the database before they are linked to other classes.

a. Prepare an integrated UML class diagram with classes, associations, and multiplicities.

b. Using the preceding information and the following attributes list, prepare a listing of the relational tables necessary to support BRMC's processes. List the tables in the following order: resources, events, agents, type images, and linking tables.

Attributes:

Actual completion date of job	Apartment square footage
Actual cost of this job	Apartment#
Actual monthly rent	Category
Agent monthly salary	Contractor name
Agent name	Contractor phone number
Apartment category#	Contractor quality rating
Apartment complex address	Contractor type

Contractor#

Count of rooms in apartment

Count of this type of contractor

Date complex was constructed

Employee#

Job type

Maintenance job#

Number of available apartments in this
category

Projected completion date of job

Rental contract date

Rental contract#

Standard cost for this job type

Standard monthly rent

Tenant credit rating

Tenant ID#

Tenant name

Total complex square footage

Vendor#

Year to date (YTD) advertising $ for this

YTD $ spent on this job type

YTD $ spent on this job type in this complex

Additional problems are available in connect only.

Chapter **Seven**

Conversion Business Process

A look at this chapter

This chapter examines the conversion process whereby manufacturing companies convert raw material into finished goods. We continue our comprehensive example to develop activity and structure models of the process. We show how the activity model in conjunction with business rules can be used to develop, implement, and monitor control activities. We show how the structure model can be used to develop a relational database to support information processing requirements.

A look back

Chapter 6 examined the purchases and payments processes. It continued the comprehensive example that we are using to examine typical process activities and data structures.

A look ahead

Chapter 8 provides a hands-on project to review Chapters 5, 6, and 7.

© Ingram Publishing/SuperStock

Starbucks roasts its coffee in roasting plants distributed around the United States. One plant is a nondescript, 320,000-square-foot warehouse building located in Kent, Washington. Other roasting plants are located in Carson Valley, Nevada; York, Pennsylvania; and Amsterdam, Netherlands. The coffee beans are stacked in 150-pound burlap bags, and each bag is marked to identify the country of origin.

The bags of green coffee beans are stacked over a large metal grate in the floor. A worker cuts open the bag and the beans pour through the grate. They are pulled into a washer that separates foreign material. After washing, the beans are weighed, sorted, and stored for roasting. They are transferred into large roasters that can hold up to 600 pounds of beans. The roasting process is carefully controlled by computer. As the beans roast, they slowly turn brown. When the beans pop, the flavor is released.

The beans are transferred to cooling vats that turn and toss them to stop further roasting. Workers test the roasted beans. Soon, they are bagged and boxed for shipment. On average, the roasted beans will be in stores within 3 days.

To keep a constant flow of quality product to their worldwide network of stores, Starbucks needs to monitor its conversion process closely. In addition to the cost information that affects its financial statements, what other information is necessary for Starbucks' management of this process?

Chapter Outline

Conversion Process

Sunset Graphics Example

Company Overview

Sunset Graphics' Conversion Process Description

Sunset Graphics' Activity Models

Basic Conversion Process Model

Refining the Model

Business Rules and Sunset Graphics' Conversion Process Controls

Sunset Graphics' Structure Models

Basic UML Class Diagram for Conversion

Refining the UML Class Diagram for Sunset's Conversion Process

Sunset Graphics' Relational Database

Relational Database Planning for Attributes

Creating the Database and Defining the Tables

Learning Objectives

After reading this chapter, you should be able to:

7-1　Describe the business activities that comprise the conversion process.

7-2　Develop an activity model of the conversion process using BPMN.

7-3　Understand and apply different activity modeling options.

7-4　Develop business rules to implement controls for the conversion process.

7-5　Develop a structure model for the conversion process using UML class diagrams.

7-6　Implement a relational database from the UML class diagram of the conversion process.

LO 7-1

Describe the business activities that comprise the conversion process.

CONVERSION PROCESS

The conversion process is inherently more complicated than the sales and collections and purchases and payments processes described in the previous two chapters, primarily because of increased recordkeeping requirements and variations in the sophistication of the process itself among companies. Many types of businesses employ conversion processes, including bakeries, wineries, breweries, restaurants, car repair shops, construction companies, equipment manufacturers, automobile manufacturers, and so on.[1] The conversion process includes business activities related to maintaining inventories of raw material and finished goods, producing finished goods from raw material, tracking direct labor and direct equipment costs, and applying overhead.

The conversion process generates accounting transactions to record the transfer of raw material to work-in-process and work-in-process inventory to finished goods. In addition to the cost of raw materials, the conversion process must also account for direct labor and other direct costs incurred in determining the cost of goods manufactured. The allocation of overhead and indirect costs to work-in-process is typically based on direct labor-hours, although overhead could be allocated based on a number of cost drivers in an activity-based costing system. More specifically, conversion costs are typically accounted for at standard, where the standard is based on management estimates, and then the costs are updated to reflect actual costs incurred. Figure 7.1 describes typical transactions resulting from the conversion process. In addition to the accounting transactions, the specific details of the conversion process are often tracked to the individual job.

In this chapter, we continue to apply the tools introduced in Chapters 2 through 6 to a comprehensive example of the conversion process. We first describe the process activities using BPMN, and then we define the typical information structure using UML class diagrams. Finally, we use the UML class diagrams to build a database to collect and report relevant process information. We also describe business rules that establish potential process controls.

SUNSET GRAPHICS EXAMPLE

Company Overview

As described in Chapters 5 and 6, Virgil and Linda B own and operate Sunset Graphics. They design and sell signs and banners, lettering and vinyl graphics for vehicles and boats, corporate promotional items, and silk-screened T-shirts and embroidered gear, among other products. Recently, Virgil and Linda decided that it was time to step back from the day-to-day operations. Before they did, they wanted to review their business processes to develop better documentation, improve processes, and establish consistency in customer service. They also wanted to be sure that effective internal controls were in place because they wouldn't be on site as often.

Sunset Graphics' Conversion Process Description

Until recently, Sunset didn't track its conversion costs. If labor was involved in preparing products for a customer's order, Sunset simply billed the customer a flat rate for the service. The company didn't assign any labor or overhead costs to its products. However, that changed when it signed a major contract to provide a variety of signs and banners to state agencies. The terms of the contract required that Sunset include direct labor, direct

---

[1]We focus on companies that use job cost accounting methods, although the models could apply generally to companies that also use process costing methods.

FIGURE 7.1
Typical Conversion
Process Accounting
Transactions

Sep 1	Work-in-Process Inventory	2,875,50		
	Raw Material Inventory		2,875.50	
	Record transfer of raw material to Work-in-process			
Sep 2	Manufacturing Wages	4,650.00		
	Cash		4,650.00	
	To record manufacturing payroll			
Sep 2	Work-in-Process Inventory	3,250.00		
	Manufacturing Wages		3,250.00	
	To record direct labor			
Sep 2	Manufacturing Overhead	1,400.00		
	Manufacturing Wages		1,400.00	
	To record indirect labor			
Sep 2	Manufacturing Overhead	1,945.25		
	Utilities Payable		1,945.25	
	To record manufacturing overhead costs			
Sep 2	Work-in-Process Inventory	4,062.50		
	Manufacturing Overhead		4,062.50	
	To allocate manufacturing overhead to			
	work-in-process at 125% of direct labor			
Sep 3	Finished Goods	10,188.00		
	Work-in-Process Inventory		10,188.00	
	Record transfer of work-in-process to finished goods			

equipment costs, and overhead in the cost of its products. Although Sunset used job costing for this contract, Virgil and Linda B began to wonder if job costing could be used to provide better information about the real costs of their products.

Virgil and Linda B explained their conversion process. Demand for products under the state contract fluctuated but often required short delivery times, so they decided to keep a safety stock of those products (**finished goods inventory**) on hand. When inventory levels dropped below certain levels, they then authorized production to replenish the inventory. To reduce delays, they also decided to maintain a **raw materials inventory,** although they wanted to keep those inventory levels as low as possible. It required some planning, but they created bills of material that identified the raw material required for each product and estimated the required inventory levels to keep production smooth and meet demand.

They summarized Sunset's conversion process as follows:

1. When the quantity on hand of a product drops below the minimum level, the item manager authorizes production to increase the quantity on hand.
2. Based on the bill of material for that item, they issue material into work-in-process.
3. Sunset partners then construct the items.
4. Upon completion, the products are placed in inventory.

LO 7-2
Develop an activity model of the conversion process using BPMN.

SUNSET GRAPHICS' ACTIVITY MODELS

Basic Conversion Activity Model

After talking with Virgil and Linda B about their conversion process, our first task was to draw a simple activity model using BPMN. As shown in Figure 7.2, the start of the process occurs when Sunset needs to replenish finished goods inventory. Then, the production authorization starts production activities, including the issue of raw material (R/M) and the use of direct labor. Work continues until the required quantity of the finished good item is prepared. At that point, production is complete, and the finished goods inventory is updated.

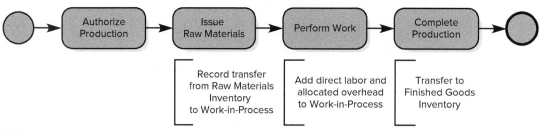

FIGURE 7.2
Basic Conversion Activity Model

LO 7-3
Understand and apply different activity modeling options.

Refining the Model

Virgil remarked that a collaboration model would not make much sense here. All the work is within Sunset. We agreed, but we said that swimlanes could show the different functions within Sunset to help clarify responsibilities. Both Virgil and Linda thought that, yes, it would clarify responsibilities. Virgil then added that sometimes they performed the work in a series of batches to make the process more manageable. Plus, they didn't necessarily issue all the raw materials at once. Sometimes, they started a batch, issued some raw materials, worked on those, and then issued more raw materials. They repeated these steps until they finished production.

We said that it would be pretty easy to add those refinements to the model, but we wondered if there was anything else to consider. Linda then added that they always inspect the work before it is added to the finished goods inventory, and if it doesn't meet quality standards, they discard the bad items and replace them. Finally, while partners place the finished items in inventory, the inventory manager updates the records.

Virgil was confident that he understood BPMN now. He suggested that the model could use multiple lanes and show the looping to reflect Sunset's conversion process. He then sketched the model shown in Figure 7.3. This model showed two lanes: (1) for the inventory manager and (2) for the Sunset employees who perform the work. This model shows the inventory manager authorizing production. Then, the conversion partners set up the batch, issue raw materials, and perform work making the finished good item. At that point, a partner inspects the work and if the work does not meet quality standards, the **intermediate error event** directs the process flow to the "discard items" activity. The sequence then loops back to issue more raw materials. If the batch is not finished, the **gateway** also directs the sequence flow back to issue more raw materials, and the steps are repeated until the batch is done. Then, a second gateway branches, depending on whether all batches are complete. If not, the sequence flow is directed back to the "set up batch" activity and the steps repeat until all batches are done. The conversion partners complete production by placing the finished items in inventory, and the inventory manager updates the inventory records.

We congratulated Virgil on his understanding of activity modeling. We said that his model would work, but we might be able to simplify it a little. We could use a looping

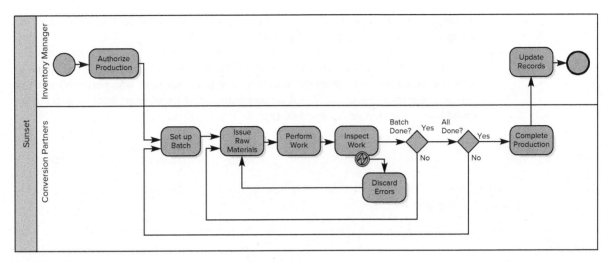

FIGURE 7.3
Conversion Process with Swimlanes and Loops

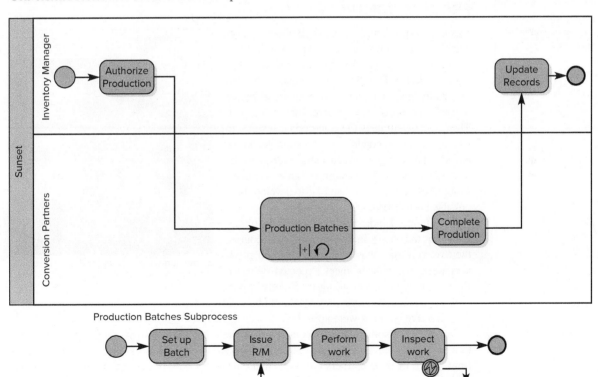

FIGURE 7.4
Conversion Process with Looping Collapsed Subprocess and Separate Production Batches Subprocess

collapsed subprocess (see Chapter 2) to represent the batch activities. The subprocess loops until all batches are done. The steps in the subprocess are then shown separately as in Figure 7.4. In this case, the original model was not that complicated, so either diagram is understandable. When certain parts of any process are complex, it can often improve understanding of the overall process if the complex parts are modeled separately. Then, one diagram shows the overall flow at a higher level, and the separate subprocess can show the more complex part of the process at a lower level of detail.

Both Virgil and Linda agreed that this model accurately describes their process. We noted that for internal control, we probably should have identified a third lane to show the separate "inspect work" function. The same partners who perform the work should not inspect the work. Virgil acknowledged that we were probably right, but we could leave that change for another day.

Progress Check

1. How would you change Figure 7.3 to show a separate organization unit performing the inspect work function?
2. Could you model the intermediate error event with a gateway instead? What would that look like?

LO 7-4

Develop business rules to implement controls for the conversion process.

BUSINESS RULES AND SUNSET GRAPHICS' CONVERSION PROCESS CONTROLS

Again, we asked Virgil and Linda B about controls over the conversion process. As with the other processes, we intended to define controls by developing business rules for the process. First, we needed to identify important business events and define Sunset's intention or objective for each event. Then, we determined the appropriate actions to take based on the conditions. For example, we've already listed important business events in the activity models, so let's examine Sunset's conversion process in Figures 7.2 and 7.3 to develop some possible business rules.

Virgil and Linda summarized their objectives for the steps in the process. Of course, their overall goal was to ensure finished products were available to meet expected demand. Because they were not going to directly supervise the process anymore, they wanted to be sure that effective controls were applied.

Inspecting work and discarding defects.
© Tetra Images/Getty Images

We outlined some standard controls over the conversion process, suggesting segregation of authorizing, issuing, and conversion work duties. We reiterated that *access controls* limit which of their partners can view and change records in the system and help implement appropriate segregation of duties. We also need *application controls* to ensure data integrity and an audit trail. For example, we need to control the assignment of production authorization and material issue numbers to make sure they are all accounted for. Plus, we need to establish appropriate ranges or limits for each value that partners can add or change in the system.

With Virgil and Linda's direction, we developed an initial set of business rules for the conversion process. They articulated their intentions for every step in the process, and then we set business rules to segregate duties and limit partner authority appropriately. Table 7.1 shows the initial set of business rules for Sunset's conversion process. We noted that we would need to set application controls for almost every attribute updated during data entry.

TABLE 7.1
Using Business
Rules to Implement
Internal Controls

Process Steps	Intention	Partner Authority/Action	Access Controls	Application Controls
Authorize Production	Partner with proper authority authorizes production to ensure finished goods are available to meet expected demand.	Supervisor must authorize production >$5,000.	Partner authorizing production cannot modify inventory records.	System must provide authorization order number control, default values, and range and limit checks; must also create audit trail.
Issue Raw Material	Issues from raw material according to bill of material recorded accurately.	Partner issuing material must not be same partner who authorized production.	Partner recording issue of material cannot modify bill of material.	System must only allow partner to enter the number of items issued based on bill of material, subject to range and limit checks on quantities; date defaults to current date.
Perform Work	Direct labor costs recorded promptly and accurately.	Partner performing direct labor must not be same partner authorizing production.	Partner recording labor costs cannot modify production authorization.	System must provide control numbers, hours, costs range, and limit checks; date defaults to current date.
Inspect Work and Discard Defects	Inspection ensures that only products meeting quality standards are allowed.	Partner inspecting work must not be a partner performing work.	Partner recording inspection cannot modify inventory records.	System must provide limit checks; date defaults to current date.
Complete Production	Finished product inventory must be updated promptly and accurately.	Partner placing products in finished inventory must not be same partner authorizing production.	Partner recording update of inventory records cannot modify production authorization.	System must default date to current date; inventory update limit is based on authorization.

LO 7-5
Develop a structure
model for the
conversion process
using UML class
diagrams.

SUNSET GRAPHICS' STRUCTURE MODELS

Now, both Virgil and Linda B looked forward to adding the conversion process features to Sunset's new database. This would mean that their database could handle their entire supply chain encompassing purchasing, making, and selling their products. We proceeded to examine Sunset Graphics' conversion information requirements. As described in Chapter 3, the primary purpose of our UML class diagram of the conversion process is to create a blueprint for the development of a relational database to support the collection, aggregation, and communication of process information. As in Chapters 5 and 6, we follow the **REA** framework (resources, events, and agents) as a proven approach to describing business processes in a way that meets both accounting and broad management information requirements.

Basic UML Class Diagram for Conversion

Based on what Virgil and Linda told us about their conversion process, we thought it was very close to a generic conversion process model shown in Figure 7.5. As indicated by numbers 1 and 2, an employee (**agent**) with supervisory responsibility authorizes

FIGURE 7.5
Generic UML Class
Diagram for the
Conversion Process

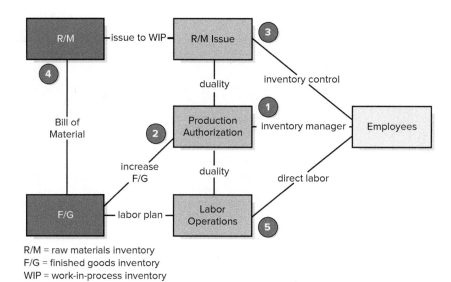

R/M = raw materials inventory
F/G = finished goods inventory
WIP = work-in-process inventory

production (**event**) of one or more finished goods items (**resources**). Next, numbers 3 and 4 denote that an employee (agent) issues (event) the raw material (resource) into **work-in-process inventory** based on the bills of material for the finished goods items. Finally, number 5 shows that production employees perform work to make sure the finished goods are items and their direct labor are recorded (**labor operations event).**

We explained that the association between finished goods and labor operations indicates the planned labor. The bill of materials association between finished goods and raw material indicates the planned material content of each finished goods item. The two duality associations link the raw material issue and labor operations events to the production authorization. Thus, the data structure captures information about both planned and actual conversion activity.

Virgil said that he understood most of the diagram, but where is the work-in-process inventory resource? We explained that we don't need to model a separate work-in-process inventory because we can calculate that value at any time. For example, the **raw material issue event** records the value of items issued into work-in-process. The labor operations event records the value of direct labor added to work-in-process. The labor plan association establishes standard overhead allocation rates. Until the job is complete, the accumulated material, labor, and overhead costs increase work-in-process inventory. When the job is complete, which would be recorded in the initial **production authorization event,** the cost of goods manufactured increase the finished goods inventory value.

Refining the UML Class Diagram for Sunset's Conversion Process

Virgil thought Sunset's bill of materials should be more than an association, although he agreed that the company's conversion process resembled the generic model. For Sunset, the bill of materials contains more than a simple link between Sunset's material (raw materials) and its final products (finished goods). He also believed that they really had no defined labor plan. Sunset just recorded direct labor incurred and used a simple overhead allocation scheme.

We replied that it was easy to modify the generic process diagram to reflect Sunset's information requirements for the conversion process. We could "promote" the bill of materials association to a **type image** class because there was more detail involved. Also, the

Updating finished goods inventory.
© Steve Cole/Getty Images

bill of materials association is typically a **many-to-many relationship** between raw materials and finished goods because each raw material item could be used for multiple finished goods items and vice versa. We would likely create a table to implement that association anyway. We could also remove the labor plan association between the finished goods resource and the labor operations event. We developed the class diagram shown in Figure 7.6 reflecting those modifications, including multiplicities, and also keeping the association between Sunset Partners and Product Categories from the sales and collection process.

Virgil and Linda both thought that the revised class diagram accurately reflected their information requirements. However, they had some hypothetical questions about modeling the conversion process to make sure they understood it perfectly. For example, they asked how we would modify the model if Sunset used equipment in the conversion process and wanted to record direct equipment costs. We replied that we would simply add an equipment resource to capture information about the equipment, and then we would add an equipment operations event to record the costs of the use of the equipment. They said that made sense; an event records costs applied to work-in-process and a resource captures permanent information about the things available for use in the process. We added that type images can specify the plan for resource use, and then the plan could be compared to the actual usage recorded in the events.

FIGURE 7.6
Revised UML Class Diagram for Sunset's Conversion Process

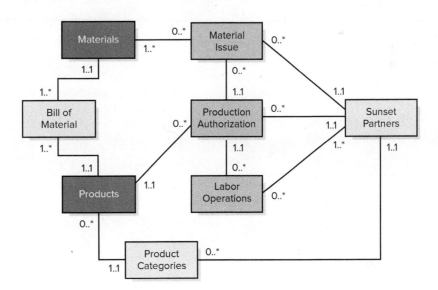

Progress Check

3. Figure 7.6 dropped the labor plan association. Could Sunset instead have "promoted" the labor plan association to a type image? How would that affect the diagram?
4. Add the equipment resource and equipment operations event to the diagram, and define the multiplicities.

LO 7-6
Implement a relational database from the UML class diagram of the conversion process.

SUNSET GRAPHICS' RELATIONAL DATABASE

Virgil and Linda B were both interested in implementing the conversion UML class diagram in a relational database for Sunset. Again, we use Microsoft Access, but the process would be similar for any database-driven system. We encourage students to use the following description to implement a relational database to support information requirements for the conversion process.

Relational Database Planning for Attributes

During the model development process, we again reviewed Sunset's existing documents to determine specific data requirements for each class/table. We then followed the guidance in Chapters 3 and 4 to determine allocation of foreign keys. This resulted in a list of tables, attributes, data types, field sizes, and primary and foreign keys as shown in Table 7.2.

Creating the Database and Defining the Tables

The next step is to create a new, blank Microsoft Access database and create the tables described in Table 7.2. Then, establish relationships between the tables as shown in Figure 7.7 following the process outlined in Chapter 5. At that point, Sunset's conversion process database is set up.

PK/FK	Attribute Name	Type	Size
	Table: tblBill_of_Material		
PK	BOM_number	Text	10
	Issue_sequence	Integer	8
	Standard_quantity	Double	8
FK	Product_number	Text	10
FK	Material_number	Text	255
	Special_handling	Memo	—
	Table: tblLabor_Operations		
PK	Labor_ops_Number	Text	10
FK	Prod_auth_number	Text	10
	Labor_ops_description	Memo	—
	Table: tblLabor_Operations_Partners		
PK	Labor_ops_number	Text	10
PK	Partner_number	Text	10
	Actual_direct_labor_hours	Long Integer	4
	Actual_direct_labor_wage	Currency	8
	Table: tblMaterial_Issue		
PK	Material_Issue_number	Text	10
	Issue_date	Date/Time	8
FK	Issued_by	Text	10
FK	Prod_auth_number	Text	255

PK/FK	Attribute Name	Type	Size
	Table: tblMaterial_Issue_Materials		
PK	Material_issue_number	Text	10
PK	Material_number	Text	10
	Qty_issued	Long Integer	4
	Table: tblMaterials		
PK	Material_number	Text	10
	Material_description	Text	255
	Material_price	Currency	8
	Material_quantity_on_hand	Integer	2
	Material_notes	Memo	—
	Table: tblPartners		
PK	Partner_number	Text	10
	Partner_first_name	Text	15
	Partner_last_name	Text	15
	Partner_hire_date	Date/Time	8
	Partner_SocSecNo	Text	11
	Partner_Address	Text	50
	Partner_Address2	Text	50
	Partner_City	Text	20
	Partner_State	Text	2
	Partner_Zip	Text	10

TABLE 7.2
Sunset Database Tables and Attribute Definitions for the Conversion Process

PK/FK	Attribute Name	Type	Size
	Partner_phone	Text	14
	Partner_cellphone	Text	14
	Table: tblProduct_Category		
PK	Product_category_number	Text	10
	Product_category_description	Text	255
FK	Product_category_manager	Text	10
	Product_category_notes	Memo	—
	Table: tblProduction_ Authorizations		
PK	Prod_auth_number	Text	255
	Prod_auth_date	Date/Time	8
FK	Partner_number	Text	10
FK	Product_Number	Text	10
	Scheduled_qty_to_produce	Long Integer	4
	Actual_qty_produced	Long Integer	4
	Scheduled_completion_date	Date/Time	8

PK/FK	Attribute Name	Type	Size
	Actual_completion_date	Date/Time	8
	Overhead_rate	Single	4
	Total_material_cost	Currency	8
	Total_direct_labor	Currency	8
	Total_overhead	Currency	8
	Total_COGM*	Currency	8
	Table: tblProducts		
PK	Product_number	Text	10
	Product_description	Text	255
	Product_price	Currency	8
	Product_unit_of_sale	Text	10
FK	Product_category_number	Text	10
	Product_quantity_on_hand	Integer	2
	Product_notes	Memo	—

*Cost of goods manufactured.

TABLE 7.2 *(continued)*

FIGURE 7.7
Linked Conversion Process Tables with Referential Integrity Enforced

© Microsoft Access

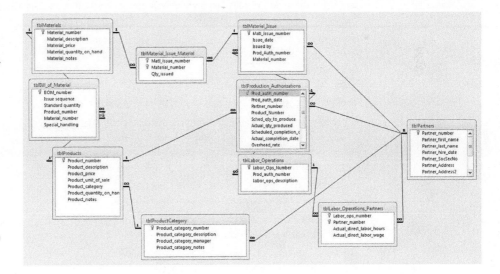

Summary

- From an accounting standpoint, we must account for transfers of raw materials into work-in-process, direct labor, allocated overhead, and the cost of goods manufactured in the conversion process.
- Sunset Graphics provides an ongoing example of how to model the conversion process.

- Activity models can show the basic steps in the process and the collaborations between the company and its customers, as well as exceptions to the process.
- Business rules implement internal control activities.
- There is a standard structure model pattern that allows for collection of accounting information for the conversion process—including issues of raw material into work-in-process and recording direct labor and allocated overhead—such that cost of goods manufactured includes material, labor, and overhead costs.
- The standard pattern is tailored to a specific organization by adding type images to collect management information.
- The structure model provides a blueprint for a relational database that will collect, store, and report sales and collection information.

Key Words

agents (*183*)   The people or organizations who participate in business events, such as customers and salespeople.

events (*184*)   Classes that model the organization's transactions, usually affecting the organization's resources, such as sales and cash receipts; Important occurrences that affect the flow of activities in a business process. BPMN includes symbols to define start, intermediate, and end events.

finished goods inventory (*179*)   For a manufacturing company, the inventory (REA resource) that has completed the manufacturing process and is held for sale to customers.

gateway (*180*)   Shows process branching and merging as the result of decisions. Basic gateways are depicted as diamonds. Usually, gateways appear as pairs on the diagram. The first gateway shows the branching, and the second gateway shows merging of the process branches.

intermediate error event (*180*)   Occurs between start and end events and affects the flow of the process. Intermediate error events represent interruptions to the normal flow of the process and start the exception flow.

labor operations event (*184*)   In the conversion process, an event that represents the recording of labor (and any associated overhead) costs applied to work-in-process.

many-to-many relationship (*185*)   Exists when instances of one class (e.g., sales) are related to many instances of another class (e.g., inventory) and vice versa. These relationships are implemented in Access and relational databases by adding a linking table to convert the many-to-many relationship into two one-to-many relationships.

production authorization event (*184*)   In a UML class model of the conversion process, an event that records the authorization to produce one or more finished good inventory items.

raw material issue event (*184*)   In a UML class diagram of the conversion process, an event that records the transfer of raw materials into work-in-process.

raw materials inventory (*179*)   For a manufacturing company, the inventory (REA resource) acquired for use (conversion) in the manufacturing process.

REA (*183*)   Resource-event-agent framework for modeling business processes, originally developed by William McCarthy.

resources (*184*)   Those things that have economic value to a firm, such as cash and products.

type image (*184*)   Class that represents management information (such as categorizations, policies, and guidelines) to help manage a business process. Type image often allows process information to be summarized by category.

work-in-process inventory (*184*)   For a manufacturing company, the value of raw materials, direct labor, and manufacturing overhead in production but not yet finished.

Answers to Progress Check

1. You could modify Figure 7.3 by creating an additional swimlane within the Sunset pool for the inspection organizational unit.

2. You could modify Figure 7.3 by adding an additional gateway following the Inspect Work activity with two branches: (a) linking to the Discard Items activity and (b) linking to the Batch Done gateway.

3. An association can be promoted to a type image if it needs to contain more information or link to other classes. Apparently, Sunset's labor operations do not vary according to the specific product. If they did, it could promote the labor plan association shown in Figure 7.6 to a labor plan class as in Figure 7.7. That type image class would link to the products class and the labor operations class.

4. An equipment class would be an additional resource. It would be linked to the products class if the equipment varied according to the specific product. The equipment operations class, like the labor operations class, would record the use of the equipment to add that cost to the costs of production.

Mc Graw Hill Education connect

Multiple Choice Questions

1. Which of the following is an activity in the conversion process? **LO 7-1**
   a. Authorize production
   b. Issue raw material
   c. Perform work
   d. Transfer completed work to finished goods
   d. All of the above are activities in the conversion process.

2. Which of the following activities results in work-in-process moving to finished goods inventory? **LO 7-1**
   a. Authorize production
   b. Inspect work
   c. Complete production
   d. Issue raw material
   e. None of the above

3. Which of the following describes the purpose of a lane within a pool in BPMN? **LO 7-2, LO 7-3**
   a. Indicates the start of the process
   b. Indicates the end of the process
   c. Identifies different activity flow options
   d. Distinguishes specific responsibilities for performing different tasks
   e. None of the above

4. Which of the following is not a purpose of using lanes to describe the conversion process? **LO 7-2, LO 7-3**
   a. Document the sequence of activities in the process
   b. Expose potential problems in the handoff between organizational units
   c. Show important decision points, and identify responsibility for those decisions
   d. Establish internal control activities, such as segregation of duties
   e. All of the above

5. Which of the following is a business rule implementing access control for the conversion process? **LO 7-4**
   a. Employee authorizing production cannot modify inventory records.
   b. System must provide control numbers.
   c. Employees preparing quotes cannot modify established prices.
   d. System must create audit trail whenever records are changed.
   e. None of the above

6. Consider a UML class diagram of the conversion process that uses the REA framework. Which of the following events begins a typical conversion process? **LO 7-5**
   a. Assign employees to departments
   b. Authorize production
   c. Issue raw material into work-in-process
   d. Sell finished goods
   e. None of the above

7. Review Figure 7.6. Which of the following describes the purpose of the Labor Operations event? **LO 7-5**
   a. Add the cost of direct labor to work-in-process inventory
   b. Control the specific labor activities
   c. Ensure that labor is performed
   d. Identify production employees
   e. None of the above

8. Review Figure 7.7. Which of the following is a correct posting of a foreign key to implement the model in a relational database? **LO 7-5**
   a. Labor Operations primary key becomes a foreign key in Production Authorization.
   b. Products primary key becomes a foreign key in Bill of Material.
   c. Product Categories primary key becomes a foreign key in Sunset Partners.
   d. Products primary key becomes a foreign key in Product Categories.
   e. All of the above are correct.

9. Review Figure 7.7. Which of the following describes the purpose of the Bill of Material class? **LO 7-1, LO 7-5**
   a. Record the invoices from suppliers for materials purchased
   b. Record the planned raw material contents of each finished good
   c. Record the authorization of production
   d. Describe the labor required for each finished good
   e. None of the above.

10. Compare Figure 7.6 with Figure 7.7. Which of the following describes the differences between those two figures? **LO 7-5**
    a. Figure 7.7 includes *tblLabor_Operations_Partners* to implement the many-to-many relationship between *tblPartners* and *tblLabor_Operations*.
    b. Figure 7.7 includes *tblMaterial_Issue_Material* to implement the many-to-many relationship between *tblMaterial_Issue* and *tblMaterials*.

c. Figure 7.6 includes the minimum multiplicities to specify data integrity requirements.

d. Figure 7.7 only shows maximum cardinalities between linked tables.

e. All of the above are differences between the two figures.

Refer to the following integrated diagram, showing part of the purchases and sales processes linked to the conversion process, for Questions 11 through 25.

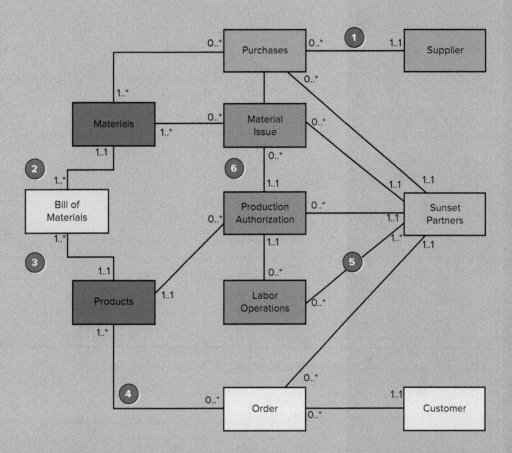

11. Refer to the association marked with the number 1 in the preceding diagram. Which of the following is the best description of the association? **LO 7-5**

    a. Each supplier participates in a minimum of zero purchases.

    b. Each supplier participates in at least one purchase.

    c. Each supplier participates in a maximum of one purchase.

    d. Supplier is the internal agent in the purchase process.

    e. None of these is a description of the association.

12. Refer to the association marked with the number 1 in the preceding diagram. Which of the following is the best description of the association? **LO 7-5**

    a. Each purchase involves one supplier.

    b. Each purchase involves multiple suppliers.

    c. Each purchase involves a minimum of zero suppliers.

    d. Some purchases are made after a production authorization.

    e. None of these is a description of the association.

13. Refer to the association marked with the number 2 in the preceding diagram. Which of the following is the best description of the purpose of the association? LO 7-5

    a. The association links finished goods to the corresponding bill of materials.

    b. The association links purchases to raw materials.

    c. The association identifies the raw materials in a bill of materials.

    d. All of these descriptions are purposes of the association.

    e. None of these are a description of the purpose of the association.

14. Refer to the association marked with the number 2 in the preceding diagram. Which of the following is the best description of the association? LO 7-5

    a. Each bill of materials entry specifies one raw material.

    b. Each bill of materials entry specifies multiple raw materials.

    c. Each bill of materials is related to a minimum of zero raw materials.

    d. Each bill of materials is related to a maximum of many raw materials.

    e. None of these is a description of the association.

15. Refer to the association marked with the number 2 in the preceding diagram. Which of the following is the best description of the association? LO 7-5

    a. Each raw material is related to a minimum of zero bills of materials.

    b. Each raw material is related to a maximum of one bill of materials.

    c. A raw material item could be related to multiple bills of materials.

    d. A raw material item could be related to no bill of materials.

    e. None of these is a description of the association.

16. Refer to the association marked with the number 2 in the preceding diagram. Which of the following is the best way to implement the association in a relational database? LO 7-5

    a. Post the primary key of bill of materials as a foreign key in raw materials.

    b. Post the primary key of raw materials as a foreign key in bill of materials.

    c. Create a linking table between raw materials and bill of materials.

    d. The location of the foreign key is optional.

    e. None of these is the best way to implement the relationship.

17. Refer to the association marked with the number 3 in the preceding diagram. Which of the following is the best description of the purpose the association? LO 7-5

    a. Links actual material costs to each finished goods item produced.

    b. Links actual labor costs to each finished goods item produced.

    c. Specifies planned material costs for each finished goods item.

    d. Specifies planned labor costs for each finished goods item.

    e. None of these is a description of the purpose of the association.

18. Refer to the association marked with the number 3 in the preceding diagram. Which of the following is the best description of the association? LO 7-5

    a. Each bill of materials is related to a minimum of zero finished goods.

    b. Each bill of materials is related to a minimum of one finished good.

    c. Each bill of materials is related to a maximum of many finished goods.

    d. Each bill of materials is not necessarily related to a finished good.

    e. None of these is a description of the association.

19. Refer to the association marked with the number 3 in the preceding diagram. Which of the following is the best way to implement the association in a relational database? LO 7-5

    a. Post the primary key of bill of materials as a foreign key in finished goods.

    b. Post the primary key of finished goods as a foreign key in bill of materials.

   c. Create a linking table between finished goods and bill of materials.

   d. The location of the foreign key is optional.

   e. None of these is the best way to implement the relationship.

20. Refer to the association marked with the number 4 in the preceding diagram. Which of the following is the best description of the purpose of the association? **LO 7-5**

   a. Shows that the conversion and sales process are integrated via finished goods.

   b. Shows that the conversion process is triggered by an order for a finished good.

   c. Links finished goods produced by the conversion process to orders (by customers).

   d. Links finished goods to subsequent cash receipts in the sales process.

   e. None of these is a description of the purpose of the association.

21. Refer to the association marked with the number 4 in the preceding diagram. Which of the following is the best description of the association? **LO 7-5**

   a. Each finished good is related to one order.

   b. Each finished good is related to many orders.

   c. Each finished good is related to a minimum of one order.

   d. Each finished good is related to a maximum of one order.

   e. None of these is a description of the association.

22. Refer to the association marked with the number 5 in the preceding diagram. Which of the following is the best way to implement the association in a relational database? **LO 7-5**

   a. Post the primary key of Sunset partners as a foreign key in labor operations.

   b. Post the primary key of labor operations as a foreign key in Sunset partners.

   c. Create a linking table between Sunset partners and labor operations.

   d. The location of the foreign key is optional.

   e. None of these is the best way to implement the relationship.

23. Refer to the association marked with the number 5 in the preceding diagram. Which of the following is the best description of the association? **LO 7-5**

   a. Each labor operation is related to one Sunset partner.

   b. Each labor operation is related to many Sunset partners.

   c. Labor operations are related to a minimum of zero Sunset partners.

   d. Labor operations are related to a maximum of one Sunset partner.

   e. None of these is a description of the association.

24. Refer to the association marked with the number 6 in the preceding diagram. Which of the following is the best description of the purpose of the association? **LO 7-5**

   a. Authorizes the issue of raw materials.

   b. Controls the transfer of raw materials to work-in-process.

   c. Relates specific raw material issues to the controlling authorization.

   d. All of these describe the purpose of the association.

   e. None of these describes the purpose of the association.

25. Refer to the association marked with the number 6 in the preceding diagram. Which of the following is the best description of the association? **LO 7-5**

   a. Each production authorization is related to a minimum of zero material issues.

   b. Each production authorization is related to a minimum of one material issue.

   c. Each production authorization is related to a maximum of one material issue.

   d. Each production authorization is related to a maximum of zero material issues.

   e. None of these is a description of the association.

Discussion Questions

1. Think about the roles of accountants presented in Table 2.1 from Chapter 2. Why should accountants be involved in developing and reviewing the bills of materials? **LO 7-1**

2. Describe some businesses that use conversion processes. Do they all use the same sequence of activities? Do they all share the same information structure? Discuss some of the differences in those conversion processes. **LO 7-1**

3. Think about the UML class diagrams for the sales and collection process described in Chapter 5 and the purchases and payments process described in Chapter 6. If you were asked to prepare an integrated model that shows those two processes as well as the conversion process, where would the models intersect/integrate? Why? What elements are unique to each process? **LO 7-5**

4. In Figure 7.6, the Labor Operations event tracks direct labor incurred in the conversion process. What event tracks indirect labor? **LO 7-1, LO 7-5**

5. Describe how you would change Figure 7.6 to implement an activity-based costing system with three different cost drivers. **LO 7-1, LO 7-5**

6. Put Figure 7.6 in the context of the overall supply chain that starts with the purchases and payments process (Chapter 6) and ends with the sales and cash receipts process (Chapter 5). How would you expand Figure 7.6 to describe Sunset's entire supply chain? **LO 7-1, LO 7-5**

7. Business rules implement internal controls. Review Table 7.1 and classify each of those business rules listed as access controls as obligatory, prohibited, or allowed, as described in Chapter 2. Select two of those business rules and rephrase them, so an obligatory rule is now a prohibited rule, a prohibited rule is now an allowed rule, and so on. **LO 7-4**

8. Compare the generic UML class diagram for the conversion process shown in Figure 7.5 with a generic sales and collection diagram, similar to Figure 5.9. Identify the similarities and differences and then explain why they exist. **LO 7-5**

Problems

connect

1. The Rubber Duck Brewing Company is a new microbrewery. Rubber Duck's brewing process converts beer raw ingredients—malt extract, malted grain, adjuncts (rice or corn), hops, yeast, and water—into brewed beer. Over time, Rubber Duck has developed a unique recipe for each of its brewed beers. The recipe describes the specific ingredients, the sequence of brewing steps, the specific equipment, and the type of employees required for each step in the brewing process for each beer. Each step in the recipe may involve multiple ingredients (e.g., barley, hops, malts, and yeast) and multiple pieces of equipment, but it only requires one type of employee.

   Rubber Duck assigns a unique ingredient number to each ingredient so it can track the quantity on hand. It tracks its brewed beer by the beer name: pale ale, amber ale, porter, stout, lager, pilsner, and so forth. When Rubber Duck decides to brew one of its beers, a supervisor issues a "Brew Order" for that beer, specifying the quantity in gallons to be brewed. Then, the brewing process begins. Several Rubber Duck employees perform each brewing step. Rubber Duck tracks the amount of each raw ingredient actually used in each step as well the time spent by each employee on each step.

   Rubber Duck tracks its brewing equipment (e.g., mash tuns, whirlpools, fermenters, and conditioning tanks) by equipment item number, and it also tracks which equipment is used and how long it is used in each brewing step. Each brewing step often requires more than one piece of equipment, and some pieces of equipment are used on multiple brewing steps, although many are used in only one step. For safety, Rubber Duck only allows employees to operate equipment that they are qualified to use.

   When the brewing process is complete, the brewed beer is stored in large copper tanks for aging. Ales require relatively little aging (less than 3 weeks), while lagers may require longer aging (up to 5 weeks). The copper tanks are tracked separately from other brewing equipment. Aging of the beer is not part of the brewing process; it takes place after the brewing process.

    a. Prepare a UML class diagram that captures Rubber Duck's brewing process.

    b. Using the preceding information and the following attributes list, prepare a listing of the relational tables, indicating the primary key (PK) and foreign keys (FK) for each table. LO 7-5

    c. (Optional) Use the UML class diagram and the listing of relational tables to prepare a relational database in Access. LO 7-6

Attributes:

Actual aging time to date for the brewed beer in this copper tank

Actual quantity of this ingredient used in this brew step

Actual time for this equipment used in this brew step

Brew order date

Brew order number (brew#)

Brew quantity in gallons

Brew step description

Brew step number (brew step#)

Brewed beer description

Brewed beer name

Brewed beer quantity on hand (QOH)

Brewing recipe step description

Brewing recipe step number (recipe step#)

Copper tank capacity in gallons

Copper tank number (tank#)

Date this employee qualified to operate this equipment

Employee name

Employee number (emp#)

Employee type

Employee type description

Equipment item description

Equipment item number (equip#)

Ingredient description

Ingredient number (ingred#)

Ingredient quantity-on-hand (QOH)

Number of employees of this type

Planned aging time for this brewed beer

Planned time for this equipment in this step

Quantity of beer in this tank (in gallons)

Standard quantity of this ingredient used in this recipe step

Time spent by this employee on this brew step

connect 2. Penny loves pastries. She wanted everyone else to love pastries, too, so she started Penny's Pastries in Orange County about 3 years ago. After a shaky start, she scored a big contract with **Starbucks** to provide pastries to all stores in southern California. This case describes Penny's daily baking process. Penny's bakery starts preparing fresh pastries every morning about 1:00 a.m. for delivery to local stores by 5:30 a.m. The selection and quantity of pastries vary according to the day of the week as well as the time of the year. LO 7-2, LO 7-3, LO 7-5

Inventories

Although Penny has a number of her own specialties, she makes many of her baked products according to Starbucks' requirements. So, every day she makes some of her own pastries for sale in her bakeries as well as all the pastries for the various Starbucks locations. Currently, her finished goods inventory can include more than 50 different kinds of pastries and baked products. Because of the volume that Penny produces, she maintains an extensive inventory of the ingredients that she uses in her baked goods, such as flour, butter, milk, chocolate, and cinnamon.

Baking Plans

Penny carefully plans the contents and preparation of each finished product (pastry and baked good). There are two parts to her formal plans—an ingredient list and a recipe—for each baked product. The ingredient list specifies the quantity of each ingredient required for each finished product. The recipe defines the sequence of steps that her bakers follow to prepare each finished product. The recipe steps also set the standard number of labor-hours, as well as the specific equipment used, to prepare a standard batch of each finished product.

Daily Baking Process

Early each morning, the supervisor prepares a daily baking order that specifies the quantities of all the different finished products to be prepared that day. As soon as the various products and quantities are known, an inventory clerk uses the ingredient list to issue all the ingredients necessary for the day, moving them from the storeroom to the baking area. In some cases, the clerk may issue ingredients several different times for each daily baking order so that none of the refrigerated items are left out longer than necessary. Penny assigns sequential issue numbers to each issue during the day, and the clerk carefully records the quantity of each ingredient issued.

Penny's bakers prepare the finished products in batches. Each batch produces one finished baked good product. A supervisor (who could be different from the supervisor who issued the baking order) issues a batch order to start the baking process for that batch. The bakers then prepare the ingredients in a series of baking steps according to the recipe for that product using the equipment and ovens specified in the recipe. Penny's bakery has an array of ovens and baking equipment, tracked by equipment number, to keep up with the daily baking production volumes. Because each oven has different characteristics, the baking time for each product can depend on the particular oven used. The baking steps usually involve mixing ingredients, preparing the pastries, placing the prepared items in an oven for baking, and then removing the products and placing them on cooling racks, ready for packing. Each actual baking step may involve the use of multiple pieces of baking equipment and multiple bakers. Penny carefully tracks actual hours of labor and equipment use for each baking step.

General Information

Penny does not separately identify employees as supervisors, inventory clerks, or bakers. There is one employee entity. Information on ingredient lists, recipes, finished products, ingredients, and employees is put into the database before those entities are linked to events or type images.

a. Draw a BPMN activity diagram that describes Penny's baking process.

b. Prepare a UML class diagram with classes, associations, and multiplicities.

c. Using the preceding case information and the following attributes list, prepare a listing of the relational tables necessary to support this conversion process. List the tables in the following order: resources, events, agents, type images, and linking tables.

Attributes:

Actual baking time for this baking step and this oven

Baking order#

Baking order date

Baking step#

Batch#

Batch finish time

Batch start time

Employee#

Employee hours worked on this baking step

Employee name

Employee pay rate

Equipment#

Equipment description

Equipment manufacturer

Finished product#

Finished product description

Finished product number of calories

Finished product price

Finished product QOH

Ingredient#

Ingredient cost

Ingredient description

Ingredient list#

Ingredient list description

Ingredient QOH

Ingredient unit of issue

Issue#

Issue date/time

Qty of this baked product ordered by this daily baking order

Qty of this baked product prepared in this batch

Qty of this ingredient issued on this issue#

Qty of this ingredient required for this finished product

Recipe step#

Recipe step description

Standard baking time for this recipe step with this oven

Standard labor hours for this recipe step

Total labor hours for this baking step

Additional problems are available in connect only.

Chapter **Eight**

Integrated Project

A look at this chapter

This chapter builds on the business process modeling and database design material in earlier chapters. It describes how to approach a business analysis and integrated systems development project involving multiple business processes. The project itself, designed as a group assignment, is available separately. To complete the project successfully, each group must plan and execute a realistic systems design and development project. The finished product will include activity and structure models of a company's business processes, which can support enhanced internal controls, more effective use of an AIS and related information technology to improve the company's performance, and the development relational database system and appropriate queries necessary to prepare financial and managerial accounting reports.

A look back

Chapter 7 completed the comprehensive example describing Sunset Graphics' business processes. It presented basic activity and structure models for the company's conversion process, as well as a description of the database to support that process.

A look ahead

Chapter 9 introduces business intelligence, data analytics, and data visualization concepts and tools.

Howard Schultz, Founder, President, and Chief Executive Officer of Starbucks.
© Kevin P. Casey/Bloomberg via Getty Images

After Starbucks implemented the Oracle E-business Suite, it had the IT backbone necessary to leverage a variety of other applications to support its business processes. As part of the Oracle implementation, Accenture worked with Starbucks to standardize business processes around the world. The Oracle ERP system resides on top of Oracle's database system, and that allows reuse and redistribution of the information collected. Starbucks' enterprise data warehouse (EDW) leverages that data to support Starbucks' internal business users.

By 2008, thousands of stores could directly access the EDW through web-based dashboards. Using a business intelligence reporting tool from MicroStrategy Inc., individual users could develop customized operational performance reports. MicroStrategy's reports can even be delivered by e-mail on preset schedules.

Although Starbucks closed a number of retail stores in response to the economic downturn, its overall revenues increased from 2008 to 2010. More importantly, its revenue per store is back above $1 million in the United States. Its operating income has almost doubled since 2008, and its operating margin increased from 8.1% to 13.8% in 2010. Clearly, Starbucks has been successful at reducing costs and increasing margins. Without standardized processes and integrated systems providing reliable and timely information for decisions, it is unlikely that it could have achieved this success.

Chapter Outline

Project Planning
Define Business Requirements
Prepare Activity Diagrams Using BPMN
Prepare Structure Diagram
Import Data into Access, Create Efficient Tables, and Set Relationships
Prepare Queries

Learning Objectives

After completing the project outlined in this chapter, you should be able to:

8-1   Plan and manage a business analysis project

8-2   Develop activity models of multiple business processes, and use those models to assess potential risks and opportunities for process improvements

8-3   Develop an integrated UML class diagram for a business

8-4   Use the UML class diagram to design and implement a relational database system in Microsoft Access™

8-5   Employ the relational database to answer a variety of business performance questions

LO 8-1

Plan and manage a business analysis project

PROJECT PLANNING

Figure 8.1 describes a suggested sequence of activities to complete an integrated business analysis project. Such projects represent "ill-structured" problems that require careful planning and attention to detail. Thus, the first step is to prepare a project plan in as much detail as possible. Develop a problem statement and the timeline to accomplish the project on time. Identify the major steps you will undertake to complete the project, when they need to be completed, and who will perform them. There are additional project planning tools, such as Gantt charts, that can help define the elements of the plan. Refer to Chapter 16 of this text for a description of project planning/management elements. Regardless of the planning tool used, the plan should identify the specific tasks necessary to complete the project, when each task must be completed, and who will complete each task. The project plan then serves as the management tool to keep progress on track to successful and on-time completion.

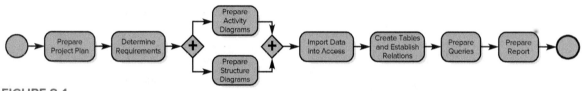

FIGURE 8.1
Suggested Project Steps

Define Business Requirements

Step 2 is to define the business requirements. The requirements discovery process involves fact-finding to determine who, what, when, where, why, and how business activities are performed. The process typically requires review of business documents as well as interviews with managers and employees. As the project team gathers requirements, they set the context of the project as shown in Figure 8.2. The focal organization is placed at the center of the diagram as an opaque pool. The external organizations that interact with "Your Company" are also shown as opaque pools. The goal is to identify all the message flows between the focal organization and the external organizations. The processes and systems within the focal organization must be able to respond to incoming message flows and efficiently deliver controlled outgoing message flows.

After establishing the context, the project team defines the activities, actors, data objects and artifacts (such as forms and documents), events, systems, and goals for the focal organization. For each activity, specify the goals of the activity and the inputs and outputs and define the actors that perform the activity, the documents created and used in the activity, and the events that affect the flow of activities. These elements will support the preparation of both your activity and structure diagrams.

LO 8-2

Develop activity models of multiple business processes, and use those models to assess potential risks and opportunities for process improvements

Prepare Activity Models Using BPMN

After gaining an understanding of the organization's business processes, document each current process with a business process activity diagram using business process modeling notation (BPMN). This is often an iterative process. First, prepare simple diagrams that show the basic steps performed in each process identified from your context diagram. Figure 8.3 shows a basic example of the sales process.

After you establish that your basic diagram is correct, then define who performs each activity and the artifacts that are created, updated, or used in the process. For example,

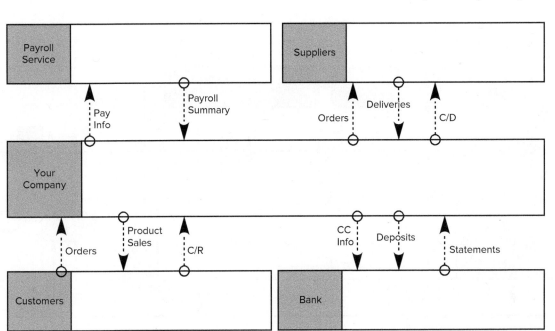

FIGURE 8.2
Project Context Diagram
C/D = cash disbursement; C/R = cash receipt; CC = credit card.

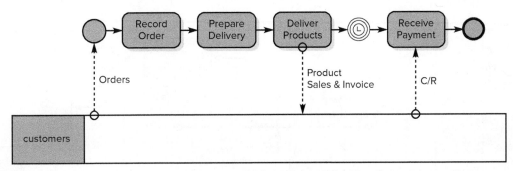

FIGURE 8.3
Basic Sales Process

Figure 8.4 expands the sales process to show that the shipping and receiving department receives the order, prepares the delivery, and delivers the products to the customer. The accounting department then receives the payment at the end of the month. Figure 8.4 also shows that the *Record Order* activity creates the Order form, which is used in the *Prepare Delivery* activity. The *Prepare Delivery* activity creates the Invoice (Inv), which is used in the *Receive Payment* process to confirm that the cash receipt matches the amount that the customer was billed.

Figure 8.4 shows the steps in the process if everything works as designed. However, it does not allow for errors or exceptions. So, the next step in the process is to include events and activities that allow for those exceptions, as shown in Figure 8.5. Figure 8.5 adds an intermediate error event to the *Prepare Delivery* activity to model circumstances where products are not available. When the error event is triggered, the process flow changes to include the *Cancel Order* activity, which then updates the Order form to record the

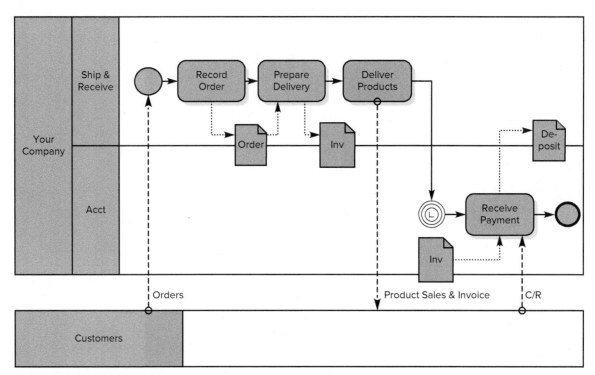

FIGURE 8.4
Expanded Sales Process

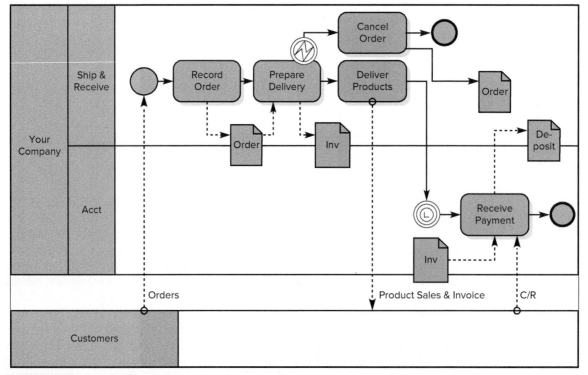

FIGURE 8.5
Expanded Sales Process with Exceptions

cancellation. Note that the Cancel Order process could also include notifying the Customer of the cancellation, although that is not modeled in this example. The project team should document the business rules that guide decisions within each activity.

Once the project team confirms the accuracy of the models, the next step is to examine the models for potential changes to increase control or improve efficiency. At this point, the team should consider material in Chapters 11 and 12 of this text to ensure effective internal controls. To improve efficiency, each activity should be examined to determine whether it adds value to the process. Value-added activities are those that are essential for production regardless of the technology used. Activities that only add cost and not value should be eliminated where possible. Cost-added activities include those that involve non-essential movements, waiting, approvals, corrections, or revisions.

Prepare Structure Diagram

LO 8-3
Develop an integrated UML class diagram for a business

Using the information gained from discovering the business requirements, the project team then prepares an integrated UML class diagram that shows the data requirements for the organization. The class diagram should articulate with the BPMN activity diagrams. The class diagram must capture information about each data object in the activity diagrams. Material in Chapters 5, 6, and 7 of this text provides standard patterns that can be the basis for the integrated diagram. Figure 8.6 shows a sample integrated UML class diagram using the REA framework. It includes four separate processes: sales, purchases of inventory, purchases of administrative expense items, and payroll. Clearly, the number of classes and associations would be very difficult to implement directly in Access without the diagram to guide the construction of the database. The diagram also helps plan the queries that will be used to prepare the financial statements. The events—sales, purchases of inventory, purchases admin, and timecards—will affect the income statement. The duality relationships between events, such as between purchases of inventory and C/D, can be used to determine items, such as payables and receivables, on the balance sheet. The inventory and cash resources will result in assets on the balance sheet. The cash disbursement (C/D) and cash receipt (C/R) events represent transactions affecting the statement of cash flows.

Import Data into Access, Create Efficient Tables, and Set Relationships

LO 8-4
Use the UML class diagram to design and implement a relational database system in Microsoft Access™

At this point, the project team is ready to create the Access database or more generally the AIS. For the purpose of the integrated project, your instructor will provide data in an Excel spreadsheet. In other projects, you might have to move data from existing systems into a new AIS. In either case, the UML class diagram will be the blueprint that you will follow. It is likely that the data will include redundancies and occasional typographical errors. You will need to correct those. After importing the data, you will need to set appropriate primary keys, check data types, and modify tables as necessary to be sure that they are efficient. Then, create the relationships among tables, enforcing referential integrity. Failing to enforce referential integrity will affect the reliability of your queries.

One common issue is dealing with information that must be split into multiple tables. For example, sales information may contain data about sales events mixed with data about the items sold on each sale. Such data would need to be split into the sales table and a sales items linking table. For example, Figure 8.7 shows sales data in a flat file before importing into Access. Although it appears that order# should be the primary key, the highlighted section shows redundant data for order #O9007. So, this table should be split so that order# is unique and the information about the inventory sold for each order is in a separate table. The table can be split in Excel or in Access. First, however, you have to determine which fields go in which table. Note that *order_date*, *customer#*, *order_emp#*, *sale_date*, and *cash_receipt#* are the same regardless of how many inventory items are included. Those

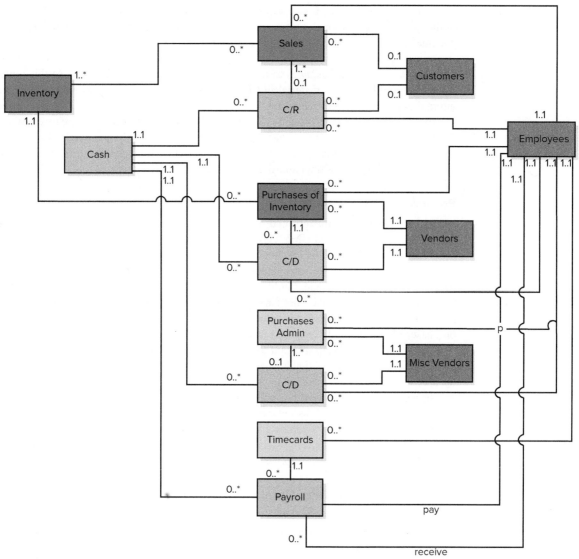

FIGURE 8.6

Sample Integrated UML Class Diagram

C/R = cash receipts; C/D = cash disbursements.

fields will go with the sales table. On the other hand, *qty_ordered*, *qty_sold*, and *sale_price* depend on both the order and the inventory item. Those fields will go in the sales items table. The primary key of the sales items table will be *order#* plus *inventory#*.

To set up the tables in Excel, select the first six columns and copy them to a new worksheet. Rename that worksheet as SALES. Then select order#, inventory#, qty_ordered, qty_sold, and sale_price to copy to a different worksheet, and rename that worksheet as SALES ITEMS. Next, to remove the duplicates in the SALES worksheet, select all six columns. Click on the DATA tab and select the Remove Duplicates icon on the ribbon bar. The Remove Duplicates box appears as shown in Figure 8.8. With all the boxes next to the column headings checked, click on the OK button. This will remove the duplicates and the data in the SALES table will look like Figure 8.9.

order#	order_date	customer#	order_emp#	sale_date	cash_receipt#	inventory#	qty_ordered	qty_sold	sale_price
O90001	12/29/2017	Atla_013	E2154	1/1/2018	CR_91117	P17008	50	52	$13.56
O90002	12/30/2017	Atla_015	E9481	1/4/2018	CR_91122	P17006	90	88	$14.44
O90003	12/31/2017	Atla_011	E8519	1/7/2018	CR_91080	P17001	90	84	$10.78
O90004	1/1/2018	Atla_010	E8519	1/8/2018	CR_91110	P17005	50	47	$13.89
O90005	1/2/2018	Atla_003	E3477	1/4/2018	CR_91091	P17013	30	27	$15.00
O90006	1/3/2018	Atla_001	E2154	1/4/2018	CR_91001	P17013	20	18	$15.00
O90007	1/4/2018	Atla_010	E9481	1/8/2018	CR_91110	P17010	100	93	$ 7.67
O90007	1/4/2018	Atla_010	E9481	1/8/2018	CR_91110	P17013	30	27	$15.00
O90007	1/4/2018	Atla_010	E9481	1/8/2018	CR_91110	P17015	80	75	$16.67
O90008	1/5/2018	Atla_008	E2154	1/10/2018	CR_91121	P17007	40	39	$10.89
O90009	1/5/2018	Atla_001	E9481	1/8/2018	CR_91001	P17007	130	129	$10.89
O90010	1/6/2018	Atla_010	E2154	1/15/2018	CR_91110	P17002	130	120	$11.11

FIGURE 8.7
Sample Mixed Sales Data

FIGURE 8.8
Removing Duplicates
in the SALES Table

© Microsoft Excel

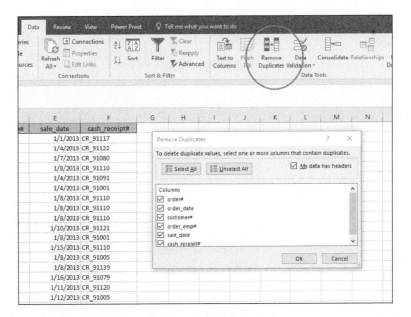

FIGURE 8.9
SALES Table with
Duplicates Removed

© Microsoft Excel

order#	order_date	customer#	order_emp#	sale_date	cash_receipt#
O90001	12/29/2017	Atla_013	E2154	1/1/2018	CR_91117
O90002	12/30/2017	Atla_015	E9481	1/4/2018	CR_91122
O90003	12/31/2017	Atla_011	E8519	1/7/2018	CR_91080
O90004	1/1/2018	Atla_010	E8519	1/8/2018	CR_91110
O90005	1/2/2018	Atla_003	E3477	1/4/2018	CR_91091
O90006	1/3/2018	Atla_001	E2154	1/4/2018	CR_91001
O90007	1/4/2018	Atla_010	E9481	1/8/2018	CR_91110
O90008	1/5/2018	Atla_008	E2154	1/10/2018	CR_91121
O90009	1/5/2018	Atla_001	E9481	1/8/2018	CR_91001
O90010	1/6/2018	Atla_010	E2154	1/15/2018	CR_91110

Import the data in the SALES and SALES ITEMS worksheets into Access. During the import, select order# as the primary key for the SALES table but no primary key for the SALES ITEMS table. After the import, open the SALES ITEMS table in design view and select both order# and inventory# as the primary key. Then, set the relationship between SALES and SALES ITEMS as shown in Figure 8.10.

LO 8-5

Employ the relational database to answer a variety of business performance questions

Prepare Queries

After importing all the data and setting the relationships to match the UML class diagram, you are ready to prepare queries for the financial statements and any other operational performance information. Each deliverable may require multiple queries. For example, to determine sales revenue for the quarter, you would first extend the SALES ITEMS table information to determine the amount for each item sold on each sale, as shown in Figure 8.11.

Then, using the query shown in Figure 8.11 and the SALES table, calculate the amount of each sale within the fiscal period, in this case the first calendar quarter, as shown in Figure 8.12. Set the criteria to constrain transactions to the first quarter. Sum the amount field, calculated as shown in Figure 8.11. Then, the summed amount from this query can be used to calculate overall sales revenue for the quarter in a subsequent query.

FIGURE 8.10

Setting Relationship between SALES and SALES ITEMS Tables

© Microsoft Excel

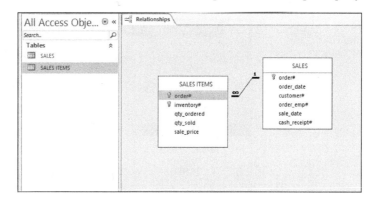

FIGURE 8.11

Calculating Amounts from the SALES ITEMS Table

© Microsoft Excel

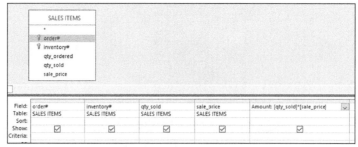

FIGURE 8.12

Summing Amounts for Each SALE

© Microsoft Excel

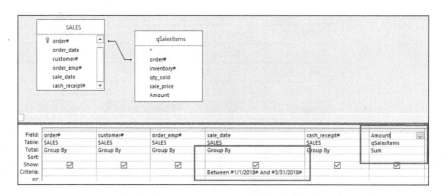

Summary

- This chapter outlines the approach to an integrated business analysis project.
- The project involves
  - Using project planning and management tools
  - Defining business requirements
  - Preparing an integrated UML class diagram
  - Preparing activity diagrams using BPMN
  - Importing data into Access from Excel
  - Cleaning and correcting data and data structures
  - Preparing queries to provide financial information

Glossary **of Models**

This glossary presents various structure and activity models to show modeling options. It is not intended to be all inclusive, but rather to provide examples of how to model common situations. For the structure models, the basic assumption is that resources, agents, and type images are added to the database before they are linked to other classes, so the minimum multiplicity is zero. Otherwise, the models show the most common multiplicities.

The glossary presents examples of structure models in the following section and then presents some generic activity models in the last section. The models are presented in the following order: sales and cash receipts process, purchases and cash disbursements process, and the conversion process, and for the structure models, it includes miscellaneous and integrated models.

Structure Models Using the REA Framework

1. Sales—Generic Model

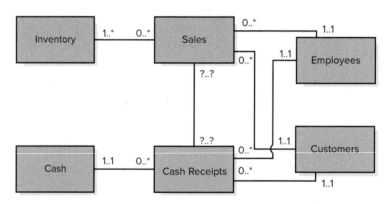

The generic model represents typical economic resources, events, and agents involved in the sales process. This model assumes that inventory items are not tracked individually (like high-value items such as automobiles and houses), but rather by UPC code such that all products with the same UPC code are considered to be the same item.

2. Sales—With Invoice Tracking

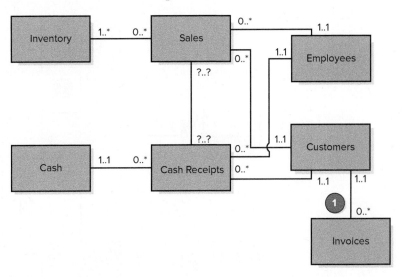

This model extends the generic model to track the invoices issued to each customer as shown in the association (1) between Customers (Agent) and Invoices (Type Image).

3. Sales—Where Employees Are Assigned to Service Particular Customers

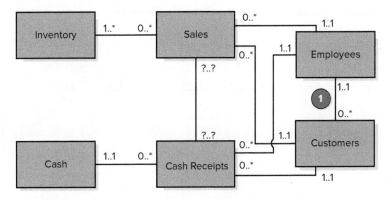

This model extends the generic model to represent assignment of employees to customers. The association (1) links customers to the assigned employee, such as when sales take place on commission. Similarly, employees can be assigned to inventory when specific employees manage specific inventory items.

4. Sales with Summary

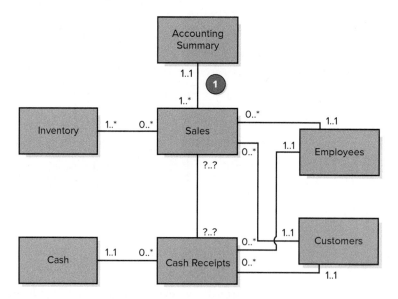

This model presents a simplified example of the summarization of economic activity by fiscal period in order to prepare financial reports. In this case, sales are summarized by fiscal period as shown in the association (1) between Accounting Summary and Sales.

5. Purchases—Generic Model

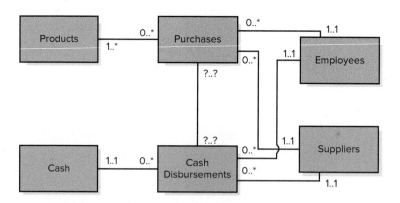

The generic model represents typical economic resources, events, and agents involved in the purchases process. Like the generic sales model, this model assumes that inventory items are not tracked individually, but rather by UPC code or similar identifier.

6. Purchases—With Commitment Event

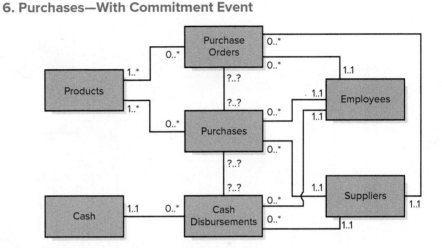

This model adds the commitment event, Purchase Orders, to the generic model. A commitment precedes the economic event. It records anticipated purchases but does not directly affect the financial statements. Note that this model requires tracking both the items ordered and the items received, which is a level of complication that many organizations avoid. Thus, they use a structure that combines the Purchase Orders and Purchases event as shown in the next model.

7. Purchases—With Combined Purchase Orders and Purchases

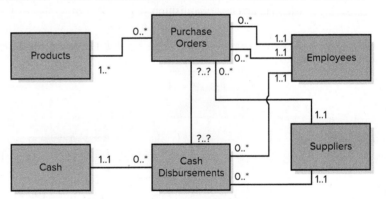

This model shows the combined Purchase Orders and Purchases event (still titled Purchase Orders). The Purchase Order class would track both the date of the order and the date of the receipt of products (the purchase date). The organization is now concerned with only one association between Purchase Orders/Purchases and the Products classes. However, there are now two associations between the Employees and Purchase Orders class, representing the requirement to track the two roles (purchasing agent and receiving agent) separately for internal control.

8. Purchases—With Type Images to Manage the Purchases Process

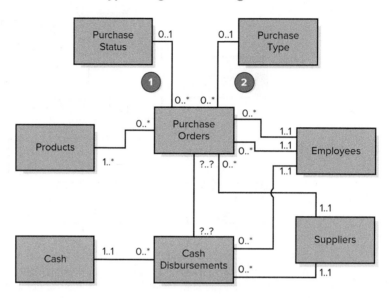

This model shows potential use of two type images to manage the purchase process. The Purchase Status type (1) would summarize information based on the point in the purchase process at the end of a fiscal period—for example, amounts on order, amounts received, amounts paid. The Purchase Type (2) would summarize information according to the type of purchase—for example, routine organizational supplies and services, inventory replenishment, and asset acquisition.

9. Purchases—With Type Images Linked for Summary Information

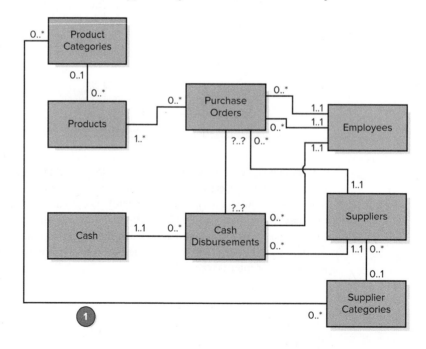

This model provides an example of the use of type images to summarize information. In this case, the organization could use the category classes to obtain summary information about supplier characteristics and activity, about product characteristics and activity, and about the common activity for each product and supplier category combination (1). For example, annual sales for each supplier category and product category combination would be recorded in the linking table between those two type images.

10. Conversion—Basic Model

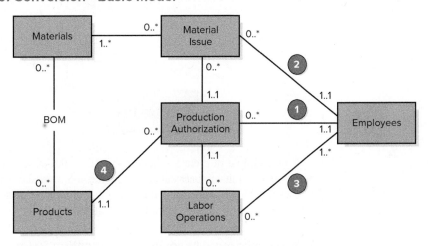

This basic conversion process model shows the structure related to (1) a supervisor authorizing production, (2) raw material issued into work-in-process, (3) labor applied to work-in-process, and (4) finished goods (products) increased when production completes.

11. Conversion—Production in a Series of Steps

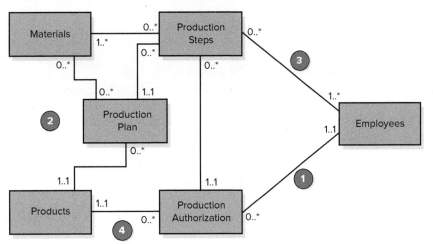

This revised conversion model shows production in a series of steps according to a production plan (a type image). The model shows (1) the supervisor authorizing production, (2) the production plan determining the raw material and labor needed to produce a specific product, (3) how employees work and materials are issued into work-in-process, and (4) how finished goods (products) increase when production completes. This model can be expanded to include accounting for equipment (a resource) use in the production steps.

12. Miscellaneous—Recursive Relationships

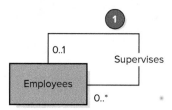

This is an example of a class related to itself. In this case, the association describes the supervisory relationship between an employee and several other employees. Similar common uses include products related to other substitute products and organizational departments that are parts of other organizational departments.

13. Miscellaneous—Associations Indicating Roles

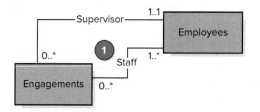

This is an example where two associations link the same two classes to indicate different agent roles in the event. In this case, each engagement (e.g., audit or consulting engagement) has one supervisor as well as several staff members. Placing the name of the role on the association can help clarify the purpose of the associations.

14. Integrated Models—Sales and Purchases

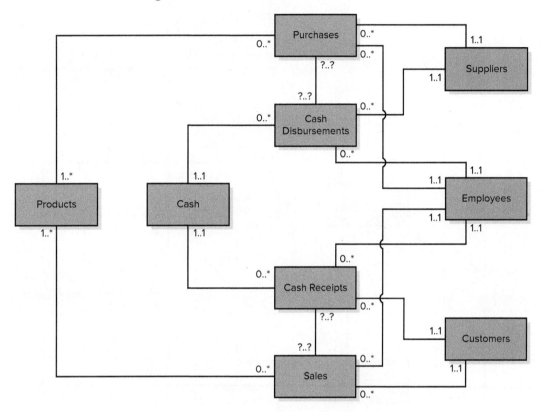

This is a basic example of a model integrating the sales (and cash receipts) and purchases (and cash disbursements) processes. Note that the two duality events (Purchases and Cash Disbursements or Sales and Cash Receipts) as well as the external agents (Customers and Suppliers) are unique to one process. However, the internal agent (Employees) and resources (Products and Cash) are shared across processes.

15. Integrated Models—Sales, Conversion, and Purchases

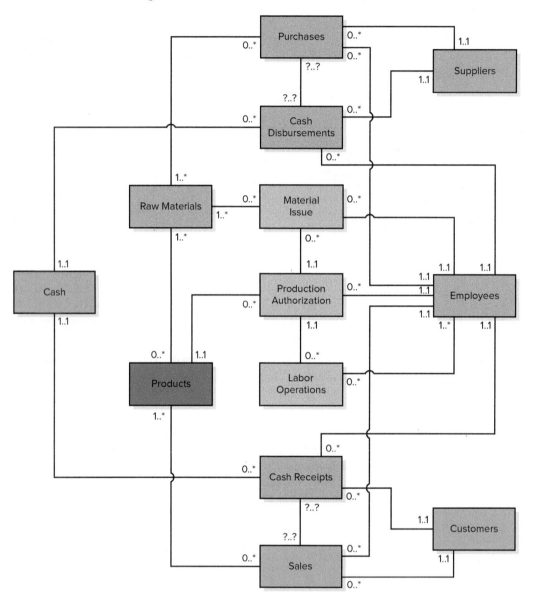

This is an example of a model integrating the sales (and cash receipts), conversion, and purchases (and cash disbursements) processes. In this case, the organization purchases raw materials that are converted into products (finished goods) that are then sold to customers. Again, the duality events (Purchases and Cash Disbursements, Sales and Cash Receipts, Production Authorization and Material Issue and Labor Operations) as well as the external agents (Customers and Suppliers) are unique to one process. However, the internal agent (Employees) and resources (Raw Materials, Products, and Cash) are shared across processes.

Activity Models Using BPMN

16. Sales—Basic Model

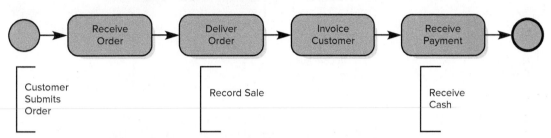

This model shows typical activity flow for a business that takes orders. Note that the steps in the model generally correspond to events in an REA diagram: commitment (receive order), sale (deliver order), and cash receipt (receive payment).

17. Sales—Basic Model with Pools and Swimlanes

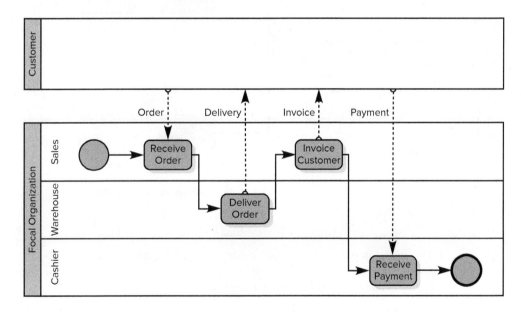

This is the basic model with pools and swimlanes to show responsibility for the various tasks. Note that there are no visible activities in the Customer pool because we are normally not interested in the specific steps they take. Instead, the focus moves to the interactions between pools, shown as message flows (dashed lines). It is good practice to put labels on the message flows to clarify the nature of the interactions. Within the pool of interest, the sequence flows connect the start and end events without any break.

18. Purchases—Basic Model

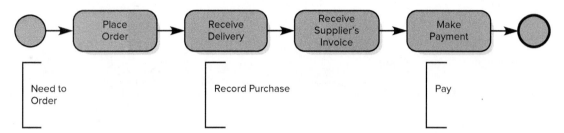

This model shows typical activity flow related to issuing purchase orders. Note that the steps in the model generally correspond to events in an REA diagram: commitment (place order), purchase (receive order), and cash disbursement (make payment).

19. Purchases—Basic Model with Gateway

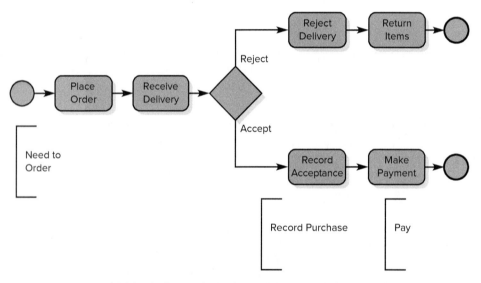

This model is similar to the basic model, except it includes the gateway to show the different flow options after the receipt of the delivery: (1) accept and make payment and (2) reject and return the items to the supplier.

20. Purchases—Basic Model with Error Event

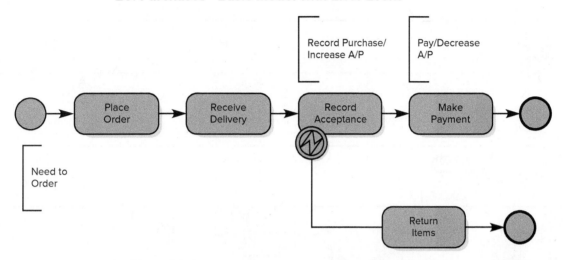

In this model, the intermediate error event shows flow when the items are rejected.

21. Purchases—With Pools and Lanes

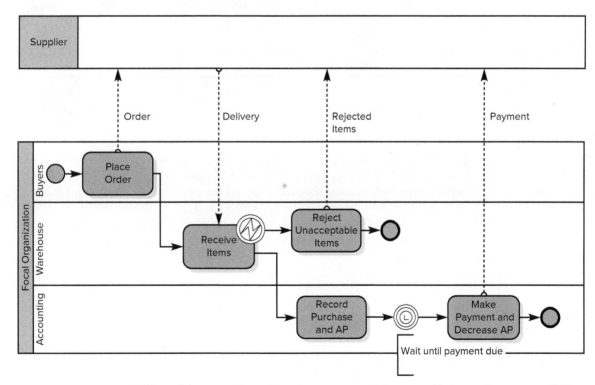

This model uses pools to show the process participants and lanes to show responsibility in the focal organization. It again employs an intermediate error event to show rejected items. It includes an intermediate timer event to show the delay until the payment to the supplier is due.

22. Purchases—With Pools and Lanes and Data Objects

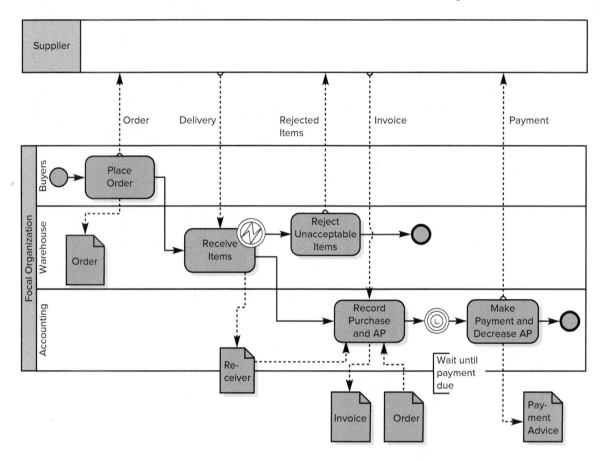

This model builds on the previous model. It also uses pools to show the process participants and lanes to show responsibility in the focal organization. It again employs an intermediate error event to show rejected items, and it includes an intermediate timer event to
show the delay until the payment to the supplier is due. It adds data objects to show the
documents/information being created or used at the various steps in the process. It assumes
a standard three-way match—matching invoices, receipts, and orders—before payments
are authorized.

23. Conversion—Basic Model with Repeated Activities or a Looping, Collapsed Subprocess

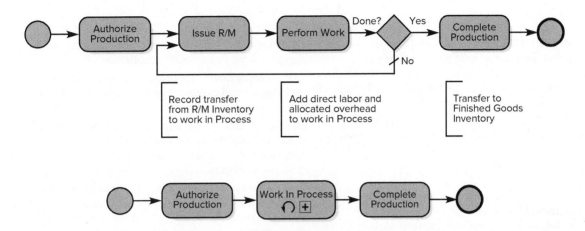

These models provide alternate descriptions of the basic conversion process. The model on top is closely related to the REA model that shows (1) the authorization, (2) raw material issue into work-in-process, (3) labor (and equipment) applied to work-in-process, and (4) completion of production and transfer to finished goods. The gateway routes the flow back until all production to carry out the authorization is complete. The model on the bottom places Work-in-Process activities in a collapsed subprocess. The looping arrow shows that the process loops until complete.

24. Conversion—Basic Model with Repeated Activities and Batches

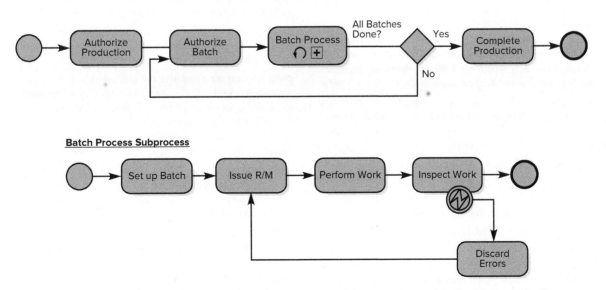

This model expands on the previous model to include batches. In this case, the flow starts with production authorization, to batch authorization, to the batch process, which then repeats until all batches are done. The contents of the collapsed Batch Process subprocess are shown separately. The subprocess also includes an intermediate error event that halts the normal process flow when items fail inspection.

Glossary

15-15 rule *(392)*   A rule suggesting that if a project is more than 15 percent over budget or 15 percent off the planned schedule, it will likely never recoup the time or cost necessary to be considered successful. At this point, a decision needs to be made on if or how to proceed.

100% rule *(393)*   A rule requiring 100 percent planning of all tasks, including all of the internal, external, and interim tasks.

A

access controls *(125)*   Limit who can use and change records in the system; for example, passwords control who can use an application.

access point *(331)*   Logically connects stations to a firm's network.

accounting information system (AIS) *(4)*   A system that records, processes, and reports on transactions to provide financial and nonfinancial information to make decisions and have appropriate levels of internal controls for those transactions.

accounting rate of return (ARR) *(373)*   The average annual income from the IT initiative divided by the initial investment cost.

accounts payable *(152)*   Amounts owed to suppliers for goods and services received. In a data modeling context, accounts payable are calculated based on receipts (purchases) from each supplier less the corresponding payments (cash disbursements) to those suppliers.

accounts receivable *(120)*   Monies owed by customers for prior sales of goods or services. In a data modeling context, accounts receivable are calculated as each customer's sales less corresponding cash receipts.

acquisition costs *(369)*   All direct and indirect costs necessary to acquire and implement the IT initiative.

activities *(37)*   In business process modeling, activities represent specific steps in a business process.

activity models *(36)*   Models that describe the sequence of workflow in a business process or processes.

agents *(126, 157, 183)*   The people or organizations who participate in business events, such as customers and salespeople.

aggregation relationship *(65)*   A special-purpose UML notation representing the relationship between two classes that are often considered together, such as when a sports league is made up of a collection of teams.

alignment risk *(370)*   The risk that an IT initiative is not aligned with the strategy of the organization.

analysis phase *(386)*   The phase of the SDLC involves a complete, detailed analysis of the systems needs of the end user as well as a proposed solution.

annotations *(37)*   Model elements that allow the modeler to add additional descriptive information to the model. Annotations are modeled with text inside a bracket connected to other model symbols with a dashed line.

application controls *(125, 274)*   Ensure data integrity and an audit trail; for example, new invoices are assigned sequential numbers; specific to a subsystem or an application to ensure the validity, completeness, and accuracy of the transactions.

association *(63)*   UML symbol that depicts the relationship between two classes; it is modeled as a solid line that connects two classes in a model.

assurance *(258)*   Independent, professional opinions that reduce the risk of having incorrect information.

asymmetric-key encryption *(304)*   To transmit confidential information, the sender uses the receiver's public key to encrypt the message; the receiver uses his or her own private key for decryption upon receiving the message. Also known as public-key encryption or two-key encryption.

attributes *(64, 73, 85)*   Data elements that describe instances in a class, very much like fields in a database table; characteristics, properties, or adjectives that describe each class.

audit around the computer (or black-box approach) *(333)*   Auditors test the reliability of computer-generated information by first calculating expected results from the transactions entered into the system. Then, the auditors compare these calculations to the processing or output results.

audit data standards *(215)*   A standard format for data files and fields typically needed to support an external audit in a given financial business process area that was developed by the AICPA.

audit through the computer (or white-box approach) *(333)*   Requires auditors to understand the internal logic of the system/application being tested.

authentication *(304)*   A process that establishes the origin of information or determines the identity of a user, process, or device.

automate *(19)*   The use of technology to replace human labor in automating business processes.

B

Balanced Scorecard framework *(346)*   Provides an integrating framework that describes organizational performance relative to its strategic objectives across four perspectives: learning and growth, process, customer, and financial. Objectives for each perspective describe the strategy in a series of cause-and-effect relationships.

Balanced Scorecard management process *(351)*   The process by which companies plan, implement, and monitor performance. It consists of five steps: formulate the strategy, translate the strategy, link the strategy to operations, monitor performance, and adapt.

benefits *(366)*   The positive consequences to the organization of an IT investment.

Big Data *(210)*   Datasets that are too large and complex for businesses' existing systems to handle utilizing their traditional capabilities to capture, store, manage, and analyze these datasets.

breach of security *(219)*   The unauthorized access to or acquisition of data in electronic form that contain personal information.

breakeven analysis *(372)*   Determines the breakeven point, where the total value of benefits equals that of total costs.

business analysis *(33)*   The process of defining business process requirements and evaluating potential improvements. Business analysis involves ascertaining, documenting, and communicating information about current and future business processes using business process modeling and related tools.

business case *(366)*   Economic justification for an IT investment or other major project.

business continuity management (BCM) *(315)*   The activities required to keep a firm running during a period of displacement or interruption of normal operations.

business intelligence *(252)*   A computer-based technique for accumulating and analyzing data from databases and data warehouses to support managerial decision making.

business model *(33)*   A simple, abstract representation of one or more business processes. A business model is typically a graphical depiction of the essential business process information.

business process *(33)*   A defined sequence of business activities that use resources to transform specific inputs into specific outputs to achieve a business goal.

business process modeling notation (BPMN) *(36)*   A standard for the description of activity models.

business rule *(70)*   Succinct statements of constraints on business processes; they provide the logic that guides the behavior of the business in specific situations.

business value *(11)*   Items, events, and interactions that determine the financial health and well-being of the firm.

C

cardinalities *(74)*   *See* multiplicities.

cash *(120, 157)*   The organization's monies in bank or related accounts. The instances of the class are individual accounts. This is considered a resource.

cash disbursements *(152)*   Record payments of cash to external agents (e.g., suppliers) and the corresponding reduction in cash accounts. This is considered an event.

cash receipts *(127)*   Record receipts of cash from external agents (e.g., customers) and the corresponding deposit of those receipts into cash accounts. This is considered an event.

Certificate Authority (CA) *(306)*   A trusted entity that issues and revokes digital certificates.

Certified Information Systems Auditor (CISA) *(10)*   The CISA designation identifies those professionals possessing IT audit, control, and security skills. Generally, CISAs will perform IT audits to evaluate the accounting information system's internal control design and effectiveness.

Certified Information Technology Professional (CITP) *(10)*   The CITP designation identifies accountants (CPAs) with a broad range of technology knowledge and experience.

Certified Internal Auditor (CIA) *(10)*   The CIA designation is the certification for internal auditors and is the standard to demonstrate competency and professionalism in the internal auditing field.

change risk *(370)*   The risk that the organization will be unable to make the changes necessary to implement the IT initiative successfully.

choreography *(122, 153)*   The interaction (message flows) between two participants (modeled as pools) in a process modeled using BPMN.

class *(62)*   Any separately identifiable collection of things (objects) about which the organization wants to collect and store information. Classes can represent organization resources (e.g., trucks, machines, buildings, cash, investments), persons (e.g., customers, employees), events (e.g., sales, purchases, cash disbursements, cash receipts), and conceptual structures (e.g., accounts, product categories, budgets). Classes are typically implemented as tables in a relational database, where individual instances of the class are represented as rows in the table.

class diagrams *(62)*   Structure models prepared using UML notation.

cloud computing *(104, 315)*   Internet-based computing, where shared resources, software, and information are provided to firms on demand; using redundant servers in multiple locations to host virtual machines.

code of ethics *(272)*   What is considered to be ethical within an organization to promote ethical behavior.

collaboration *(122, 153)*   A BPMN model showing two participant pools and the interactions between them within a process.

Committee of Sponsoring Organizations (COSO) *(274)* Composed of several organizations (AAA, AICPA, FEI, IIA, and IMA); studies the causal factors that lead to fraudulent financial reporting and develops recommendations for public companies, independent auditors, the SEC and other regulators, and educational institutions to improve the quality of financial reporting through internal controls and corporate governance.

composition relationship *(65)*   A special-purpose UML notation representing the relationship between two classes that are often considered together, similar to aggregation relationships, except in composition relationships, one class cannot exist without the other, such as a book and the chapters that compose the book.

computer-assisted audit techniques (CAATs) *(332)*   Essential tools for auditors to conduct an audit in accordance with heightened auditing standards.

constraints *(64)*   Optional or mandatory guidance about how a process should perform in certain situations.

continuous audit *(334)*   Performing audit-related activities on a continuous basis.

control objectives for information and related technology (COBIT) *(275)*   An internationally accepted set of best IT security and control practices for IT management released by the IT Governance Institute (ITGI).

control risk *(281)*   The threat that errors or irregularities in the underlying transactions will not be prevented, detected, and corrected by the internal control system.

corporate governance *(273)*   A set of processes and policies in managing an organization with sound ethics to safeguard the interests of its stakeholders.

corrective controls *(274)*   Fix problems that have been identified, such as using backup files to recover corrupted data.

cost/benefit analysis *(281)*   Important in determining whether to implement an internal control.

critical path *(393)*   The longest path for a project and represents the minimum amount of time needed for the completion of the project when sufficient resources are allocated.

customer *(121)*   The external agent in the sales and collection process.

customer perspective *(348)*   The Balanced Scorecard perspective that describes the organization's customer-related objectives and corresponding customer measures; it views organization performance from the customers' perspective.

customer relationship management (CRM) software *(16)* Software used to manage and nurture a firm's interactions with its current and potential clients. CRM software often includes the use of database marketing tools to learn more about the customers and to develop strong firm-to-customer relationships.

D

data *(6)*   Raw facts or statistics that, absent a context, may have little meaning.

DATA (2009) *(217)*   Data Accountability and Trust Act of 2009 (DATA) creates a national standard for privacy and data protection.

data analytics *(210)*   The science of examining raw data (now often Big Data), removing excess noise from the dataset, and organizing the data with the purpose of drawing conclusions for decision making.

data dictionary *(85)*   Describes the data fields in each database record such as field description, field length, field type (e.g., alphanumeric, numeric), etc.

data flow diagram (DFD) *(52)*   Another type of activity model that graphically shows the flow of data through a system and also incorporates elements of structure models.

data governance *(327)*   The convergence of data quality, data management, data policies, business process management, and risk management surrounding the handling of data in a firm.

data integrity *(305)*   Maintaining and assuring the accuracy and consistency of data during transmission and at storage.

data mart *(250)*   A subset of the information from the data warehouse to serve a specific purpose.

data mining *(253, 327)*   A process of using sophisticated statistical techniques to extract and analyze data from large databases to discern patterns and trends that were not previously known.

data models *(62)*   A graphic representation of the conceptual contents of databases; data models support communication about database contents between users and designers of the database.

data warehouse *(250, 327)*   A collection of information gathered from an assortment of external and operational (i.e, internal) databases to facilitate reporting for decision making and business analysis.

database *(84, 327)*   A shared collection of logically related data for various uses.

database administrator *(85)*   The person responsible for the design, implementation, repair, and security of a firm's database.

database management system (DBMS) *(84)*   A computer program that creates, modifies, and queries the database. Specifically, the DBMS is designed to manage a database's storage and retrieval of information.

database system *(327)*   A term typically used to encapsulate the constructs of a data model, database management system (DBMS), and database.

decision support system (DSS) *(251)*   A computer-based information system that facilitates business decision-making activities.

design phase *(386)*   The phase of the SDLC that involves describing in detail the desired features of the system that were uncovered in the analysis phase.

detective controls *(274)*   Find problems when they arise.

digital certificate *(306)*   A digital document issued and digitally signed by the private key of a Certificate Authority that binds the name of a subscriber to a public key.

digital dashboard *(254)*   A display to track the firm's process or performance indicators or metrics to monitor critical performance.

digital signature *(305)*   A message digest of a document (or data file) that is encrypted using the document creator's private key.

disaster recovery planning (DRP) *(315)*   A process that identifies significant events that may threaten a firm's operations and outlines the procedures to ensure that the firm will resume operations when the events occur.

discretionary information *(7)*   Information that is generated according to one's own judgment.

documentation *(33)*   An information transmission and communication tool that explains how business processes and business systems work.

E

economic justification process *(367)*   The process by which an organization creates a business case for an IT investment or other major project.

embedded audit module (EAM) *(334)*   A programmed audit module that is added to the system under review.

encryption *(303)*   Using algorithmic schemes to encode plaintext into nonreadable form.

enterprise IT (EIT) *(350)*   A type of information technology that restructures interactions within an organization and with external partners, such as customer relationship management systems.

enterprise risk management (ERM) *(278)*   A process, affected by the entity's board of directors, management, and other personnel, applied in strategy setting and across the enterprise, designed to identify potential events that may affect the entity, and manage risk to be within the risk appetite, to provide reasonable assurance regarding the achievement of objectives.

enterprise system (ES) *(13, 102)*   A centralized database that collects data from throughout the firm. Commercialized information system that integrates and automates business processes across a firm's value chain located within and across organizations.

entities *(73)*   The people, things, and events in the domain of interest; in UML notation, entities are modeled as classes.

entity integrity rule *(87)*   The primary key of a table must have data values (cannot be null).

error event *(123)*   An intermediate event in a BPMN model showing processing for exceptions to the normal process flow.

events *(36, 126, 157, 184)*   Important occurrences that affect the flow of activities in a business process. BPMN includes symbols to define start, intermediate, and end events.

Excel pivot table *(223)*   A pivot table is a dynamic summary report generated from a range or table in Excel or an external data file. It allows cross-tabulations and summary reporting of multiple dimensions and levels of detail. In conjunction with Slicers, it offers a powerful data analysis tool.

Excel table *(220)*   A rectangular range of structured data in one Excel worksheet specifically identified as a table. The table usually has one row of text headings that indicate the contents of each column. Designating a range of data as a table provides access to a set of formatting and analysis tools.

extract, transform, and load (ETL) *(211)*   The process of cleaning and scrubbing the data before data analysis can take place.

F

fault tolerance *(315)*   Redundant units providing a system with the ability to continue functioning when part of the system fails.

financial perspective *(348)*   The Balanced Scorecard perspective that describes the organization's financial objectives and corresponding financial measures of performance; it views organizational performance from the shareholders' perspective.

financial risk *(370)*   The risk that the IT investment will not deliver expected financial benefits.

finished goods inventory *(179)*   For a manufacturing company, the inventory (REA resource) that has completed the manufacturing process and is held for sale to customers.

firewall *(329)*   A security system comprised of hardware and software that is built using routers, servers, and a variety of software.

firm infrastructure *(12)*   Activities needed to support the firm, including the CEO and the finance, accounting, and legal departments.

flowcharts *(47)*   Visualizations of a process activity; they are activity models much like models using BPMN.

foreign key (FK) *(65, 86)*   Attribute that allows database tables to be linked together; foreign keys are the primary keys of other tables placed in the current table to support the link between the two tables.

form *(87)*   Forms are utilized by users to enter data into tables and view existing records.

fraud triangle *(307)*   Three conditions exist for a fraud to be perpetrated: incentive, opportunity, and rationalization.

function IT (FIT) *(350)*   A type of information technology that performs/supports a single function, such as spreadsheet applications.

G

Gantt chart *(394)*   A graphical representation of the project schedule that maps the tasks to a project calendar.

gateways *(37, 154, 180)*   Show process branching and merging as the result of decisions. Basic gateways are depicted as diamonds. Usually, gateways appear as pairs on the diagram. The first gateway shows the branching, and the second gateway shows merging of the process branches.

general controls *(274)*   Pertain to enterprisewide issues such as controls over accessing the network, developing and maintaining applications, and documenting changes of programs.

generalization relationship *(65)*   A special-purpose UML symbol that supports grouping of things that share common characteristics; it reduces redundancy because the shared characteristics need only be modeled once.

generalized audit software (GAS) *(334)*   Frequently used to perform substantive tests and used for testing of controls through transactional data analysis.

H

hierarchical data model *(84)*   Organizes data into a tree-like structure that allows repeating information using defined parent/child relationships.

hub *(328)*   Contains multiple ports.

human resource management *(12)*   Activities include recruiting, hiring, training, and compensating employees.

I

implementation phase *(387)*   The phase of the SDLC that involves development, testing, and implementation of the new proposed system.

inbound logistics *(11)*   Activities associated with receiving and storing raw materials and other partially completed materials and distributing those materials to manufacturing when and where they are needed.

informate-down *(19)*   The use of computer technology to provide information about business activities to employees across the firm.

informate-up *(19)*   The use of computer technology to provide information about business activities to senior management.

information *(6)*   Data organized in a meaningful way to the user.

information capital *(349)*   An intangible asset that reflects the readiness of the company's technology to support strategic internal processes. It includes computing hardware, infrastructure, applications, and employees' abilities to use technology effectively.

information overload *(6)*   The difficulty a person faces in understanding a problem and making a decision as a consequence of too much information.

Information Technology Infrastructure Library (ITIL) *(275)*   A set of concepts and practices for IT service management.

information value chain *(7)*   The overall transformation from a business need and business event to the collection of data and information to an ultimate decision.

inherent risk *(281)*   The risk related to the nature of the business activity itself.

input controls *(283)*   Ensure the authorization, entry, and verification of data entering the system.

integrated test facility (ITF) *(334)*   An automated technique that enables test data to be continually evaluated during the normal operation of a system.

intermediate error event *(180)*   Occurs between start and end events and affects the flow of the process. Intermediate error events represent interruptions to the normal flow of the process and start the exception flow.

intermediate event *(155)*   Occurs between start and end events and affects the flow of the process.

intermediate timer event *(155)*   Intermediate events that indicate a delay in the normal process flow until a fixed amount of time has elapsed.

internal rate of return (IRR) *(372)*   The discount rate (return) that makes a project's net present value equal to zero.

International Organization for Standardization (ISO) 27000 series *(275)*   This series contains a range of individual standards and documents specifically reserved by ISO for information security.

IT application controls *(283)*   Activities specific to a subsystem's or an application's input, processing, and output.

IT controls *(283)*   Involve processes that provide assurance for information and help to mitigate risks associated with the use of technology.

IT general controls (ITGC) *(283)*   Enterprise-level controls over IT.

K

key performance indicator *(350)*   Those measures that the organization feels best indicate the performance of a particular activity.

L

labor operations event *(184)*   In the conversion process, an event that represents the recording of labor (and any associated overhead) costs applied to work-in-process.

learning and growth perspective *(347)*   The Balanced Scorecard perspective that describes the organization's objectives and corresponding measures related to improvements in tangible and intangible infrastructure, such as human, information, and organizational capital.

local area network (LAN) *(328)*   A group of computers, printers, and other devices connected to the same network that covers a limited geographic range such as a home, small office, or a campus building.

M

MAC (media access control) address *(328)*   A designated address that is connected to each device via the network and only sees traffic.

macro *(88)*   Macros are defined by Access users to automate processes such as opening a specific form.

maintenance phase *(387)*   The final phase of the SDLC that includes making changes, corrections, additions, and upgrades (generally smaller in scope) to ensure the system continues to meet the business requirements that have been set out for it.

mandatory information *(7)*   Information that is required to be generated or provided by law or regulation.

many-to-many relationship *(126, 158, 185)*   Exists when instances of one class (e.g., sales) are related to many instances of another class (e.g., inventory) and vice versa. These relationships are implemented in Access and relational databases by adding a linking table to convert the many-to-many relationship into two one-to-many relationships.

marketing and sales activities *(11)*   Activities that identify the needs and wants of their customers to help attract them to the firm's products and buy them.

message digest (MD) *(305)*   A short code, such as one 256 bits long, resulting from hashing a plaintext message using an algorithm.

message flows *(39)*   BPMN represents exchanges between two participants (pools) in the same process as message flows, which are modeled as dashed arrows.

module *(88)*   Some Microsoft applications come with modules built in that will be automatically added onto Access.

multiplicities *(63)*   UML symbols that describe the minimum and maximum number of times an instance of one class can be associated with instances of another class for a specific association between those two classes; they indicate whether the two classes are part of one-to-one, one-to-many, or many-to-many relationships.

N

net present value (NPV) *(372)*   The sum of the present value of all cash inflows minus the sum of the present value of all cash outflows related to an IT investment or other capital investment.

network data model *(84)*   A flexible model representing objects and their relationships; allows each record to have multiple parent and child records or M:N mapping, also known as many-to-many relationships.

network IT (NIT) *(350)*   A type of information technology that allows people to communicate with one another, such as e-mail and instant messaging.

O

one-to-many relationship *(126)*   Exists when instances of one class are related to multiple instances of another class. For example, a customer can participate in many sales, but each sale involves only one customer.

one-to-one relationship *(158)*   Exists when instances of one class (e.g., sales) are related to only one instance of another class (e.g., cash receipts) and each instance of the other class is related to only one instance of the original class.

operating system (OS) *(326)*   Performs the tasks that enable a computer to operate; comprised of system utilities and programs.

operation cost *(369)*   The recurring cost necessary to operate, maintain, and administer an IT initiative.

operational database *(327)*   Often includes data for the current fiscal year only.

operations *(11)*   Activities that transform inputs into finished goods and services.

orchestration *(122, 153)*   In BPMN, the sequence of activities within one pool.

outbound logistics *(11)*   Activities that warehouse and distribute the finished goods to the customers.

output controls *(284)*   Provide output to authorized people and ensure the output is used properly.

P

pages *(88)*   Access pages allow data to be entered into the database in real time from outside of the database system.

parallel simulation *(333)*   Attempts to simulate the firm's key features or processes.

payback period *(372)*   The amount of time necessary to recoup a project's initial investment.

perceived ease of use *(396)*   The extent to which a person perceives that the use of a particular system will be relatively free from effort.

perceived usefulness *(395)*   The extent to which users believe the system will help them perform their job better.

personal identifying information *(218)*   An individual's first name or initial and last name, or address, or phone number, in combination with Social Security number, driver's license number, passport number, military identification number, or other similar number issued on a government document used to verify identity and financial account number and passcodes.

physical controls *(283)*   Mainly manual but could involve the physical use of computing technology.

planning phase *(386)*   The phase of the SDLC that summarizes the business needs with a high-level view of the intended project.

pools *(38)*   BPMN symbols used to identify participants, actors, or persons that perform activities and interact with other participants in a process.

Power Pivot *(228)*   Excel add-in that can create an integrated database from various Excel tables and external data sources, such as Access and SQL databases. It supports the creation of calculated fields and the use of pivot tables for the integrated database.

preventive controls *(274)*   Deter problems before they arise.

primary key (PK) *(64, 85)*   An attribute or a combination of attributes that uniquely identifies an instance of a class in a data model or a specific row in a table.

private key *(304)*   A string of bits kept secret and known only to the owner of the key.

process maps *(48)*   Simplified flowcharts that use a basic set of symbols to represent a business process activity.

process perspective *(347)*   The Balanced Scorecard perspective that describes the organization's internal, process-related, objectives and corresponding measures; it views organizational performance from an internal perspective.

processing controls *(284)*   Ensure that data and transactions are processed accurately.

procurement *(12)*   Activities that involve purchasing inputs such as raw materials, supplies, and equipment.

product *(120, 157)*   Class representing the organization's goods held for sale, that is, the organization's inventory. This is considered a resource.

production authorization event *(184)*   In a UML class model of the conversion process, an event that records the authorization to produce one or more finished goods inventory items.

Program Evaluation Review Technique (PERT) *(393)*   A project management tool used to help identify all tasks needed to complete a project. It is also helpful in determining task dependencies.

project *(389)*   A series of tasks that are generally performed in a defined sequence to produce a predefined output.

project management *(386)*   The process of carrying out the systems development life cycle to achieve an intended outcome.

project manager *(390)*   The lead member of the project team who is responsible for the project.

project risk *(370)*   The risk that the project will not be completed on time or within budget.

project sponsor *(390)*   Generally a senior executive in the company who takes responsibility for the success of the project.

Public Company Accounting Oversight Board (PCAOB) *(272)*   Established by SOX to provide independent oversight of public accounting firms.

public key *(304)*   A string of bits created with the private key and widely distributed and available to other users.

public-key infrastructure (PKI) *(306)*   A set of policies, processes, server platforms, software, and workstations used for the purpose of administering certificates and public-/private-key pairs, including the ability to issue, maintain, and revoke public-key certificates.

purchase discount *(152)*   An offer from the supplier to reduce the cost of a purchase if payment is made according to specified terms, usually within a specified time.

purchase order *(152)*   A commitment event that precedes the economic purchase event. It records formal offers to suppliers to pay them if the supplier complies with the terms of the purchase order.

purchases *(152)*   Records the receipt of goods or services from a supplier and the corresponding obligation to pay the supplier. These are considered events.

Q

query *(87)*   Query in Access is a tool used to retrieve and display data derived from records stored within the database.

quote *(121)*   Description of the products and/or services to be provided to a customer if ordered.

R

raw material issue event *(184)*   In a UML class diagram of the conversion process, an event that records the transfer of raw materials into work-in-process.

raw materials inventory *(179)*   For a manufacturing company, the inventory (REA resource) acquired for use (conversion) in the manufacturing process.

REA *(126, 157, 183)*   Resource-event-agent framework for modeling business processes, originally developed by William McCarthy.

receipt *(157)*   Same as the purchases event.

referential integrity rule *(87)*   The data value for a foreign key must either be null or match one of the data values that already exist in the corresponding table.

relational data model *(84)*   Stores information in the form of related two-dimensional tables.

relationship *(73)*   The business purpose for the association between two classes or two database tables; *see* association.

relevance *(5)*   Information that is capable of making a difference in a decision.

relevant costs *(369)*   Those costs that will change as a result of an IT initiative or other major project.

reliability *(5)*   Information that is free from bias and error.

remote access *(330)*   Connection to a data-processing system from a remote location, e.g., through a virtual private network.

report *(88)*   Reports in Access are used to integrate data from one or more queries and tables to provide useful information to decision makers.

residual risk *(281)*   The product of inherent risk and control risk (i.e., Residual risk = Inherent risk × Control risk).

resources *(126, 157, 184)*   Those things that have economic value to a firm, such as cash and products.

risk assessment *(280)*   The process of identifying and analyzing risks systematically to determine the firm's risk response and control activities.

router *(329)*   Software-based intelligent device that chooses the most efficient communication path through a network to the required destination.

S

sales *(120)*   Events documenting the transfer of goods or services to customer and the corresponding recognition of revenue for the organization.

sales order *(121)*   Event documenting commitments by customers to purchase products. The sales order event precedes the economic event (sale).

Sarbanes-Oxley Act of 2002 (SOX) *(9, 272)*   A federal law in the United States that set new and enhanced standards for all U.S. public companies, management, and public accounting firms; a response to business scandals such as Enron, WorldCom, and Tyco International. It requires public companies registered with the SEC and their auditors to annually assess and report on the design and effectiveness of internal control over financial reporting.

scope creep *(392)*   The change in a project's scope after the project work has started.

sequence flows *(37)*   BPMN symbols that show the normal sequence of activities in a business process. Sequence flows are modeled as solid arrows, with the arrowhead showing the direction of process flow.

service activities *(11)*   Activities that provide the support of customers after the products and services are sold to them (e.g., warranty repairs, parts, instruction manuals, etc.).

session key *(304)*   A symmetric key that is valid for a certain timeframe only.

solution risk *(370)*   The risk that the proposed solution will not generate expected benefits.

station *(331)*   A wireless endpoint device equipped with a wireless network interface card.

strategy map *(349)*   A one-page representation of the firm's strategic priorities and the cause-and-effect linkages among those strategic priorities.

structure model *(62)*   A conceptual depiction of a database, such as a UML class model or an entity-relationship model.

Structured Query Language (SQL) *(96)*   A computer language designed to retrieve data from a relational database.

subprocess *(122, 154)*   Represents a series of process steps that are hidden from view in BPMN. The use of subprocesses in modeling helps reduce complexity.

suppliers *(152)*   In the UML diagram of the purchases and payments process, the external agents from whom goods and services are purchased and to whom payments are made.

supply chain *(14)*   The flow of materials, information, payments, and services from raw materials suppliers, through factories and warehouses, all the way to the final customers of the firm's products.

supply chain management (SCM) software *(15)*   Software that connects the focal firm with its suppliers. It generally addresses segments of the supply chain, including manufacturing, inventory control, and transportation.

swimlanes (or lanes) *(38)*   BPMN symbols that provide subdivisions of pools to show, for example, functional responsibilities within an organization.

switch *(328)*   An intelligent device that provides a path for each pair of connections on the switch by storing address information in its switching tables.

symmetric-key encryption *(304)*   Both the sender and the receiver use the same key to encrypt and decrypt messages.

systems analyst *(9, 386)*   Person responsible for both determining the information needs of the business and designing a system to meet those needs.

systems development life cycle (SDLC) *(386)*   The process of creating or modifying information systems to meet the needs of its users. It serves as the foundation for all processes people use to develop such systems.

T

Tableau Desktop *(233)*   Software application that supports data analytics and visualizations. It integrates data from multiple data sources. It provides easy-to-use and powerful summary reporting and charting capabilities. It allows users to build dashboards and create stories from their data.

technological risk *(370)*   The risk that the technology will not perform as expected to deliver the planned benefits.

technology *(12)*   Supports value-creating activities in the value chain. These technologies also include research and development to develop new products or determine ways to produce products at a cheaper price.

technology acceptance model (TAM) *(395)* A model that predicts when users will adopt a new system to the extent they believe the system will help them perform their job better.

test data technique *(333)* Uses a set of input data to validate system integrity.

timer events *(155)* Indication of a delay in the flow of a process to a specific date, an elapsed time (for example, 30 days), or a relative repetitive date, such as every Friday.

transform *(19)* The use of computer technology to fundamentally redefine business processes and relationships.

triple constraints *(391)* Three factors that constrain information technology and other projects: cost, scope, and time. Also known as Dempster's triangle.

type image *(128, 159, 184)* Class that represents management information (such as categorizations, policies, and guidelines) to help manage a business process. Type image often allows process information to be summarized by category.

U

uninterruptible power supply *(314)* A device using battery power to enable a system to operate long enough to back up critical data and shut down properly during the loss of power.

V

Val IT *(353)* An IT investment framework developed by the IT Governance Institute.

value chain *(11)* A chain of critical business processes at a company that creates value.

value proposition *(348, 372)* Represents the product and service characteristics, such as price, quality, selection, and brand image, that the firm attempts to deliver to customers to meet or exceed its customers' expectations and thereby result in customer retention and new customer acquisition; summarizes the costs and benefits of a preferred alternative IT investment, describing (1) the relevant time frames in which the costs will be incurred and benefits realized, (2) the corresponding discount rates to apply to future cash flows, and (3) the sensitivity of the results to assumptions.

virtual private network (VPN) *(330)* Securely connects a firm's WANs by sending/receiving encrypted packets via virtual connections over the public Internet to distant offices, salespeople, and business partners.

virtualization *(315)* Using various techniques and methods to create a virtual (rather than actual) version of a hardware platform, storage device, or network resources.

W

wide area network (WAN) *(329)* Links different sites together; transmits information across geographically dispersed LANs; and covers a broad geographic area such as a city, region, nation, or an international link.

wireless network *(331)* Comprised of two fundamental architectural components: access points and stations.

work breakdown structure (WBS) *(393)* The process of identifying all tasks needed to complete a project.

work-in-process inventory *(184)* For a manufacturing company, the value of raw materials, direct labor, and manufacturing overhead in production but not yet finished.

X

XBRL (eXtensible Business Reporting Language) *(255)* An open, global standard for exchanging financial reporting information.

XBRL Global Ledger Taxonomy (XBRL GL) *(259)* Serves as a ledger using the XBRL standard for internal purposes.

XBRL instance document *(258)* A document containing XBRL elements.

XBRL specification *(256)* Provides the underlying technical details of what XBRL is and how it works.

XBRL style sheet *(258)* Adds presentation elements to XBRL instance documents to make them readable by people.

XBRL taxonomy *(256)* Defines and describes each key data element (e.g., total assets, accounts payable, net income, etc.).

XML (Extensible Markup Language) *(255)* Open, global standard for exchanging information in a format that is both human- and machine-readable.

Index

Bold page numbers indicate definitions or key discussions of terms; page numbers followed by *n* indicate footnotes or source notes.

A

AAA (American Accounting Association), 274
Accenture, 60, 198
Acceptable use policy (AUP), 311
Access controls
    computer fraud schemes, 310
    conversion process, 182
    IT general controls, 283
    purchases and payments process, 156
    sales and collections process, **125**
    wireless LAN, 331
Access point, 331
Accountability, documentation for, 34
Accountants
    business process documentation, 32–33
    role in AIS, 8–9
    specific accounting roles, 8–9
Accounting, data analytics, in accounting
    (*See* Data analytics)
Accounting information systems (AIS)
    attributes of useful information, 5–6
    Balanced Scorecard framework, 349–351
    as business analysts, 4
    certifications in, 9–10
    data versus information, 6–7
    definition, 4
    digital dashboards, 254
    discretionary versus mandatory information, 7
    and external business processes, 14–17
    and firm profitability, 17–18
    and internal business processes, 13–14
    role of accountants, 8–9
    simple information system, 5
    stock prices, 18–19
    value chain and, 10–13
Accounting rate of return (ARR), 373
Accounts payable, **150**
Accounts receivable, 120
Acquisition costs, **369**–370

Activities
    definition, 37
    notation in BPMN diagrams, 37
Activity-based costing (ABC) system, 7
Activity models
    business process modeling notation, 36–46
    collaboration model, 153–155
    conversion process, 180–182
    integrated project, 200–203
    purchases and payments process, 153
    sales and collections process
        basic sales activity model, 121
        collaboration model, 121–122
        exceptions, 122–124
Agents, **183**
    relational database, 85
    sales and collections process, 126
Aggregation relationship
    notation in UML class diagrams, 65
Alignment risk, **370**
Amazon.com, **12**, 40
American Accounting Association (AAA), 274
American Express, 70
American Institute of Certified Public Accountants (AICPA), 9, 10, 257, 272, 274
Analysis phase, systems development life cycle (SDLC), 386
Annotations
    definition, 37
    in flowchart, 50
    notation in BPMN diagrams, 37
Apple, 252
Apple iPad, 21
Application controls, 274
    conversion process, 182
    purchases and payments process, 156
    sales and collections process, **125**
Applications, 349
ARR (Accounting rate of return), 373
Arraj, V., 288*n*
Associations
    notation in data flow diagram, 45
    notation in UML class diagrams, 63
    purchases and payments process, 165
Assurance, **258**
Asymmetric-key encryption, **304**
Attributes
    notation in ERDs, 73

    notation in UML class diagrams, 64, 67
    relational database
        conversion process, 186
        purchases and payments process, 159–160
        sales and collections process, 131–132
    relational databases, 85
    sales and collections process, 131–132
Audit Command Language (ACL), 334
Audit data standards, 214–217
Auditing, 213–214
    continuous, 334–336
Auditing, documentation for, 34
Audit Standard Library, 215*n*
AUP (Acceptable use policy), 311
Australian Prudential Regulatory Agency (APRA), 257
Authentication, **304**
Automate, **19**
Availability
    of information, 302
    wireless LAN, 331

B

Bachman, Charles, 62
Bachman diagrams, 62
Backing up data, 314
Baer Belly Bikinis comprehensive exercise
    company overview, 134–135
    purchases and payments process, 160–163
    sales and collections process, 134–136
Bain and Company, 347
Balanced Scorecard framework, **346**
    customer perspective, **348**
    financial perspective, **348**
    learning and growth perspective, 347
    process perspective, **347–348**
    role of ASI/IT, 349–351
    strategy map, **349**
    using Balanced Scorecard management process, 351–353
Bank of America, 88
Batch processing, 284
Batch totals, 284
Beasley, M. S, 278*n*, 280*n*
Bed Bath & Beyond, 85
Benefits, **366**

430   Index

Best Buy, 6, 252
BETWEEN operator, SQL (Structured
    Query Language), 100
Big Data
    data analytics, 210
    definition, **210**
BI Pros, 211*n*
Black-box approach, 333
Borthick, F., 3*n*
Botnet (bot), 303
Brancik, K.C., 308*n*
Branson, Bruce C., 278*n*, 280*n*
Breach of security, **219**
Breakeven analysis, 372
Business analysis, **33**
Business analysts
    accountants as, 4
    business process documentation,
        33–35
    changing roles in business, 32–33
Business case, **366**
Business continuity management (BCM),
    315–316
Business intelligence
    data mining, 253
    definition, 252
Business intelligence (BI), 32
Business models. *See also* Activity models;
    Data models
    definition, 33
    value of, 34–35
Business process. *See* Conversion process;
    Purchases and payments process;
    Sales and collections process
    definition, 33
    types of, 34
Business process analysis, 121
Business process documentation
    definition, 33
    purposes, 33–34
Business process modeling notation
    (BPMN), 36
    integrated project, 200–203
    messages, 39–40
    purchases and payments process, 153
Business rules, 70–71
    conversion process, 182–183
    purchases and payments process,
        155–156
    sales and collections process, 124–125
Business value, **11**
    accountants as business analysts, 8–9
    accounting information systems
    external business processes, 14–17
    firm profitability, 17–18
    internal business processes, 13–14
    stock prices, 18–19
    value chains, 10–13

C

Cadbury, Adrian, 273, 273*n*
Capital budgeting techniques, 366
Cardinalities
    definition, 74
    notation in ERD, 73
Cash, 120, 138
Cash disbursements
    association between purchases and,
        166
    definition, **150**
    in purchases and payments process,
        158
Cash receipt, 89, 138, 139
    in sales and collections process, 127
    UML Class Model, 127
Cash resource, 139
CERT Coordination Center, 310
Certificate Authority (CA), **306**
Certified Information Systems Auditor
    (CISA), 10
Certified Information Technology
    Professional (CITP), 10
Certified Internal Auditor (CIA), 10
Change management controls, IT general
    control, 283
Change risk, **370**
Chen, Peter P., 62, 73*n*
Chen's notation (ERD), 74
Chief executive officer (CEO), 280
Choreography
    purchases and payments process, 153
    sales and collections process, 122
Class, 85
    notation in UML class diagrams, 67
Class diagrams
    definition, 62
    UML class diagrams, 62
Cloud computing, **104, 315**
COBIT Framework, 285–286
Code of ethics, **272**
Cole, J., 346*n*
Collaboration model
    purchases and payments process, 153
    sales and collections process, 122
Collapsed subprocess, 122
Columbus, Louis, 212*n*
Committee of Sponsoring Organizations
    (COSO), 274
Communication, 276
Competitive intelligence, 252
Composition
    notation in UML class diagrams, 65
Composition relationship
    notation in UML class diagrams, 65
Computer-assisted audit techniques
    (CAATs), 332–334
Computer fraud and abuse

computer fraud schemes, 309–310
    fraud triangle, **307**
    prevention and detection, 310–311
    risk assessment, 308
    vulnerability assessment and
        management, 311–314
Computer fraud schemes, 309
Computer hardware and software
    database systems, 327
    LANs, 328–330
    operating system (OS), 326–327
    WANs, 328–330
    wireless networks, 331–332
Computer operations controls, 283
Computer Sciences Corporation, 346*n*
Computerworld, 328
Computing hardware, 349
Concurrent update control, 284
Confidentiality
    information, 302
    wireless LAN, 331
ConocoPhillips, 10
Constraints
    definition, 64
    factors, 391–393
    notation in UML class diagrams, 66
Continual service improvement (CSI), 287
Control activities, 276, 277. *See also*
    Internal controls
    conversion process, 182–183
    input controls, **283**–284
    IT application controls, **283**
    IT controls, **283**
    IT general controls (ITGC), **283**
    output controls, **284**
    physical controls, **283**
    processing controls, **284**
Control environment, 276, 277
Control objectives for information and
    related technology (COBIT), 275,
    387
Control risk, **281**
Conversion process
    activity models, 180–182
    business rules, 182–183
    relational database, 186–187
    structure models, 183–185
    Sunset Graphics example, 178–179
Corporate governance, **273**
    commonly used frameworks, 274–275
    overview and control concepts, 274
Corrective controls, 274
COSO ERM Framework, 278–284
COSO Internal Control Framework,
    275–278
Cost avoidance, 368
Cost/benefit analysis, **281**
    cost of IT projects, 392

information technology (IT)
    projects, 369–370
Cost savings, 368
Couger, D.J., 36*n*
Critical path, 393
Cross-footing balance test, 284
Customer, 121
Customer information, computer fraud
    schemes, 309
Customer perspective, **348**
Customer relationship management, 16–17,
    350
Customer relationship management (CRM)
    software, **16**
Customers, 138
Cyphertext, 303

D
Data
    definition, **6**
    vs. information, 6–7
Data Accountability and Trust Act of 2009
    (DATA), 217, 217*n*
Data analytics
    audit data standards, 214–217
    auditing, 213–214
    benefits and costs, 210–211
    Big Data, 210
    definition, **210**
    financial reporting, 212–213
    impact on business, 211–212
    managerial and tax accounting, 214
    privacy and data protection, 217–219
        compromise of information, 219
        National Standard for Privacy and
            Data Protection, 217–218
        personal identifying information,
            218–219
    Tableau desktop, for data visualization
        and analysis, 233–238
    using Excel
        Excel pivot tables, **223–233**
        power pivot, **228–233**
        table in Excel, **220–223**
Database, **327**
Database administrator, **85**
Database management system (DBMS), **84**
Databases
    definition, 84–85
    hierarchical data models, 84
    network data model, 84
    relational (*See* Relational databases)
Database system, **327**
Data dictionary, **85**
Data entry control, 284
Data flow diagrams (DFD)
    definition, 52

    example, 53
    nesting/exploding, 53
    practices for, 53
    system documentation, 54
Data flows, 52
Data governance, **327**
Data import, 203–206
Data integrity, **305**
Data marts, **250–252**
Data mining, **253, 327**
Data models
    business rules and decision tables,
        70–71
    definition, 62
    entity-relationship diagrams, 73–75
    hierarchical data models, 84
    network data model, 84
    relational data model, 84
    structure models, 62
    UML class diagrams, 62–69
Data objects, 45
Data stores
    notation in BPMN diagrams, 45
    notation in data flow diagram (DFD),
        52
Data visualization, 233–238
Data warehouses, **250–252, 327**
Davis, C., 287*n*
Davis, F., 395
Debreceny, Roger S., 210*n*
Decisions, flowcharts, 48
Decision support systems (DSSs), 251
Decision tables, 70–71
Dehning, B., 15*n*
DELETE FROM operator, SQL (Structured
    Query Language), 100
Dell Computer, 15
Deloitte & Touche, 336*n*
Delta Airlines, 252
Denial-of-service (DoS), 303
Designer of accounting information, 9
Design phase, systems development life
    cycle (SDLC), 386
Detective controls, 274
Diageo, 278
Digital certificate, **306**
Digital dashboards, **254–255**
Digital signature, **305**
Disaster recovery planning (DRP),
    315, 317
Discretionary information, 7
Documentation
    business process, 33–34
    definition, 33
    purposes, 33–34
Document flowcharts, 48
Dropbox, 252
Dunkin' Donuts, 82, 252, 253

E
Eavesdropping, 331
eBay, 314
Ebbers, Bernard, 272
Economic justification process, **366**
EDGAR (Electronic Data Gathering,
    Analysis and Retrieval), 258
Embedded audit module (EAM), 334
Employees, 138
Encryption, **303**
    asymmetric-key encryption, **304**
    symmetric-key encryption, **304**
End-user computing policy, 311
Enron, 272
Enterprise IT (EIT), **350**
Enterprise resource planning (ERP) systems,
    32, 291–293
Enterprise risk management (ERM), 275,
    278
    computer fraud risk assessment, 308
Enterprise system (ES), 13
    cloud computing, 104–105
    implementation challenges, 103–104
    XBRL use by, 259
Entities
    notation in ERDs, 73
    relational databases, 85
Entity integrity rule, 87
Entity-relationship diagrams (ERD),
    73–75
    basic notation, 73–74
    cardinality options, 74–75
    Chen's notation, 74
    information engineering notation, 74
ERP systems, 335
ESPN, 253
Ethics, need for, 272
Evaluation of IT projects
    benefits of large projects, 366
    business case IT initiatives, 366–368
    capital budgeting techniques, 366
    estimating benefits, 368–369
    estimating costs, 369–370
    risk assessment, 370–371
    value proposition, 372–374
Evaluator of accounting information, 9
Event identification, 280
Events, **184**
    definition, 36
    notation in BPMN diagrams, 36
    relational database, 85
    sales and collections process, 126
Event types, 42
Everson, Miles E. A., 278*n*
Excel pivot tables, **223–233**
Extensible Business Reporting Language
    (XBRL), 335
Extensible Markup Language (XML), 335

432   Index

Extensible Stylesheet Language (XSL), 258
External business processes
    customer relationship management,
        16–17, 350
    supply chain, 14–15
Extract, transform, and load (ETL)
    process, 211

F

Fault tolerance, **315**
Federal Information Processing Standards
    (FIPS), 332*n*
FedEx, 18
15-15 rule, 392
Financial Executives Institute, 346
Financial Executives International (FEI),
    274
Financial Executives Research Foundation,
    346*n*
Financial perspective, **348**
Financial reporting, 212–213
Financial risk, **370**
Finished goods inventory, 179
Firewalls, 329
Firm infrastructure, **12**
Firm profitability, 17–18
Flowchart
    business process flowchart, 48–49
    definition, 47
    document flowcharts, 48
    elements of, 48
    opportunity, 50
    responsibilities, 50, 51
    symbols, 49–50
    systems flowcharts, 48
Ford, 12
Foreign key (FK)
    notation in UML class diagrams, 65,
        67
    relational databases, 86
Forms
    relational database, 87–88
Fox Meyer, 104
Fraud detection program, 311
Fraud triangle, **307**
FROM clause, SQL (Structured Query
    Language), 97–98
Function IT (FIT), **350**

G

Gantt chart, 394
Gartner Inc., 315*n,* 366, 369
Gateways
    conversion process, 180
    definition, 37
    notation in BPMN diagrams, 37, 41

purchases and payments process, 154
Geerts, G., 128*n*
GEICO, 253
General controls, 274
Generalization
    notation in UML class diagrams, 65
Generalized audit software (GAS), 334
Generally accepted auditing standards
    (GAAS), 333
General Motors, 85, 102
Global Corporate Governance Forum, 273
Global Technology Audit Guides (GTAG),
    308
GoDaddy, 252
Google, 6
GoPro, 253
Gray, Glen L., 210*n*
GROUP BY operator, SQL (Structured
    Query Language), 98–99

H

Hancock, Bonnie V., 278*n*
Hashing, **305**
Hendricks, K. B., 18*n*
Hershey's Corp., 104, 371
Hewlett-Packard (HP), 104
Hierarchical data models, 84
Hoffman, Charles, 257
Hoogduin, Lucas, 210*n*
HTML format, 258
Hubs, 328
Human resource management
    definition, **12**
    value chain, 11

I

Inbound logistics
    definition, **11**
    value chain, 11
IndustryWeek, 346
Informate-down, **19**
Informate-up, **19**
Information
    attributes of useful, 5–6
    availability, 302
    confidentiality, 302
    definition, **6**
    vs. discretionary information, 7
    input, 5
    integrity, 302
    internal control, 276
    output, 5
Information capital, **349**
Information overload, **6**
Information security. *See also* Computer
    fraud and abuse

authentication, 303–307
business continuity management
    (BCM), 315–316
disaster recovery planning (DRP),
    315–316
encryption and authentication,
    303–307
risks and attacks, 302–303
system availability, 314–315
Information Systems Audit and Control
    Association (ISACA), 10, 272, 311,
    326*n,* 333, 387
Information technology (IT)
    Balanced Scorecard framework,
        349–351
    evaluation of IT projects
        benefits of large projects, 366
        business case IT initiatives,
            366–368
        capital budgeting techniques, 366
        estimating benefits, 368–369
        estimating costs, 369–370
        risk assessment, 370–371
        value proposition, 372–374
    omnipresent, 9
    project management, 386–387
    value chain, 11
Information Technology Infrastructure
    Library (ITIL), 275
Information value chain, **7**
Infrastructure, 349
    value chain, 11
Inherent risk, **281**
Input
    information, 5
    input controls, **283**, 283–284
Input/output journal/ledger, flowchart, 49
Input/Output of Document(s)/Report(s),
    flowcharts, 49
INSERT INTO operator, SQL (Structured
    Query Language), 99
Institute of Internal Auditors (IIA), 10, 272,
    274, 307, 333, 333*n*
Institute of Management Accountants
    (IMA), 272, 274
Integrated project, 200–206
Integrated test facility (ITF), 334
Integrity
    information, 302
    wireless LAN, 331
Interactive Data Extraction and Analysis
    (IDEA), 334
Intermediate error event, 123
    conversion process, 180
Intermediate event, 155
Intermediate timer boundary event, 123
Intermediate timer event, 155
Internal business processes

enterprise system (ES), 13
managerial accounting
    information, 7
Internal controls, 156
    comparing frameworks, 290
    control and governance frameworks
        COBIT Framework, 285–286
        COSO ERM Framework, 278–284
        COSO Internal Control
            Framework, 275–278
        Information Technology
            Infrastructure Library
            (ITIL), 287–288
        ISO 27000 Series, 288–289
    conversion process, 183
    Sarbanes-Oxley Act of 2002 (SOX),
        272–273
Internal environment, 279
Internal rate of return (IRR), 372–373
Internal Revenue Service, 2
International Data Corporation, **369**
International Federation of Accountants
    (IFAC), 8, 9, 366
International Organization for
    Standardization (ISO), 275
International Organization for
    Standardization (ISO) 27000 series,
    275
International Professional Practices
    Framework (IPPF), 307, 307n
International Red Cross, **11**
Internet Protocol (IP), 330
Inventory, 138
    purchases and payments process, 166
IT application controls, **283**
IT controls, **283**
IT general controls (ITGC), **283**
IT Governance Institute (ITGI), 275

J
JPMorgan Chase, 327–328
Juniper Networks, 249

K
Kaplan, R.S., 351
Kennedy, Joseph, 212n
Key performance indicators, **350**
Kickbacks, 310
Knight Vale and Gregory, 257
Kogan, Alexander, 210n
Kuhn, J. R, 335n

L
Labor operations event, **184**
Landauer Inc., 389

Learning and growth perspective, **347**
Local area network (LAN), 328
London Ambulance Service (LAS), 397

M
MAC (media access control) address, 328
Mackey, Richard, 218n
Macros, relational database, 88
Magnetic disc storage, flowchart, 50
Maintenance phase, systems development
    life cycle (SDLC), 387
Management controls, 332
Managerial accounting information, 7
Manager of accounting information systems,
    9
Mandatory information, 7
Man-in-the-middle, 331
Manual task/activity, flowchart, 50
Many-to-many relationship
    conversion process, 185
    notation in ERDs, 74
    notation in UML class diagrams, 67
    purchases and payments process, 158
    sales and collections process, 126
Marketing and sales activities
    definition, **11**
    value chain, 11
Martens, Frank J., 278n
Masquerading, 331
McAfee, A., 350n
McCarthy, W., 128n
McDonald's Corporation, 7, 253
McKinsey Global Institute, 211
Membership Operator (IN), SQL (Structured
    Query Language), 100
Message digest (MD), **305**
Message flows, 121
    definition, 39
    notation in BPMN diagrams, 39
    purchases and payments process, 153
Message modification, 331
Message replay, 331
Metro, Karen, 60
Microsoft, 67, 249
Microsoft Access, 132
    creating and defining new tables,
        92–94
    creating relationships, 95–96
    form for data entry and display,
        107–111
    introduction, 87–88
    Steve's Stylin' Sunglasses, 88–96
Microsoft Corporation, 258, 370n
Microsoft Excel, 258, 372
Microsoft Surface Book, 7
Microsoft Word, 258
Microsoft XBox, 7

MicroStrategy Inc., 198
Misappropriation, 331
Modules, relational database, 88
Monitoring, internal control, 276
Morgan Stanley, 252
Multiplicities
    notation in UML class diagrams, 63
    relational database, 138–139
Muthukrishnan, R., 316

N
National Institute of Standards and
    Technology (NIST), 331n
Net present value (NPV), 372
Network data model, 84
Network interface card (NIC), 331
Network IT (NIT), **350**
Nike, 104
Norton, D., 351
Nottingham, Lucy E., 278n

O
Objective setting, 279–280
Object Management Group (OMG), 36,
    62, 69
Office of Government Commerce (OGC;
    UK), 275
100% rule, 393
One-to-many relationship
    notation in ERDs, 74
    sales and collections process, 126
One-to-one relationships, 158
Online analytical processing (OLAP), **327**
Online keying, flowchart, 50
On/Off Page Connectors, flowchart, 50
Operating costs, 370
Operating system (OS), 326–327
Operational controls, 332
Operational databases, **327**
Operation cost, **369**
Operations
    definition, **11**
    value chain, 11
Oracle, 60, 198, 249
Oracle ERP, 102, 259
Orchestration
    purchases and payments process, 153
    sales and collections process, 122
ORDER BY clause, SQL (Structured Query
    Language), 99
Organizational change, 34
Outbound logistics, **11**
    value chain, 11
Output
    information, 5
    output controls, **284**

P

Pages, relational database, 88
Panko, J., 329*n*
Panko, R., 329*n*
Parallel simulation, 333
Pässler, Jörg, 280
Passwords, 310
Payback period, 372
Payments. *See* Purchases and payments
    process
PayPal, 88
PDF format, 259
Perceived usefulness, **395**
Personal identifying information, **218**
Physical controls, **283**
Plaintext, 303
Plan-do-check-act model (PDCA), 288
Planning phase
    effective information technology
        planning, 388–389
    systems development life cycle
        (SDLC), 386
Pools, 38, 121
    purchases and payments process, 153
Power pivot, 228–233
Prenumbered documents, 284
Preventive controls, **274**
Primary key (PK)
    notation in UML class diagrams, 64
    relational databases, 85
Private key, **304**
Process description
    conversion process, 178
    purchases and payments process,
        152–153
    sales and collections process, 121
Processes, notation in data flow diagram
    (DFD), 52
Processing controls, 284, **284**
Processing, in information systems, 5
Process maps, 48
Process perspective, **347–348**
Procter & Gamble, 212
Procurement
    definition, **12**
    value chain, 11
Product categories
    purchases and payments process, 159
    sales and collections process, 128
Production authorization event, **184**
Products
    purchases and payments process, 157
    in sales and collections process, 120
Program Evaluation Review Technique,
    393
Project development and acquisition
    controls, IT general controls, 283

Project management
    challenges of IT project management,
        390–391
    constraining factors of IT projects,
        391–393
    IT project evaluation, 364–375
    tools, 393–394
    usefulness of system, 395–397
Project manager, **390**
Project plan
    activity models, 200–203
    business requirements, 200
    data import, tables and set relation-
        ships, 203–206
    queries, 206
    structure diagram, 203
Project risk, **370**
Projects, **389**
Projects/examples
    Sunset Graphics example, 152–153
Project sponsor, **390**
Public Company Accounting Oversight
    Board (PCAOB), 34*n*, 258, **272**
Public key, **304**
Public-key infrastructure (PKI), **306**
Purchase discounts, **150**
Purchases
    association between suppliers and, 165
    definition, **150**
Purchases and payments process
    activity model, 153–155
    Baer Belly Bikinis comprehensive
        exercise, 161–163
    business rules, 155–156
    generic pattern with multiplicities,
        165–166
    process description, 152–153
    process steps, 156
    relational database, 159–160
    structure models, 156–159

Q

Quality of service (QoS), 329
Queries
    integrated project, 206
    relational database, 87
Quote, 121

R

Raw material issue event, **184**
Raw materials inventory
    conversion process, 179
    definition, 179
REA framework
    conversion process, 183

purchases and payments process, 157
    sales and collections process, 126
Receive Payment process, integrated
    project, 201
Record, 85
Referential integrity rule, 87
Relational databases
    conversion process, 186–187
        creating and defining new tables,
            186–187
        planning for attributes, 186
    entities and attributes, 85
    Microsoft Access implementation,
        87–96 (*See also* Microsoft
        Access)
    purchases and payments process
        planning for attributes,
        159–160
    requirements of tables, 87
    Sunset Graphics example, 131–133
    UML class diagrams, 66–69
Relational data models, 84
Relationships, notation in ERDs, 73
Relevance, **5**
Relevant costs, **369**
Reliability, **5, 6**
Remote access, 330
Reports, relational database, 88
Residual risk, **281**
Resources, **184**
    sales and collections process, 126
Revenue enhancement, 368
Revenue protection, 368
Richardson, V. J., 15*n*
Risk assessment, 277, 280–281
    computer fraud prevention and
        detection, 308
Risk response, 280
Rogue access points, 331
Role designation, notation in UML class
    diagrams, 66
Romney, M. B., 281*n*
Routers, 329
Royal Bank/Royal Bank of Canada,
    17, 17*n*

S

Saint Exupéry, Antoine de, 366
Sales, 120, 138
Sales and collections process
    activity model, 121
    Baer Belly Bikinis Inc. comprehensive
        exercise, 134–136
    business rule, 124–125
    generic pattern with multiplicities,
        138–139

process description, 121
relational database, 131–133
structure models, 126–130
Sunset Graphics' activity models,
    121–124
Sunset Graphics example, 120–121
Sales order, 121
Sales process, 202
SAP, 259, 384, 397
SAP/ERP, 102
SAP modules, 102
Sappi Group Treasury, 280
Sarbanes-Oxley Act of 2002 (SOX), 9, **272,**
    388
Sayana, S. A., 332*n*
Schemas, 67*n*
Schiller, M., 287*n*
Schrock, D., 346*n*
Schultz, Howard, 118, 249
Scope creep, **391**
Security control, 332
Segregation of duties (SOD), 283*n*
SELECT DISTINCT clause, SQL (Structured
    Query Language), 100
SELECT operator, SQL (Structured Query
    Language), 97
"Semantics of Business Vocabulary and
    Business Rules" (SBVR), 70
Sequence checks, 284
Sequence flows, 122
    definition, 37
    flowcharts, 48
    notation in BPMN diagrams, 37
Service activities
    definition, **11**
    value chain, 11
Service design (SD), 287
Service operation (SO), 287
Service strategy (SS), 287
Service transition (ST), 287
Session key, **304**
Shaffer, J., 346*n*
Shane Co., 104
Singhal, V. R., 18*n*
Social engineering, 303
Solution risk, **370**
Spam, 303
Specification, 256, 396
Spoofing, 303
Spyware, 303
Starbucks, 5, 82, 139, 253, 344–355
    computer fraud and abuse, 300
    control of market, 384
    conversion process, 176
    CRM, 16
    data analytics, 208
    data models, 60

data warehouse and data marts,
    250–252
integrated project, 198
purchases and payments process, 150
sales and collections process, 118
Start/End, flowcharts, 48
Station, 331
Steinbart, P. J., 281*n*
Steinberg, Richard M., 278*n*
Steve's Stylin' Sunglasses (SSS), 88–96
    access to implementation, 91–96
    data model and attributes, 88–89
    multiplicities, 89–91
Stock prices, 18–19
Storage offline, flowchart, 50
Storey, V. C., 210*n*
Strategy map, **349**
Strategy Maps (Kaplan and Norton), 347
Stratman, J. K., 18*n*
Strickland, A. J., 15*n*
Structure diagram, 203
Structured Query Language (SQL), 96–102
Structure models, **62**
    conversion process, 183–185
    purchases and payments process,
        156–159
    sales and collections process,
        126–130
    Unified Modeling Language (UML)
        class diagrams, 62–66
Subprocess
    purchases and payments process, 154
    sales and collections process, 122
Sunset Graphics example
    company overview, 120–121, 152
    conversion process, 178–179
    purchases and payments process,
        152–153
    sales and collections process
        business rules, 124–125
        description, 121
        process description, 121–123
        sales activity model, 121
Suppliers
    association between purchases and,
        165
    definition, **150**
Supply chain, **14**–15
Supply chain management (SCM), 350
Supply chain management (SCM) software,
    15
Sutton, S. G., 335*n*
Swimlanes, 38
Switches, 328
Symmetric-key encryption, **304**
System documentation, 54
Systems analyst, 9

Systems development life cycle (SDLC),
    283, 310
    analysis phase, 386
    definition, 386
    design phase, 386
    implementation phase, 387
    maintenance phase, 387
    planning phase, 386
Systems flowcharts, 48
Systems integrity, 302

T

Tableau desktop, 233–238
Table in Excel, **220**–223
Tables
    creating in Microsoft Access, 67, 87
    integrated project, 203–206
    relational database, 67–69, 85, 87
    Target, 19
Task dependency, 394
Tasks/Activities, flowcharts, 48
Task types, 43
Tax accounting, 214
Taxonomies
    XBRL GL (XBRL Global Ledger
        Taxonomy), 259
    XBRL taxonomy, 256–257
Tax returns, 32
Taylor, Frederick W., 36*n*
Technical controls, 332
Technological risk, **370**
Technology, **12**
Technology acceptance model
    (TAM), **395**
Terminators, notation in data flow diagram
    (DFD), 52
Tesla, 252
Test data technique, 333
Thompson, A. J., 15*n*
Threat assessment and management, 313–314
Time issues, project management, 392
Timer events, 155
Token concept, notation in BPMN diagrams,
    40
Traffic analysis, 331
Training, documentation for, 34
Transform, **19**
Treadway Commission, 274
Triple constraint, **391**
Trojan horse, 303
Tuttle, Brad M., 210*n*
Tyco International, 272
Type images, 126
    conversion process, 184
    purchases and payments process, 159
    sales and collections process, 128

U

Ucuzoglu, Joe, 214*n*
Unified Modeling Language (UML) class
    diagrams
    associations, 63
    attributes, 64
    best practices, 66
    classes, 62–63
    conversion process, 183–185
    foreign keys, 65
    multiplicities, 63
    other relationships, 65–66
    purchases and payments process,
        158–159
    relational database design, 66–69
    sales and collections process, 127–130
Uninterruptible power supply, 314
UPDATE operator, SQL (Structured Query
    Language), 99
U.S. Census data, 220
User of accounting information, 9
U.S. Secret Service, 310
U.S. Securities and Exchange Commission
    (SEC), 33, 255
    EDGAR (Electronic Data Gathering,
        Analysis and Retrieval), 258

V

Val IT, 353–354
Val IT (ISACA), 285
Value chain
    definition, **11**
    information value chain, **7**

W

WaferGen Bio-Systems Inc., 389
Wallgum, T., 17
Walmart, 6, 15, 384, 397
Walsh, Paul, 278
Wayfair, 12
WHERE clause, SQL (Structured Query
    Language), 97
White-box approach, 333
Wide area networks (WANs), 329
Wi-fi protected access (WPA), 332
Wired equivalent privacy (WEP) algorithm,
    332
Wireless networks, 331
Work breakdown structure (WBS), 393
Work-in-process inventory
    conversion process, 184
    definition, **184**

Value proposition, **348,** 372, 374
Varian, Hal, 6
Variety, 210
Vasarhelyi, Miklos A., 210*n*
Velocity, 210
Vendor information, computer fraud
    schemes, 309
Virtualization, **315**
Virtual private network (VPN), 330
Viruses, computer, 302
Volume, 210
Vulnerability assessment and management
    overall framework, 313–314
    types of, 312

World Bank, 273
WorldCom., 272, 335
Worms, 302

X

XBRL (eXtensible Business Reporting
    Language)
    history and development, 256
    XBRL assurance, 258
    XBRL GL (XBRL Global Ledger
        Taxonomy), 259
    XBRL instance documents, 258
    XBRL style sheets, 258
    XBRL taxonomy, 256–257
XBRL assurance, 258
XBRL GL (XBRL Global Ledger
    Taxonomy), 259
XBRL instance documents, 258
XBRL International, 255
XBRL style sheets, 258
XBRL taxonomy, 256–257
XML (Extensible Markup Language), 255

Z

Zhang, Li, 210*n*
Zmud, R. W., 15*n*